Porte Ouverte

Tony Mais
Alan Proffitt
Helen Silverstone

H·E·B

HEINEMANN EDUCATIONAL BOOKS

Heinemann Educational Books Ltd
22 Bedford Square, London WC1B 3HH

LONDON EDINBURGH MELBOURNE AUCKLAND
SINGAPORE KUALA LUMPUR NEW DELHI
IBADAN NAIROBI JOHANNESBURG PORTSMOUTH (NH)
KINGSTON

© Tony Mais, Alan Proffitt and Helen Silverstone
First published 1987

British Library CIP Data
Mais, Tony
    Porte ouverte.
    1. French language—Textbooks for
       foreign speakers—English
       I. Title II. Proffitt, Alan III. Silverstone, Helen
       448   PC2112

       ISBN 0−435−37825−2

Designed and typeset by Oxprint Ltd, Oxford
Printed by Butler and Tanner Ltd, Frome and London

Acknowledgements
The authors and publishers would like to thank the following for permission
to use their material:
Liz Somerville; Jumelages et Relations Internationales de la Ville de Lyon;
Office de Tourisme de Lyon; West Wales Trust for Nature Conservation;
SATIS Promotion; Agence Commerciale de Télécommunications de
Courbevoie; New Enterprise Publications Ltd; Le Petit Malin; Le Petit Futé;
Le Point; CISL; Club Praia da Oura; British Rail; SNCF French Railways;
Editions La Route Robert; British Tourist Authority; Radio Times; Agora;
Hôtel de Ville, Vaulx-en-Velin; Ombres Vives; Centre de l'Epervière; Télé 7
Jours; Department of Tourism, York; Office de Tourisme, Sedan; Michelin
Tyre Public Limited Company; Le Progrès; FNAC; Le Figaro; Coastal Cottages
of Pembrokeshire; Parke Davis and Company; The Shakespeare Birthplace
Trust; France Soir; Château d'Ussé; Les 3 Toques: Pâtisseries Fines,
Tourcoing; Mairie de Saint-Valéry-sur-Somme; Pomme: Les Informations
Dieppoises; Friskies: Gloria S.A.; Syndicat d'Initiative d'Apremont; Christiane
Charillon; Crédit Agricole de l'Isère; Société Lyonnaise de Transports en
Commun; Vision International; Bayard-Presse; Bristol Myers Co. Ltd; Lyon
Matin; Gendarmerie Nationale Française; Office Départemental de Tourisme
de la Dordogne.

It has not been possible in all cases to trace copyright holders; the publishers
would be glad to hear from any such unacknowledged copyright holders.

Note for Teacher
The **Teacher's Resource Pack** contains the teaching notes for each
chapter, a full transcript of the recorded material and 70 pages of
photocopy masters.
These photocopy masters include the answer grids, forms, diary pages,
floor plans, maps, street plans and timetables that are reproduced in
miniature in the Pupil's Book, plus all the role play cards, cue cards and
sets of picture cards that are needed for pupils to complete the tasks.
ISBN 0–435–37826–0

Contents

1

Premières rencontres

 LISTENING

1 Your class receives a cassette letter from a group
of French teenagers. Your teacher gives you a grid
on which to jot down details of each person as they
speak. From this grid you are told you will decide
to whom you would like to write. You hear the
cassette twice.

Name	Age	Likes	Dislikes
Guy			
Sophie			
Jean-Marc			
André			
Robert			
Marie			
Colette			
Nathalie			
Alain			
Michèle			

2 Your penfriend who does not like writing very
much has hit on the idea of sending you
cassette letters. She has just moved to a new
town and in part of her cassette letter this time
she tells you about some of her new friends. As
several people in your class are looking for
penfriends, you take a few notes to see if any
might be suitable matches.

Name	Age	Likes	Dislikes	Type of person
Claire				
Florence				
Marc				
Agnès				
Roland				

3 Your penfriend's mother is on the committee of
an organisation whose purpose is to visit and cheer up people
in the local old people's home. She has been asked to find out
when each old person's birthday is so that a card and small
present can be sent at the right time. She asks you to go with
her and make a note of the birthdays whilst she chats to the
old people. There are twelve old people in the home.

Name	Date	Month
Mme Chenu		
Mme Lafitte		
Mme Brelli		
M. Lesanges		
Mlle Jacquot		
Mme Leowicz		
Mme Robert		
Mme Coriche		
M. Rondeau		
Mme Bonvoisin		
Mlle Ragôt		
Mme Cloche		

4 You have sent off your name and address to a
penfriend agency in France. One day you receive this
cassette letter. Your family are anxious to know all
about your new penfriend so you make notes under
the following headings in order to give them details.

- Name
- Age
- Where he lives
- What he likes doing
- What he doesn't like
- Information about brothers
  and sisters
- Information about parents
- Information about pets
- School subjects he enjoys
- His hopes for the future

5 You have applied to a penfriend bureau for a penfriend and they send you a cassette with five people speaking. You make notes under the following headings about each one and then decide which one you will choose to write to.

- Name
- Age
- Interests
- Dislikes
- Hopes for the future

6 You and four friends are meeting your penfriends for the first time at Heathrow airport. They have each sent a cassette letter in which they describe themselves. Below are pictures of some girls of the right sort of age who come through the barrier. Which ones will you approach?

7 Whilst staying with your penfriend in France you take part in a treasure hunt organised by the Parents' Association of his school. During the course of this hunt there are five mysterious strangers who hold clues and who will hand them over when the password is given. At the start of the treasure hunt each group listens to a cassette on which the strangers are described. Because you are a good artist you are asked to draw identi-kits from the descriptions.

8 Your uncle, who lives in France, has to go to the Middle East for a few months on business. Your French aunt decides to take the opportunity to come to England and meet you all for the first time. One evening, she phones to say she is arriving the next day. She describes herself so that whoever meets her at the airport will recognise her. Make notes, in order to describe her to your father, who is the person who will be going to meet her.

9 Your penfriend's parents are coming to London on a work's outing. Your penfriend phones to describe them to you as you are to meet them at their hotel for lunch. Make notes so that you will recognise them.

10 Whilst travelling by car with your parents in France you hear a message on the radio about three escaped convicts. You fancy yourself as an amateur detective and you make notes about their descriptions so that if you see them you can inform the police.

SPEAKING

1 1 Working with your partner introduce yourselves giving the following information:

- Name
- Where you live
- One special interest
- Age
- One thing you dislike

2 Now turn and introduce yourselves to another pair. Work with each one of the other pair in turn.

3 Now introduce your partner to the other pair and allow him/her to introduce you.

4 Get up and move around the classroom introducing yourself to as many people as possible and letting them introduce themselves to you.

5 Introduce your partner to as many people as possible and let him/her introduce you.

2 Play this game in a large group (ten or more) or as a class game. One person is blindfolded and then the group decides on someone who is to be introduced as Monsieur/Mademoiselle 'X'. Another person performs the introduction and the blindfolded person has to guess who is being described. If he/she guesses correctly then it is his/her turn to perform the introduction next time round.

3 You ring the telephone number given to you by your prospective penfriend, to give a few details of yourself. The phone is answered by your penfriend's mother and you tell her about yourself. She notes down the details you give and checks them back to you.

You should give at least six or seven details about yourself. Your partner will play the part of your penfriend's mother who takes the call. Then reverse the roles.

4 Working in a group of about six people, each person takes it in turn to throw the dice. You then have to give as many items of information about yourself as the number you throw. You can go round the group several times but no-one should give the same information as they did on the last round. (This is difficult if you keep throwing sixes.)

5 Your penfriend has asked you to find someone who would like to write to a friend of hers. You phone her to give details of your friend and compare his likes with those of your penfriend's friend. Take it in turns with your partner to play the role of the penfriend.

Your Friend	*Your Penfriend's Friend*
• Is a boy named Peter aged 16.	• Is a girl named Nathalie aged 15½.
• Likes—dancing, discos, football and films.	• Likes—dancing, discos, tennis, watching football and reading.
• Dislikes—school.	• Dislikes—doing homework.
• Ambition—to play football for England.	• Ambition—to be a pop singer.

6 Repeat the previous exercise with your partner this time making up your own descriptions of the two friends. Repeat this as many times as you can with different descriptions each time.

7 Starting with your partner, go round the classroom and interview as many people as possible asking the following questions. Note down their answers.

1 Comment t'appelles-tu?

2 Quel âge as-tu?

3 Où habites-tu?

4 Combien de frères as-tu?

5 Combien de sœurs as-tu?

6 Quels sports aimes-tu?

7 Qu'est-ce que tu aimes faire le soir et le week-end?

8 Quels programmes aimes-tu à la télé?

9 Qu'est-ce que tu n'aimes pas?

10 Quelle est ton ambition?

Remember!

• Use the 'vous' form to your teacher when interviewing him/her.

8 If you have interviewed two people with similar tastes, introduce them to each other explaining to them what they have in common. (They should get on well together.)

9 Ask your partner a further ten questions about him/herself and answer his/her questions to you.

On a piece of paper, jot down details about an imaginary (or real) person and then answer all your partner's questions as if you were that person.

10 You have been asked to send a cassette from your class to your link school in France. In a group, decide the order in which you are going to speak and record the cassette. Say as much as you like about yourself.

11 Working with a partner, play this game where you must never answer 'oui' or 'non'. Ask your partner questions about him/herself, eg. "Tu aimes le sport?" or "Tu as quinze ans n'est-ce pas?". Your partner must answer with expressions like "C'est exact, ce n'est pas vrai, c'est ça" or by repeating the question as a statement.

As soon as you catch your partner out, let him/her ask you questions. See who can answer the most questions without saying 'oui' or 'non'.

📖 READING

1 You have received details from a French boy called Jean-Marc Peyrolles who is looking for a penfriend. As you are writing your first letter to him that evening your younger sister comes in and wants to know all about Jean-Marc. Using the information on the form answer her questions as well as you can.

1 Where does Jean-Marc live?
2 Has he got any brothers?
3 Has he got any sisters?
4 What are their ages?

5 What does he like doing?
6 Does he like dancing?
7 What else do you know about him?

Age. 15 ans

Nom. Peyrolles

Prénom(s). Jean-Marc

Adresse. 10 avenue de la grace
08800 Montherme

Age(s). 10, 13

Nombre de frères. 2

Age(s). 17

Nombre de soeurs. 1

Goûts. Sport, cinéma, Bandes dessinées, danser, vélo

Ce que l'enfant n'aime pas. Collection de timbres. Rester sur place

Autres observations. Aime beaucoup bouger.

bandes dessinées (f.) comic strips

2 Your class has received an envelope full of requests for penfriends from your link school in France. Your teacher asks for your help in sorting out a penfriend for your friend Susan who is absent. She gives you three possible forms. Try to sort out which one will be best for Susan.

Nom. Adobati

Prénom(s). Clémentine

Age. 15 ans

Adresse. 30 rue de la Victoire
69 008 Lyon

Goûts. la nature, les animaux, la musique

Ce que l'enfant n'aime pas. le sport

D'autres observations. très timide

l'équitation (f.) horse-riding

Nom. Laroche

Prénom(s). Sylvie

Age. 15 ans

Adresse. 8, boulevard Legros, 69 002 Lyon

Goûts. l'équitation, le théâtre la danse corporelle, lire regarder la télé

Ce que l'enfant n'aime pas. Rester trop enfermée

D'autres observations. très ouverte

Nom. Abime

Prénom(s). Martine

Age. 16 ans

Adresse. 5, avenue Henri Pasteur
69500 BRON

Goûts. la lecture, la peinture, les arts

Ce que l'enfant n'aime pas. trop sortir

D'autres observations. calme

Susan is 15 and likes reading, collecting postcards, going to the cinema, watching television and painting. She is a quiet girl who does not like discos or going out a lot.

Write a few lines saying which penfriend you have chosen for Susan and why.

3 You have written to a penfriend organisation asking for a penfriend in France. You get the following letter back.

Your mother wants to know what the person you intend writing to is like. Try to answer her questions.

1 Is it a boy or a girl and what's the name?

2 How old is he/she?

3 Where does he/she live?

4 What kinds of things interest him/her?

5 What kinds of things does he/she dislike?

6 What sort of person is he/she?

7 What does he/she want to be in later life?

8 Does he/she like school?

Calais, le dix-sept novembre

Cher ami,

J'ai reçu ton nom de France-Corres ; J'espère que tu vas bien vouloir correspondre avec moi.

Je m'appelle Jean-Luc Gallet et je suis âgé de quinze ans. J'habite au Bâtiment C, allée des Bégonias à Calais. C'est un appartement, et ce n'est pas loin du Hoverport de Calais. J'adore regarder, et partir les aéroglisseurs arriver. au Hoverport.

Je suis un garçon assez calme et j'aime collectionner les choses, les timbres, la monnaie des cartes postales. Ce que je n'aime pas c'est le sport. Je ne suis pas sportif du tout.

J'aime assez l'école et je m'intéresse pour les langues étrangères - je fais de l'anglais et de l'italien. Plus tard j'aimerais beaucoup voyager, peut-être comme marin sur un grand paquebot ou comme steward dans un avion.

Alors j'espère que tu vas bientôt m'écrire.

Ton ami,

Jean-Luc.

---

un aéroglisseur   hovercraft
un marin   sailor
un paquebot   liner

4 You are going to France soon to stay with your penfriend. Her mother will be meeting you at the airport in Paris as she has a day off work that day. Your penfriend writes to describe her mother so that you will recognise her. Make a few notes to help you when you arrive.

- Age
- Height
- Colour of hair and eyes
- Distinguishing features
- Clothes

châtain ⎫
marron ⎭ chestnut brown

> *Versailles le neuf mai*
>
> Cher Peter,
>
> Alors tu arrives comme prévu le 19 mai à midi. Je m'impatiente de te voir après toutes les lettres qu'on s'est écrites.
>
> C'est maman qui viendra te chercher à l'aéroport car elle a la journée libre ce jour-là, je lui ai donné ta photo - celle où tu es en tenue de foot. J'espère qu'elle va te reconnaître.
>
> Cependant je vais te décrire maman pour que tu puisses la reconnaître. Elle est assez grande, elle a 40 ans et elle a les cheveux châtains et les yeux marrons. Elle porte des lunettes. Ce jour-là elle sera habillée d'une robe rouge et d'une veste noire, m'a-t-elle dit.
>
> Alors à bientôt Peter.
>
> Je te salue,
>
> Jacky.

5 Working with a partner play the following game.

Read the descriptions and draw pictures of each of the people described plus a few more. Give your partner *one* description and all the pictures. He or she must then choose the right picture. Your partner will also have drawn some pictures for you to choose from. Do this with each of the descriptions.

1 C'est une fille blonde avec les cheveux longs. Elle porte une robe rouge et blanche et des sandales. Elle est très belle.

2 C'est une fille brune avec les cheveux frisés. Elle porte des lunettes. Elle aime beaucoup les pantalons et les grands pulls.

3 C'est une fille blonde avec les cheveux courts. Elle est petite et ronde et elle porte une jupe noire et un chemisier rouge et blanc.

4 C'est un garçon avec les cheveux bruns et plutôt longs. Il porte un T-shirt et un blue-jean.

5 C'est un garçon très sportif. Il porte un jogging et des tennis. Il a une petite moustache.

6 C'est un garçon sérieux qui a les cheveux courts et qui porte des lunettes. Il travaille dans une banque et il porte une chemise blanche, une cravate et un complet gris.

frisé curly

6 You have applied to go on the exchange organised between Birmingham and Lyon. You receive the form below from a partner in Lyon. Your mother and father ask you questions about what the form contains.

VILLE DE LYON

JUMELAGES ET RELATIONS INTERNATIONALES DE LA VILLE DE LYON
Christian GELPI, Adjoint au Maire de Lyon

Hôtel de Ville - B.P. 1065 - 69205 LYON Cédex 01
Tél. 78.27.71.31 - Poste 30.92
Télex : COMLYON 305-666

Coller une

photo récente

VILLE A VISITER _____   ANNÉE DE L'ÉCHANGE _____   198___

VEUILLEZ COMPLÉTER CHAQUE RUBRIQUE DE CE FORMULAIRE EN LETTRES MAJUSCULES D'IMPRIMERIE. LES FORMULAIRES ILLISIBLES OU INCOMPLETS VOUS SERONT RENVOYÉS.

NOM _CLAUDEL_

PRÉNOMS _Marie-Christine_

NOM DES PARENTS OU TUTEUR _CLAUDEL LOUIS._

DATE DE NAISSANCE _9-6-74_ (garçon/fille) _fille_

ADRESSE _72 boulevard des Anglais._

CODE POSTAL/VILLE _69100 VILLEURBANNE_

TÉL. : DOMICILE : _897-43-21._

TRAVAIL PERE _842-47-0l_/TRAVAIL MERE _256-31-21_

SI VOUS N'AVEZ PAS LE TÉLÉPHONE, INDIQUEZ LE Nº D'UN VOISIN OU D'UN AMI OU L'ON PUISSE VOUS JOINDRE EN CAS D'URGENCE.

NOM DE L'ÉTABLISSEMENT SCOLAIRE _Cdl. Maurois_

DEPUIS COMBIEN D'ANNÉES ÉTUDIEZ-VOUS LA LANGUE DU PAYS CHOISI _4 années._

NOM DU PROFESSEUR DE LANGUE ÉTRANGÈRE _JACQUOT._

▸ ATTESTATION DU PROFESSEUR :

1) Sur le caractère de l'enfant _douce, sérieuse._

2) Niveau d'études envisagé : _bac._

SIGNATURE DU DIRECTEUR :

- -

RUBRIQUE A REMPLIR PAR TOUS LES CANDIDATS

CARACTERE DE L'ENFANT : (Veuillez rayer les mots qui ne correspondent pas).

Sociable – ~~expansif~~ – réservé – ~~timide~~ – ~~bavard~~ – calme – patient – ~~impatient~~ – d'égale humeur – ~~impulsif~~ – ~~mûr~~ – pas mûr – s'adapte facilement – ~~s'adapte avec difficulté~~ – ~~s'ennuie rapidement~~ – ne s'ennuie jamais – ~~actif~~

REMARQUES PARTICULIÈRES (religion, environnement, activités sociales, faites-vous partie d'une famille de non-fumeurs ?, etc...) _non-fumeur_ _fait partie des scoutes._

DÉSIREZ-VOUS RENOUVELER UN ÉCHANGE AVEC QUELQU'UN EN PARTICULIER ? ~~OUI~~/ NON.

(Si OUI, veuillez compléter la rubrique au verso de la feuille).

TAILLE DE L'ENFANT _1m66._ cm

SANTÉ DE L'ENFANT (Allergies, medicaments, problèmes médicaux habituels...)

Rhume des foins.

(Des détails peuvent être envoyés sous pli séparé).

SITUATION DE FAMILLE

PERE : OUI/~~NON~~   MERE : OUI/~~NON~~

PROFESSION DU PERE _professeur_

PROFESSION DE LA MERE _Comptable_

NOMS ET AGES DES FRERES ET SOEURS (Veuillez marquer d'une astérisque ceux qui vivent à la maison)

1. _Renaud_ AGE _19_
2. _Jean-Louis_ * AGE _17_
3. _Sylviane_ * AGE _12_
4. _____ AGE _____

Toute autre personne vivant dans la famille. Par ex. les grands-parents. _grand'mère_

- -

Veuillez indiquer (sous pli séparé si vous le désirez) toute situation de famille exceptionnelle.

ANIMAUX DOMESTIQUES _chat, chien, ~~lapin~~_

ACTIVITÉS - LOISIRS - DISTRACTIONS -

1) qui intéressent votre enfant (Veuillez compléter le plus clairement possible). _lecture, télé, patinage à glace. Scoutisme._

2) Activités que votre enfant n'aime pas. _danser aller au disco._

3) Sports auxquels votre enfant participe activement. _basket, natation_

4) Sports qui intéressent votre enfant. _equitation_

5) Sports que votre enfant n'aime pas. _football sports violents par ex. boxe._

---

un comptable bookeeper, accountant	*les loisirs* leisure activities/spare time	*participer* to take part
un rhume des foins hay fever	*le patinage à glace* ice skating	*faire partie de* to belong to

1 What work do her parents do?
2 How long has she been learning English?
3 What kind of person is she?
4 Has she got any health problems?
5 How many brothers and sisters has she and how old are they?

6 Are there any animals in the house?
7 What kinds of things does she like doing?
8 What doesn't she enjoy?
9 Is she sporty?
10 Is there anything else we should know?

7 You have received the following details of the partner you are going to stay with on exchange. You write to tell your cousin about the trip and include details about your partner. Write that part of the letter.

VILLE A VISITER

ANNÉE DE L'ÉCHANGE

198 7

VEUILLEZ COMPLÉTER CHAQUE RUBRIQUE DE CE FORMULAIRE EN LETTRES MAJUSCULES D'IMPRIMERIE. LES FORMULAIRES ILLISIBLES OU INCOMPLETS VOUS SERONT RENVOYÉS.

NOM _LEROY_

PRÉNOMS _ANNICK_

NOM DES PARENTS OU TUTEUR _LEROY_

DATE DE NAISSANCE _9 - 12 - 74_ (garçon/fille) _FILLE_

ADRESSE _14 BOULEVARD DES ETAS-UNIS_

CODE POSTAL/VILLE _FRANCHEVILLE 01001_

TÉL. : DOMICILE : _50 - 29 - 41 - 77_

TRAVAIL PERE _96-35-02_ TRAVAIL MERE _____

NOM DE L'ÉTABLISSEMENT SCOLAIRE _C.E.S. JACQUOT_

DEPUIS COMBIEN D'ANNÉES ÉTUDIEZ-VOUS LA LANGUE DU PAYS CHOISI _2 ANS_

NOM DU PROFESSEUR DE LANGUE ÉTRANGÈRE _Mlle. TINTEY_

ATTESTATION DU PROFESSEUR :

1) Sur le caractère de l'enfant _SÉRIEUSE, BONNE ÉLÈVE_

2) Niveau d'études envisagé : _B. Et/BAC_

SIGNATURE DU DIRECTEUR :

RUBRIQUE A REMPLIR PAR TOUS LES CANDIDATS

CARACTERE DE L'ENFANT :

SOCIABLE, CALME, ACTIVE

TAILLE DE L'ENFANT _1 · 65_ ____ cm

SANTÉ DE L'ENFANT (Allergies, médicaments, problèmes médicaux habituels...)

(Des détails peuvent être envoyés sous pli séparé).

SITUATION DE FAMILLE

PERE : OUI/NON   MERE : OUI/NON

PROFESSION DU PÈRE _Fonctionnaire_

PROFESSION DE LA MÈRE _SANS_

NOMS ET AGES DES FRERES ET SOEURS

1. _PATRICE_ AGE _11 ANS_
2. _LÉONIE_ AGE _5 ANS_
3. _____ AGE _____
4. _____ AGE _____

Toute autre personne vivant dans la famille. Par ex. les grands-parents. _AUCUNE_

Veuillez indiquer (sous pli séparé si vous le désirez) toute situation de famille exceptionnelle).

ANIMAUX DOMESTIQUES _NÉANT_

ACTIVITÉS · LOISIRS · DISTRACTIONS ·

1) qui intéressent votre enfant (Veuillez compléter le plus clairement possible).
CINÉMA, SPORT, COLLECTION DE TIMBRE

2) Activités que votre enfant n'aime pas.
JEUX DE SOCIÉTÉ

3) Sports auxquels votre enfant participe activement.
TENNIS, NATATION

4) Sports qui intéressent votre enfant.
FOOTBALL, EQUITATION

5) Sports que votre enfant n'aime pas.
KARATE, CATCH, BOXE

Coller une photo récente

---

les jeux de société board games
le catch wrestling

un fonctionnaire civil servant
néant none (emphatic)

8 You are going to Lyon to stay with a penfriend. He sends you a pamphlet about the city. You are writing to your grandmother and decide to tell her a bit about the place. Jot down some notes under the following headings ready for when you write your letter:

- Situation of city
- Size of city
- Museums etc.

LYON vous étonnera...

... d'abord par son site que charpentent avec vigueur deux fleuves et deux collines,

puis par son âge et la qualité de sa mémoire : cette ville bimillénaire, que vous embrasserez d'un seul coup d'oeil depuis Fourvière, peut vous parler de l'époque romaine [1] aussi bien que de la Renaissance [2] ou encore du siècle qui a produit les grands bâtiments publics de Lyon tels que l'Hôtel de Ville [3] ou le Palais St-Pierre [4] .

Des souvenirs rares, Lyon en a conservé pour vous dans vingt quatre Musées dont le Musée Gallo-Romain [5] ,le Musée des Tissus [6] ,le Musée des Hospices [7] , le Musée des Beaux Arts [4] , le Musée Historique de Lyon [8] , le Musée de l'imprimerie [9] etc.

Et si le Vieux Lyon [2] ,au pied de Fourvière est un Musée vivant, à la Croix Rousse [10] , sur l'autre colline, flotte encore dans les traboules nostalgiques le souffle du peuple de "canuts" qui fit naître ici tant de merveilles. Aujourd'hui la soierie a besoin d'autres espaces...

Mais Lyon n'est pas qu'un livre d'histoire. Cette métropole de 1 200 000 habitants est aussi une ville moderne : vous le constaterez partout : dans les quatiers neufs de la Duchère [11] ou au Tonkin [12] à Villeurbanne où déjà se manifestait avant guerre le nouvelle urbanisme des Gratte-Ciel [16] . Du neuf encore à Montessuy (Caluire) [13] et

à la Part-Dieu [14] nouveau Centre d'Affaire, d'Administration, de Commerce et d'Activités artistiques.

Vous y verrez notamment l'Auditorium Maurice Ravel devenu un haut lieu européen pour la Musique et qui, avec l'Opéra [15] , le Théâtre National Populaire [16] à Villeurbanne et vingt autres scènes ou lieux de concerts ou d'expositions, structurent la vie culturelle de la cité.

Lyon vous étonnera encore par ses rues piétonnes [17] , "sentiers de la presqu'île" entre Rhône et Saône, par la perspective de ses quais [18] et par le sompteux tapis de velours coloré et odorant que le mois de juin déroule à la Roseraie du Parc de la Tête d'Or [19] . En définitive, sur un seul point Lyon ne pourra vous étonner : sa cuisine que le monde entier connaît si bien !

A VOTRE SERVICE :

L'OFFICE DE TOURISME DE LYON/COMMUNAUTE

- Accueil - Documentation - Renseignements
- Central hôtelier - Réservations
- Hôtesses - Interprètes
- Visites commentées de la ville

3 bureaux :

(A) **Place Bellecour**   Tél. : **(7) 84 22 57 5**
(B) **Centre d'échanges de Perrache**   **(7) 84 22 07**
(C) **A Villeurbanne, 25, Cours Emile Zola** **(7) 88 96 44 2**

un *fleuve* river

9 Whilst on holiday with your parents in a French seaside resort, you see a poster advertising a competition. It tells you that the first person each day to recognise a mysterious stranger will win a prize. The description of each day's stranger is available from the tourist office.

You go and collect all six descriptions (Monday to Saturday) and study them carefully.

Either

Make notes about each day's stranger so that you will recognise them if you meet them. What should you do if you do recognise someone?

or

Make the whole exercise into a game. With a partner take three descriptions each and quickly draw five pictures for each description *one* of which will actually fit the description. Give one description and the five pictures to your partner who has to work out which drawing fits the description. (You could see who gets all three right first.)

Fête de Belleville-sur-mer
Concours de l'étranger mystérieux

1 L'étranger mystérieux de lundi portera un imperméable beige et un vieux chapeau. Il est brun avec des lunettes. C'est un monsieur.

2 L'étranger mystérieux de mardi portera un complet gris avec une chemise blanche, une cravate bleu marine et une rose jaune à la boutonnière. C'est un monsieur.

3 L'étranger mystérieux de mercredi est féminin. Elle portera une robe multicolore et des lunettes de soleil. Elle sera accompagnée d'un caniche noir.

4 Jeudi notre étranger mystérieux vient du Japon. C'est un touriste avec un appareil-photo et qui sera habillé en short. Il portera un grand chapeau de paille.

5 L'étranger mystérieux de vendredi est étudiant. Il portera l'uniforme des étudiants, c'est-à-dire un blue-jean et un T-shirt. Il est blond et barbu. Le message sur son T-shirt n'est pas du français.

6 Encore une étrangère mystérieuse. Elle est très chic avec une coiffure soignée. Elle portera une robe noire et blanche avec un petit sac en cuir noir.

Si vous reconnaissez un étranger mystérieux abordez-le en disant "Vous êtes l'étranger mystérieux de (lundi, mardi, etc.). J'ai gagné le prix." Bonne chasse!

WRITING

1 You receive this form from an organisation in France who offer to find you a penfriend with a lot in common with you. Fill in the details about yourself on your copy of the form *in French*.

2 Your friend has asked you to find him/her a penfriend. Jot down details to send to your penfriend who will pass your friend's name on to one of his/her classmates.

FRANCE CORRES

Nom ....

Prénoms ....

Date de Naissance ....

Adresse ....

Ville ....

Activités/Distractions que vous aimez ....

....

Activités/Distractions que vous n'aimez pas ....

....

Sports auxquels vous participez activement ....

....

Sports qui vous intéressent ....

3 Since you got a penfriend through *France Corres* some of your classmates also want penfriends and ask you to help them. Fill out similar forms in French for two friends whose personal details are as follows:

Kathy Markam, 15 years old, date of birth: 7-9-73, of 63 Laurel Avenue, Derby. Likes computers, watching TV, records and reading. Dislikes sewing, knitting and collecting things. Plays tennis and table-tennis and is interested in football and ice-skating.

David Brookes, 14 years old, date of birth: 17-7-74, of 94 School Lane, Derby. Likes all sports, watching TV and discos. Dislikes reading and board games. Plays football, tennis, rugby and basketball. Likes swimming and is interested in skiing.

4 You have received the letter opposite from the classmate of your friend's penpal. Write back giving similar details about yourself and answering the questions asked.

5 Your teacher wants to send off a photograph of your class to your link school in France. She asks you all to write about yourselves in French under the following headings:

- Name   - Age   - Likes   - Dislikes   - Ambitions

so that she can send this information with the photo. Do not write more than about 100 words.

6 You have received the name of Marie-Claire Latallette from your teacher as someone who wants a penfriend. You know nothing about her. Write and introduce yourself and ask her some questions about herself.

7 You decide to send a photo of your family to your penfriend. Write a few lines in French about each person who appears on the photo. Use headings such as:

- Moi   - Mon père   - Ma mère

8 Your penfriend will be arriving at Manchester airport in ten days time. Unfortunately, you have a music exam that day so cannot meet him. Write a brief letter explaining the problem and saying that your uncle will meet him from the plane (give time and date). Describe your uncle so that your penfriend will recognise him.

9 You are staying with a penfriend and are spending some time at school with him/her. You decide to conduct a survey amongst the pupils in your penfriend's class. You have decided on the following headings for what you want to know:

- Name
- Age
- Address
- Number of brothers
- Number of sisters
- Their names and ages
- Likes
- Dislikes
- Sports played
- Future ambitions

Prepare the list of questions you will ask.

Carcassone le dix octobre

Chère amie,

Ma copine florence qui correspond avec ta camarade Katie m'a donné ton nom et ton adresse en me disant que tu cherchais une correspondante française.

Je m'appelle Nathalie forestier et j'ai 14 ans ½. J'habite Carcassone 10 Boulevard du château. J'ai deux frères, Bernard qui a 18 ans et Jérôme qui a 13 ans. Mes soeurs Catherine et Chantal sont jumelles ; elles ont 16 ans. As-tu des frères et des soeurs?

Nous habitons une grande maison avec 5 chambres en haut et un salon, une salle à manger et une cuisine en bas ainsi qu'un bureau pour papa. Nous avons aussi un grand jardin.

J'adore nager et faire de la danse. J'aime aussi les animaux. Je n'aime pas trop l'école. Comme sports, j'aime le volley-ball et le tennis. Et toi? Qu'est-ce que tu aimes faire? Est-ce que tu aimes l'école?

J'espère qu'on va correspondre. Veux-tu m'envoyer une photo de toi s'il te plaît!

A bientôt,

Nathalie.

IN THE PEMBROKESHIRE COAST NATIONAL PARK

Only yards from the Coast Path and beautiful sandy cove

Camrose **MARINERS' INN** 710469

AA & RAC ★★

Quality Bar Meals daily

A la Carte Restaurant

2 Bars overlooking bay

Children's Room

Traditional Sunday lunch

CAMRA - Good Beer Guide
Les Routiers - Good Food Guide
Morning coffee, Cream teas

RESIDENTIAL
All rooms en suite
with colour television

Peter, Margaret, Nick
Skudder

THE VILLAGE SHOP

General Store and Off-Licence

Groceries and Provisions

Gifts, Souvenirs, Post-cards,

Beachwear, Ice-cream, Gift shop

200 yards from sea

Maureen and Dave
Canton

710298

ATTRACTIVE

HOLIDAY BUNGALOWS

on
FOLKESTON HILL
for
Holidays & Weekend
breaks

400 yds from the sea
and beach.

Perfect for walking the Coastal Path, bird-watching, riding, surfing, visiting offshore Islands, pub-lunching or relaxing on lovely sandy beaches.

Ken and Pam Miller

Haverfordwest 2093

NOLTON HAVEN

NOLTON HAVEN FARM
710263

Accommodation in double, family and single bedrooms. Just yards from sandy beach. Sports facilities. Pets welcome. Open all year. Horse riding holidays.

Jim and Joyce Canton

NOLTON HAVEN COTTAGES

30 yards from sandy beach
Fully equipped, open plan
two bedrooms
shwr/bath.

Open all year

Dave & Jim
Canton
710263

BOAT HIRE

Mirror,

canoes,

fishing, etc.

from

Capt. Kenyon.

******

HOLIDAY COTTAGE AND BUNGALOWS

in a rural location
in the heart of
the national park.

Anne Kenyon 710621

Folkeston Hill Farm,
Folkeston Hill.

NOLTON CHILDREN'S PLAYGROUND

ART & CRAFTS EXHIBITION
Nolton Church Schoolroom
From 24th July to 10th August
Open daily from 10 a.m.

SPORTS & SANDCASTLES
For all the family Tuesday 5th August
Sandcastles a.m.
Sports p.m.

NOLTON HAVEN UR CHURCH
Sunday — see notice board
Rev. E. Jones

EAST NOLTON RIDING SCHOOL

John and Ruth Owen
710360

Experienced riders
and beginners welcome.

Hourly and ½ day rides.

Riding holidays for all
with accommodation available.

Beach side cottage.

P.O.B. and BSHAI staff.

C.C. site for members.
Listed C.L.

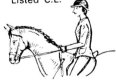

ST MADOC'S CHURCH IN WALES
Sunday 9.30 a.m.
Rev. A. Craven.

ON THE PEMBROKESHIRE COAST PATH   Telephone Exchange — CAMROSE

10 You decide to write and tell your penfriend a little about an area you will be visiting when she comes to stay with you in the near future. Use the details on the brochure opposite to help you.

11 Get some information about your *own* home town and region and write giving a penfriend details about it.

MULTI-SKILL TASK

In the French magazine to which your school subscribes you see this advertisement for a penfriend agency.

1 You decide to write off requesting information and an application form.

2 This form is returned to you and you complete it and send it off.

"LES AMIS PAR LETTRES"

Tu cherches un correspondant/une correspondante? Alors, nous, on peut t'aider.

On a des centaines de jeunes gens dans beaucoup de pays et partout en France qui désirent correspondre avec quelqu'un de sympa—peut-être toi! Ecris-nous pour demander un dossier à remplir et pour nous envoyer 10F d'inscription. On te mettra en contact avec le correspondant/la correspondante que tu cherches.

"Les Amis par lettres", 19 boulevard de Saumur, 75100 PARIS

"LES AMIS PAR LETTRE"

Demande de Correspondance

Nom _____

Prénom(s) _____

Adresse _____

Ville/code postal _____

Date de naissance _____

Ce que tu aimes faire _____

_____

_____

_____

Ce que tu n'aimes pas faire _____

_____

_____

Signé _____

le _____

---

3 After a while you receive a cassette from a prospective penfriend.
Having listened to it you decide to write/send a cassette back to her. Make sure that you give plenty of information about yourself and answer any questions asked.

Fais comme chez toi

 LISTENING

1 Your penfriend's family is going to move to a new flat. Whilst you are staying with them your penfriend shows you a plan of the new flat and describes what each room will be used for. On your copy of the plan you mark, in English, what each room is so that you can send the plan home to your mother.

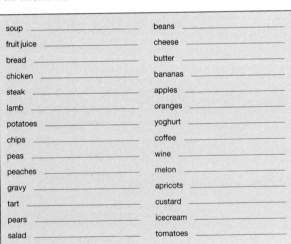

front door

2 You receive a cassette letter from your penfriend on which each member of his family introduces him/herself. Your parents want to know a bit more about them all too, so you make notes under the following headings to help you remember all the details:

- Name
- Age
- Relationship to penfriend
- What he/she does

3 You are staying in your penfriend's house and are finding everything a bit confusing at first. During dinner on the first evening your penfriend and his parents offer you various items of food. Listen carefully to what they say and then, on your copy of the list of food, tick what you think you heard.

soup		beans	
fruit juice		cheese	
bread		butter	
chicken		bananas	
steak		apples	
lamb		oranges	
potatoes		yoghurt	
chips		coffee	
peas		wine	
peaches		melon	
gravy		apricots	
tart		custard	
pears		icecream	
salad		tomatoes	

4 The first evening at your penfriend's house you did not eat much. Your penfriend's mother is worried and checks with you what food you like. Listen to what she says and jot down in English the names of the various foods she asks you about.

5 Your penfriend has just arrived to stay with you and your father is anxious to establish exactly what she likes to eat. You have asked her about various foods which your father has suggested. Mark on your copy of the chart, for your father's benefit, whether she likes each of the items very much, a little or not at all. If there are any other bits of information jot those down too.

Food	Likes a lot	A little	Not at all	Other information
soups				
chicken				
beef				
green veg.				
other veg.				
fruit				
cakes				
biscuits				
fruit tart				
cheese				
pasta				
stew				
rice				

6 Your penfriend and his sister are discussing what they will do on Wednesday afternoon when they are free. As the plans include you too, you listen carefully to the conversation and to what your penfriend tells you of what has been decided. You make a few notes to help you remember what has been planned. Make the notes under these headings:

- Time   - Place   - Activity   - Other information

7 Your penfriend's sister is extremely popular. Whilst in France you are alone in the flat one afternoon when she receives no fewer than five phone calls. You take the messages to pass on to her. Make the notes in English.

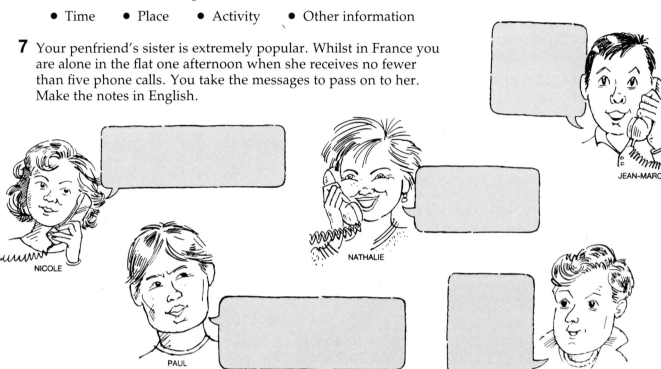

NICOLE

PAUL

NATHALIE

JEAN-MARC

PHILIPPE

8 You are staying with your penfriend. One morning she is not feeling very well so her father decides to take her to the doctor. As the rest of the family are all out your penfriend's father asks you to stay in the flat, in case the TV repairer comes. He does and so do several other people. Jot down the information to give your penfriend's father when he comes back.

Caller	Message
1 TV Repairer	
2	
3	
4	
5	

9 Whilst your penfriend is staying with you her mother phones. Unfortunately your penfriend has gone out with your parents to do 'late-night' shopping at the supermarket. You explain to her mother and offer to take a message.

10 Whilst staying with your penfriend you hear the following news item on the early news. Realising that it refers to the town where you are, you hastily jot down the details to tell your penfriend who is still asleep.

11 Whilst you are staying with your penfriend a few of her friends come round one evening. Whilst they are talking the conversation turns to the problems of young people. This sounds a lot like some of the things which concern you so you listen in. Later you write to your sister and in the letter you tell her what was discussed. Write that part of the letter.

💬 SPEAKING

1 1 Working with a partner greet each other and ask after each other's health. You could say something like this:

—Bonjour John.
—Bonjour Mary, ça va?
—Ça va bien merci et toi?
—Ah oui ça va bien.

2 Turn and each of you do the same thing with each of another pair.

3 Get up and greet as many people as you possibly can.

4 Introduce your partner to each of the other pair in your group. You could say something like this:

You   Kate, je te présente mon amie Mary. Mary, voici Kate.
Kate   Bonjour, Mary ça va?
Mary   Bonjour, Kate, oui ça va bien et toi?
Kate   Ça va bien merci.

5 Now move around the room introducing your partner to as many people as possible.

2 Work in a group with three other people.

1 You arrive at your penfriend's home and he/she introduces you to his/her parents. Take it in turns within your group to take each role. Don't forget to use M. and Mme and use the 'vous' form.

2 Your penfriend introduces you to other members of the family. Take it in turns within the group to play each role. Use 'vous' to adults and 'tu' to other young people.

3 You are at breakfast in your penfriend's home. Your partner will play the part of your penfriend. Working with the cards your teacher gives you, ask your penfriend to pass you various items e.g. the bread, butter, sugar, jam and coffee. Don't forget to say please and thank you. Now swap roles.

4 Work in a group with four or five people.

You are at lunch in your penfriend's home with him/her and other members of the family. Decide who is to play which role i.e. British person, penfriend, mother, father, brother, sister etc. Using the cards your teacher gives you ask each other to pass various items e.g. bread, salt, meat, chips, peas etc.

You may like to draw some cards of your own to extend the number of things you ask for. Remember to be very polite.

5 This game is played like 'Happy Families' with at least four people. There are eight meals and four pieces of information on each (you may only ask for an item for a meal if you hold the master card for that meal). The first player asks any one of the others something like ''Passe-moi le poulet s'il te plaît''. If the

---

> **Remember!**
>
> - Always shake hands when greeting each other.
> - Use the 'vous' form to your teacher as you would to any adult whom you do not know well.

answer is "oui bien sûr" the chicken must be handed over and the first player can ask for something else. If the answer is "Non, je regrette mais je n'en ai pas" then that player has a turn. The winner is the person with most 'meals' at the end of the game.

6 Whilst you are staying with a penfriend from your link school you spend time at the school. As you come out of class one day you are stopped by a younger child who explains that he is doing a survey about family life in England and would like to ask you some questions. You agree. Your partner will play the role of the child and you answer the questions, then swap around.

  1 Où habites-tu?

  2 Combien y a-t-il dans ta famille?

  3 Nomme les membres de ta famille.

  4 Comment est ta maison?

  5 Décris ta chambre.

  6 Qu'est-ce que tu manges le soir chez toi?

  7 Qu'est-ce que tu manges pour le petit déjeuner?

  8 Que fais-tu d'habitude le soir?

  9 As-tu des animaux domestiques?

  10 Raconte un dimanche typique chez toi.

7 You have arrived at your penfriend's house and his father is showing you round. On the plan provided mark the names of the rooms mentioned. Your partner will play the part of your penfriend's father. Then swap round and you play the role of the father. Don't forget that:

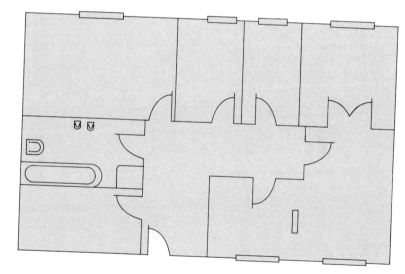

  • You can describe the flat any way you like.

  • You would probably address your penfriend's father as 'vous'.

8 Play this game in a group of about six people. Everyone should throw a dice in turn.

  1 Each person should give as many items of information about where they live as the number they throw. See how many 'rounds' you can do before someone runs out of information.

  2 Each person should give information about their daily routine. Proceed as above.

9 **1** Here are two photos belonging to an English boy called Darren Hartfield. Pretend that you are Darren and that your partner is Darren's penfriend. Describe the house and the family. Make up any details you need.

2 Using some photos of your family that you have brought in, show them to a partner and explain who the people are. You could say things like "Voici mon frère, Michael. Il a 14 ans". Then look at your partner's photos. You could ask questions like "Qui est-ce?", "Quel âge a-t-il/elle?" etc.

3 If you have a photo of your house describe that to your partner too. You could say things like "Ça, c'est la fenêtre de ma chambre", "Ma chambre est assez grande" etc. If you don't have a photo draw a rough sketch and use it in the same way.

10 You are staying with a French family and you find that you need certain things. You ask your penfriend's mother. Your partner will play the mother.

You	Your Penfriend's Mother
1 Say excuse me but you need a towel.	Say certainly and apologise.
Say it doesn't matter and thank her very much.	
2 Say excuse me but you're cold in bed and could you have another blanket.	
	Say of course and agree that it is cold now. Give him/her a blanket.

Now make up a few requests of your own and try out the dialogue. Remember to take it in turns to play each role.

11 Your penfriend has been asked to do a survey about domestic routine in Britain. He sends you a list of the questions he wants answered. You decide to be very helpful and interview at least five people on his behalf. Here are the questions he wants you to ask:

1 A quelle heure te lèves-tu le matin?

2 A quelle heure te couches-tu le soir?

3 Où mangez-vous d'habitude, à la cuisine, dans la salle à manger ou dans la salle de séjour?

4 Est-ce que ta famille regarde souvent la télévision?

5 Quels programmes préfères-tu?

6 Quels programmes préfèrent tes parents?

7 Est-ce que tu sors souvent le soir (a) pendant la semaine (b) le week-end?

Remember!

- You may need to modify the questions if you are asking your teacher or the assistant.
- Record the assistant's answers separately as he or she is not British.

8 Est-ce que tes parents travaillent? Si oui, quel travail font-ils?

9 Est-ce que toi, tu travailles à temps partiel?

10 Est-ce que vous sortez souvent en famille?

Make a note of the answers you are given. Interview at least five people, more if you have time, and allow yourself to be interviewed too.

12 See how well you can express a point of view in French. Take a topic such as 'Les jeunes gens aujourd'hui sont paresseux' or 'Pour ou contre le divorce'. With a partner discuss the topic trying to each take a different point of view. Your teacher will help you think up topics. You could then discuss the topic in a group and perhaps eventually have a mini-debate as a class.

READING

1 You are going to France to stay with a penfriend. In one of his letters he sends you this plan of his flat with all the rooms labelled and a brief note under it.

As you are writing to your grandmother you decide to send a copy of the plan with the rooms labelled in English. Also tell your grandmother what your penfriend noted under the plan.

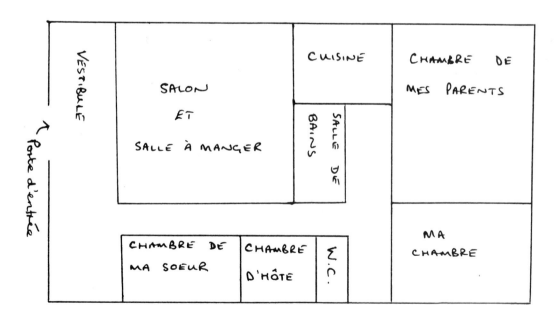

Voici un plan de notre appartement. Tu vas avoir la chambre d'hôte mais si tu préfères on peut partager la mienne (j'ai ma télé à moi dans la chambre - c'est super! La musique pop tous les soirs!)

2 You receive the following letter from a penfriend telling you about his daily routine. As you are making a folder at school about French Daily Life you make some notes under the following headings in order to write it up.

- Time he gets up, goes to school, has meals
- Parents' activities, his after-school activities
- How the family spends the evening

Lille le 6 mars.

Chère Caroline,

dans ta dernière lettre tu m'as demandé ce que je fais pendant mes journées. alors voilà:

En général, le matin je me lève à 7 heures et demie. Une heure plus tard, je pars à l'école en vélo.

Je prends mes repas à la cantine à midi car mes parents travaillent tous les deux. Mon père est professeur et ma mère est architecte. L'après-midi, après l'école, comme mes parents rentrent assez tard, je reste avec mon amie Laurence. Nous faisons du théâtre ensemble. Nous sommes dans un groupe théâtral et nous montons une pièce que nous avons écrite.

Nous passons la soirée en famille. Nous ne regardons pas la télé puisque nous l'avons cassée, il y a trois mois; et nous n'avons pas pensé à la faire réparer. Nous lisons, nous causons et nous jouons aux cartes. Bien sûr j'ai mes devoirs à faire aussi.

Voilà. Dis moi ce que tu fais, toi aussi.

A Bientôt.

Pierre.

causer to chat

3 You are staying with your penfriend in France. His brother comes home with this piece of advertising. He tries to persuade you and your penfriend to join him at the gymnasium. You read the information in order to decide if it appeals to you. Make some notes by answering the following questions.

1 Where is the gymnasium?

2 When is it open (a) during the week (b) at the weekend?

3 Which activities are you told will take place in a group?

4 Your penfriend's brother is interested in body-building. Would he do this in a group?

5 You have always wanted to try out an exercise bike. Is there provision for this?

6 Will you have to pay individually for each activity?

les conseils advice
le cours lesson
une carte membership card

PENSEZ FORT PENSEZ FORME!

YOGA, VÉLOS SANTÉ, MASSAGES MÉCANIQUES, SAUNA, HAMMAM, BAIN CALIFORNIEN, DOUCHE HYDROTHERAPIQUE, ROCK, MODERN JAZZ, BODY-BUILDING, GYMNASTIQUE AEROBIQUE (cours collectifs), GYMNASTIQUE TRADITIONNELLE (cours collectifs), SALLES DE MUSCULATION (conseils personnalisés), STRETCHING, TAI JI TSU, BOXE FRANÇAISE.

Nous serons heureux de vous accueillir de 9 h à 21 h non-stop du lundi au vendredi et de 9 h à 18 h le samedi

SANTÉ

14, Rue de Paris   DIJON

4 Your penfriend's older sister has now finished her training as a secretary and has quite a well-paid job. She is looking to her future. She brings home some leaflets from the *Crédit Agricole de l'Isère* which talk about loans. She shows you the information. As you are studying economics for your exams you make some notes about the information.

1 She is thinking of buying a car. How is it suggested she might find the car she wants?

2 How could the loan system help her in her plans for a winter sports holiday?

3 She is hoping to find her own flat. How would the loan plan help her there?

4 What should she do if she does want to borrow money?

O.K. POUR O.K. POUR LE PRET LE PRET

AUTO-MOTO   LOISIRS

DEMARRAGE DANS LA VIE

Quand on est jeune, on a des projets plein la tête.

Pour passer du rêve à la réalité en tenant compte des nécessités…

Alors… OK POUR LE PRÊT* !

Venez nous en parler.

PRÊTS JEUNES
CRÉDIT AGRICOLE DE L'ISÈRE

* PRÊTS AFFECTÉS.

PRÊTS JEUNES
CRÉDIT AGRICOLE DE L'ISÈRE

PRÊT AUTO-MOTO
D'occasion ou neuve, elle sera bientôt à vous. Vous l'avez trouvée chez un garagiste, dans les petites annonces ou par l'intermédiaire d'un copain.
Vous serez prochainement en possession de cette voiture ou de cette moto, sans mettre vos économies en péril… sans attendre… grâce au PRÊT AUTO MOTO qui vous aidera à la financer.
Votre voiture ou votre moto sera d'ici peu garée devant votre porte.

PRÊT LOISIRS
Si vous êtes une véliplanchiste acharnée, un mélomane averti, un amateur de sports d'hiver, LE PRÊT LOISIRS a été conçu spécialement pour vous.
Ce prêt vous permettra de disposer d'une somme d'argent destinée à vous offrir l'équipement de vos rêves et donc de profiter ainsi pleinement de votre temps libre !

PRÊT DEMARRAGE DANS LA VIE
Vous avez trouvé l'appartement ou le studio de vos rêves, ou bien vous êtes déjà installé chez vous, mais vous souhaitez acquérir le canapé, le réfrigérateur ou le mobilier qui vous manque.
Pour vivre indépendant, en toute liberté, facilement et rapidement… LE PRÊT DEMARRAGE DANS LA VIE, vous aidera à financer les frais occasionnés par votre installation ou par l'amélioration de votre intérieur.

le prêt   loan
les petites annonces   small ads
les loisirs   leisure or free time
le mobilier   furniture
acquérir   to acquire

5 Whilst on a business trip to France your father bought some carwash. Back at home he asks you to wash his car. You read the instructions on the bottle.

1 What proportions of carwash to water do you want?

2 What three stages do you have to carry out?

3 What must you avoid when washing the car?

4 What particular safety precautions should you take?

5 From whom should you keep the product?

6 You are staying with your penfriend's family in France. They have all gone off to a friend's wedding. You are not feeling well and have stayed behind. The cat keeps crying and you realise that she has not been fed. You find a fresh packet of cat food and prepare to feed the cat.

1 How much food should you give her?

2 Where should you put the packet once it has been opened?

3 What else must you give the cat?

SHAMPOOING AUTO

Produit destiné au nettoyage des carrosseries.

Mode d'emploi:

S'utilise mélangé à l'eau (1 cuillère à soupe pour 5 litres d'eau).
Nettoyer la carrosserie au moyen d'une éponge trempée dans le mélange.
Rincer ensuite à grande eau.
Essuyer à la peau de chamois.

Précautions d'emploi:

Ne pas laver la voiture au soleil.
Pour les sièges et housses en plastique, imbiber une éponge humide de shampooing et essuyer avec un chiffon sec.

ATTENTION: *le produit non dilué peut irriter les yeux. En cas de contact, laver abondamment à l'eau et consulter un médecin.*

TENIR HORS DE PORTÉE DES ENFANTS.
Taux de biodégradabilité supérieur à 90%.

la carrosserie   body work
un mélange   mixture
une éponge   sponge
la peau   skin, hide

Friskies au Poulet

Les croquettes pour chats préparées avec des morceaux de viandes.

Les chats raffolent de la viande. Pour eux Friskies a mis au point ces succulentes croquettes. Elles sont préparées avec des morceaux de viandes mélangés à des céréales, des sels minéraux et des vitamines.

Grâce à ce procédé de fabrication, les croquettes Friskies constituent un aliment complet et équilibré au délicieux goût de viandes.

Parce que votre chat aime aussi croquer, et que c'est bon pour lui, les croquettes Friskies ont une forme et une taille spécialement étudiées. Elles sont ainsi délicieusement croustillantes.

—— mode d'emploi ——

Les quantités journalières conseillées pour un chat adulte de 4 kg sont de 70 à 85 g (une assiette bien pleine). Ces quantités suffisent à satisfaire tous ses besoins nutritionnels. Un paquet de 400 g représente 5 à 6 repas pour un chat adulte de 4 kg. Une fois ouvert, s'il est bien fermé et placé dans un endroit frais et sec, le paquet peut se conserver pendant plusieurs semaines. Les croquettes étant une nourriture sèche, il est indispensable que votre chat boive beaucoup.
Veillez bien à ce qu'il ait toujours à proximité de son assiette un bol d'eau fraîche ou de lait. La plupart des chats raffolent de cette nourriture croustillante. Si le vôtre n'est pas habitué à cette alimentation, accoutumez-le en mélangeant les croquettes Friskies à sa nourriture habituelle pendant une quinzaine de jours.

journalier   daily
conseiller   to recommend
frais/fraîche   cool, fresh

7 Whilst you are staying with your penfriend in France you get your new jeans very dirty. As it is a lovely day you want to wash them and hang them out to dry. Your penfriend's mother leaves you these instructions for the use of the washing machine.

Branche la machine
Jets le tuyau dans l'évier
Jets un goblet de poudre dans le tiroir de la machine compartiment 3.
Tourne le bouton au n°4 et retire-le.
Quand la machine s'arrête attends 2 minutes avant d'ouvrir la porte.

1 What must you do first?
2 Where does the waste pipe go?
3 How much washing powder will you need?
4 What do you do after turning the knob to No.4?
5 What must you do before opening the door?

brancher to plug in and switch on
retirer to pull out

8 Whilst you are staying with your penfriend in France it has been arranged that you will all go with his mother to a place called Pra-Loup where she will be attending a medical conference. Your penfriend shows you the programme for the conference. You write to tell your parents all about it and so make some notes to help you.

1 What sporting activity will you be undertaking for most of your stay?
2 When will your penfriend's mother be able to join you?
3 Where can you get the necessary equipment?
4 What kinds of activities are organised during the stay?
5 Would you need to pay full price for the chair-lift?
6 Your party will consist of your penfriend's parents, your penfriend and yourself. Assuming that your penfriend's parents have a few days to spare before the conference starts, where would be the best place to stay?
7 At the end of the conference your penfriend's parents are anxious to get home before Sunday. Why do you think this is?

sur place on the spot
une ballade excursion
une remontée ski-lift

CHANGEZ DE **MEDECINE**

PRA Loup
ALPES DE HAUTE PROVENCE
DU 12 AU 15 MARS 1986

4èmes **Rencontres Thérapeutiques**
Les Médecines Naturelles au service des Traumatismes
Conférences et travaux pratiques

AGENDA

MERCREDI 12 MARS 1986	JEUDI 13 MARS 1986	VENDREDI 14 MARS 1986	SAMEDI 15 MARS 1986
9	9	10 _Séances de travail (avec pauses)_	9
10	10 _Séances de travail_	11	10
11	11	12	11
12 _Départ pour Praloup_	12	13	12
13	13	14	13
14	14 _Ski_	15 _Animation Ballades_	14 _Voter demain ??_
15	15	16 _Ski de fond_	15
16	16 _Séances de travail_	17	16
17	17	18	17
18	18	19	18
19 _Cocktail de Bienvenue_	19	20 _Remise des prix Repas de Gala_	19
20	20 _Dîner_		20

QUELQUES RENSEIGNEMENTS

TRANSFERT :
Possibilité de navette entre Gap et Pra-Loup.

HEBERGEMENT :
Choix d'hôtel ou de studio allant de F 450 à F 700 par personne pour 3 nuits, petit déjeuner inclus. Possibilité de louer des studios pour 4 personnes du 8 au 15 mars pour F 1.450.

FRAIS DE PARTICIPATION :
Ils sont fixés à F 800 par Congressiste (comprenant le droit d'accès à toutes les séances, travaux pratiques et pauses).

ANIMATION :
Diverses animations seront proposées durant le séjour, avec moniteurs, slaloms, jeux organisés, ballades, leçons pour débutants, encadrement enfants, etc.
Remontées gratuites pour les Congressistes et importantes réductions pour les Accompagnants.

EQUIPEMENT :
Location de matériel sur place (skis, chaussures, bâtons, etc.).
Conditions avantageuses réservées aux Congressistes et Accompagnants aux Rencontres Thérapeutiques.

9 Your penfriend's parents have come into some money. They decide to place it in a savings account which will later enable them to borrow money for things they need. They show you some of the information they have. You rather like the look of this one and compare it with what you know of English mortgage accounts.

1 How much will they need to open an account?

2 On what condition do they draw money out?

3 How much tax-free interest does the account attract?

4 What is the maximum they can hold in the account?

5 How long will it be before they can borrow money?

6 How much can they borrow?

7 Name three improvements to their property they could finance in this way.

8 Your penfriend's parents want to buy a holiday home. Can they borrow money for this purpose?

9 If *they* decide not to borrow money who else could?

10 What is the only condition of this?

Compte Epargne Logement

Pour mieux vivre,
pour améliorer plus vite votre confort,
ouvrez un Compte Epargne-Logement
au Crédit Agricole de l'Isère.
Au bout de 18 mois seulement,
il vous permet d'obtenir un prêt immobilier
à un taux très avantageux.

une formule pratique

● Vous faites un premier dépôt de 750 F.
● Vous pouvez procéder à tout moment,
soit à des versements,
soit à des retraits (le solde de votre compte doit rester supérieur à 750 F).
● Vous profitez ainsi d'une épargne toujours disponible et rémunérée.

un placement intéressant

qui vous rapporte 5,50 % exonérés d'impôts*, c'est-à-dire :
● un intérêt de 3,25 % net
● et une prime d'épargne de 2,25 % nette, égale au montant des intérêts en cas de demande et d'obtention de prêt. Cette prime peut atteindre 7500 F.
● Vous pouvez épargner jusqu'à 100 000 F.

un prêt pour votre logement

18 mois après l'ouverture de votre compte :
● Vous pouvez obtenir pour votre logement un prêt proportionnel à votre épargne.
● à un faible taux : 4,75 % (frais de gestion compris)*, pour une durée de 2 à 15 ans.
● Vous pouvez emprunter jusqu'à 150 000 F.

de nombreuses utilisations

● Vous pouvez utiliser le prêt immobilier
  - pour acquérir une résidence principale ou aménager la vôtre :
    • réfection d'une toiture
    • mise en place du chauffage central
    • installation d'une salle de bain...
  - pour financer une résidence secondaire (sous certaines conditions).
● Si vous n'utilisez pas votre prêt, vous pouvez céder vos droits à vos enfants ou à un membre de votre famille s'ils possèdent déjà un Compte Epargne-Logement ou un Plan Epargne-Logement.

Taux au 1er Août 1985

Septembre 1985

le solde   balance
exonérés d'impôts   tax-free
emprunter   to borrow
épargner   to save
céder les droits   to surrender rights

10 Whilst you are staying with a penfriend in France this piece of publicity from the French Post Office arrives. You read it and are very interested in what is being done to help people and to combat vandalism and theft. You decide to mention some of this in your next letter home. Make the following notes to help you remember details.

1 What two things are being done to help combat unemployment?

2 What three services are available in 1986 to old people?

3 What is being done about (a) vandalism (b) hold-ups?

4 What special pieces of equipment are available to help (a) the visually handicapped (b) the hard of hearing?

5 Out of all the helpful services offered by the PTT which would you consider the most useful and why?

Solidarité **S**et sécurité avec les PTT

Les 20 mesures et programmes mis en oeuvre depuis 1981

Contre le chômage:

• les 21 800 agents nouveaux en fonction aux PTT;
• les 4 000 jeunes employés à des travaux d'utilité collective (TUC) d'ici la fin de l'année dans le cadre des associations et sociétés mutualistes des PTT.

Pour les personnes âgées:

• La création du service de téléalarme publique. 2 500 personnes âgées, isolées ou malades bénéficient ainsi d'une sécurité renforcée. Plus de 10 000 transmetteurs pourront être mis en service par les PTT en 1986 dont 7 500 avec télécommandes radio. Un simple geste et la personne en difficulté entre en liaison avec le centre de secours chargé d'intervenir rapidement.
• Le poste téléphonique à 2 boutons... une pression sur l'un de ces boutons vous met directement en relation avec l'un ou l'autre des 2 correspondants de votre choix.
• le maintien et le développement de toutes les prestations de la poste au domicile des usagers, notamment des mandats et versement des pensions. La poste est le seul établissement financier français qui rend ces services, indispensables à nos concitoyens âgés, malades, handicapés ou isolés.

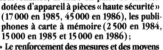

Face au vandalisme et aux agressions:

• la campagne d'information nationale par affichage contre le vandalisme grandissant dont font l'objet les cabines de téléphone public, a été diffusée sur tout le territoire;
• la protection des publiphones avec notamment le renvoi d'alarme, la télésurveillance, la mise en place de cabines dotées d'appareil à pièces «haute sécurité» (17 000 en 1985, 45 000 en 1986), les publiphones à carte à mémoire (2 500 en 1984, 15 000 en 1985 et 15 000 en 1986);
• Le renforcement des mesures et des moyens de sécurité dans les bureaux de poste: aujourd'hui une grande majorité de guichets est dotée d'une protection renforcée. Des liaisons instantanées sont établies avec la police ou la gendarmerie. Les locaux détenant des fonds sont systématiquement munis de caméras automatiques et de systèmes sophistiqués anti-effraction.
• le renouvellement complet du parc de véhicules destinés aux transports de fonds de la Poste.

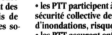

En direction des handicapés:

• Le recrutement et l'insertion des travailleurs handicapés: ils sont plus de 2 000 aujourd'hui alors qu'ils n'étaient que 250 en 1981;
• l'aménagement systématique des accès aux bureaux des PTT nouvellement construits ou rénovés et l'implantation de 3 000 cabines téléphoniques spéciales;

• les 40 000 avertisseurs lumineux couplés avec la sonnerie du téléphone, les 30 000 disques à gros chiffres, les cadrans à repères en braille, les 135 000 capsules et les 50 000 combinés téléphoniques pour malentendants, etc.;
• le minitel «dialogue» qui permet aux sourds et aux handicapés de la parole de communiquer par écrit ou en phonie avec toute autre personne disposant d'un minitel ordinaire.
• la rédaction des chèques par les non-voyants: 2 guides, l'un en plastique, l'autre métallique comportant des lignes en relief délimitant les emplacements à remplir, sont actuellement testés. La poste remet gratuitement des «guide-mains» aux titulaires de CCP;
• le sous-titrage de plus en plus d'émissions de télévision pour les mal-entendants grâce au système «Antiope» mis en œuvre par TDF.

Pour l'accueil du public:

• la levée de l'anonymat des agents: désormais les agents des PTT indiquent leur nom sur les correspondances, les affaires traitées et au guichet. Un badge ou un chevalet nominatif permet aux usagers d'identifier leur interlocuteur dans les services qui reçoivent le public;
• la possibilité de se faire appeler dans une cabine téléphonique: 160 000 sur 170 000, soit 95 %, sont aujourd'hui équipées d'un numéro d'appel;
• les bureaux de poste de l'an 2 000: sur le modèle de celui inauguré à Mézidon en 1984, les nouveaux bureaux de poste sont entièrement conçus pour faciliter l'accueil des usagers et garantir leur sécurité comme celle des agents des PTT.

Au service du pays:

• les PTT participent à des missions nationales de sécurité civile: sécurité collective des populations habitant les zones à risques d'inondations, risques d'incendies et à proximité des barrages;
• les PTT assurent enfin par l'intermédiaire des stations côtières les liaisons téléphoniques, télégraphiques et télex entre les abonnés à terre et les marins en mer. Les télécommunications contribuant ainsi à la sauvegarde des vies humaines: diffusion d'informations urgentes et de bulletins météorologiques, veille permanente sur les fréquences de sécurité, et transmission des appels de détresse et alerte.

Denis-Beaumont et Associés conseil en stratégie de communication Imprimé en France par J. Didier

Agence Commerciale des Télécommunications de Courbevoie

---

le chômage unemployment	*une effraction* break-in	*un usager* user
une prestation benefit, allowance	*l'aménagement* equipping	*l'accueil* welcome
l'affichage the posting of notices	*avertir* to warn	*une inondation* flood
la mise en place positioning	*sourd* deaf	*un incendie* fire
le renforcement intensification	*la rédaction* writing, drawing up	*un barrage* dam
dôté(e) supplied with	*la levée* removal	*un abonné* subscriber
les fonds funds, money	*désormais* from now on	*une veille* watch

11 Whilst you are staying with your penfriend in France some information about the forthcoming elections arrives. Amongst the papers is a booklet on the electoral system which is aimed at young people who are going to vote for the first time. You read the booklet and are particularly interested by the last page which explains the French system of proportional representation quite simply. As your sister is studying electoral reform in one of her examination courses you decide to write and tell her about this system.

un siège   seat
un suffrage   vote
un bulletin de vote   voting slip
pourvoir   to provide for
la répartition   distribution
la moyenne   the average

annexe
exemple concret de répartition des sièges
pour un arrondissement de 75 000 habitants

Imaginons un arrondissement de 75 000 habitants, avec 49 sièges à pourvoir. Sur 30 275 suffrages exprimés (le total des bulletins de vote d'où l'on retire les bulletins blancs ou nuls):
● la liste A obtient 18 240 voix (60,2 %)
● la liste B obtient 5 489 voix (18,1 %)
● la liste C obtient 6 546 voix (21,6 %).
La liste A a la majorité absolue des suffrages exprimés. Elle obtient donc la moitié des sièges (arrondie à l'unité supérieure), soit 25 sièges.
Pour procéder ensuite à la "représentation proportionnelle", il faut d'abord déterminer le "quotient électoral". Il est égal au nombre de suffrages exprimés (30 275) divisé par le nombre de sièges qui restent à pourvoir (24). Soit 30 275 : 24 = 1 261.
Pour calculer la répartition des 24 sièges restants entre les trois listes, il suffit maintenant de diviser les voix de chaque liste par le "quotient électoral".
Soit:
● pour la liste A : 18 240 : 1 261 = 14 sièges
● pour la liste B : 5 489 : 1 261 = 4 sièges
● pour la liste C : 6 546 : 1 261 = 5 sièges.
14 + 4 + 5 = 23. Il reste un siège à attribuer. Pour cela, on calcule "la moyenne" de chaque liste en divisant le nombre de ses voix par le nombre de sièges qu'elle a obtenus + 1 (c'est-à-dire le siège restant à pourvoir). Soit:
● liste A : 18 240 : (14 + 1) = 1 216
● liste B : 5 489 : (4 + 1) = 1 097
● liste C : 6 546 : (5 + 1) = 1 091.
La plus forte moyenne est celle de la liste A. Elle obtient donc le dernier siège. En définitive:
● la liste A obtient 40 sièges
● la liste B obtient 4 sièges
● la liste C obtient 5 sièges.

✎ WRITING

1 Your penfriend is coming to stay with you for two weeks and during that time you are spending a few days camping with a friend. Whilst you are planning what you need to take with you, you realise that your penfriend may not bring the necessary equipment. Using the picture of the things you have assembled to help you, make a list of the items your penfriend needs to bring along ready to send off to France.

2 You are sending a photo of your family to your French penfriend. Draw a quick sketch to indicate your family or stick a real photo, if you have one, in your book. Label each person in French e.g. moi, mon père, Roger 9 ans etc.

3 You are writing to your penfriend who is coming to stay with you and you decide to enclose a rough sketch of the layout of your home. Draw this and label the rooms in French.

4 Whilst you are staying with your penfriend, a friend of hers phones to invite you both round for the evening. As the time to leave has come and your penfriend still hasn't come home you decide to go on without her. You leave a note saying where you are, giving the address and asking her to follow on as soon as she can.

5 You are staying with your penfriend in the country in France. You send a postcard to another penfriend in Paris telling him what you are doing. Write the postcard in French saying what time you get up, what the weather is like, that the food is good and adding one or two things that you have been doing.

6 You have just helped your mother to re-decorate your bedroom. In a letter to your penfriend you describe the 'new look' room. Write that part of the letter, in French, and if you like put in a labelled plan of the room.

7 Whilst in France on a visit to your link school, your teacher has asked you to conduct a survey about homes and families. In order to do this, you make up ten questions to ask which would cover the following points:

- Size of family
- Ages of children
- Whether they live in flats or houses
- How much TV they watch
- What time they eat in the evening
- Whether the family returns home for lunch
- What they have for breakfast
- Whether they have a second home in the country, mountains or by the sea

Write out in French the ten questions you would ask.

8 Your class receives a letter from your link school asking for details of television programmes which the British enjoy watching. Each person is asked to write about 100 words in French on their favourite TV programme.

9 Your penfriend will be coming shortly to stay with you and you want to warn her a little of what to expect. Write a letter in French giving details of your family, the kinds of things they like doing and describe a typical weekend at your home. Do not write more than about 200 words.

10 Whilst you are spending a term at your link school in France it is suggested to you that all English families:

- Eat their meals in front of the TV all the time
- Allow the children too much freedom
- Have cats and dogs sleeping on all the beds
- Live in terraced houses
- Eat terrible food

You decide to write an article in French for the school magazine putting the record straight. You can agree or disagree with the points above.

MULTI-SKILL TASK

One morning, whilst you are staying with your penfriend Jean-Pierre, he has to go to the dentist. Everyone else is out and you decide to stay in and read a book. However, your morning is anything but peaceful . . .

1 Suddenly the phone rings and you answer it.

 At each bleep the tape should be stopped and, pretending your partner is the caller, answer the questions. (You can make up any details you like.) You note down any message(s) in French to give to Jean-Pierre.

 2 You settle down to read again when the door bell rings. You answer it and one of the neighbours is there.

You agree to pass the message on and again make a note, in French, for Jean-Pierre's mother.

3 A short while later one of your English friends who is also on an exchange visit comes round and together you start to get things ready for the midday meal, following the instructions left by Jean-Pierre's mother.

Your friend is not very good at French and asks you to tell her what you have to do. Pretend your partner is your friend and explain, in English, what the instructions tell you to do.

1. Éplucher les pommes de terre (à peu près 500g)

2. Les faire sauter dans un peu d'huile pendant 3 ou 4 minutes, puis les mettre de côté.

3. Battre les œufs (6) et les mettre de côté

4. Raper les carrottes et les mélanger avec une vinaigrette.

éplucher to peel
râper to grate
une vinaigrette French salad dressing

3

Vous désirez?

 LISTENING

1 You are waiting to meet a friend in a *brasserie*. As always, you are trying to brush up on your French. You listen attentively to the shouts and requests of the barman, customers etc. Each time you understand, write down in English what has been called for.

2 You are in the cafeteria of a big department store waiting for your penfriend to finish her shopping. You hear the following announcements, and in order to while away the time you jot down roughly what each one was about.

   1 This advertisement was about ....

   2 This advertisement was about ....

   3 .... of all sizes and prices were offered in this advertisement.

   4 People who were going .... would be interested in this advertisement.

   5 .... were offered in this advertisement.

3 During a camping holiday in France, you are waiting one day for your mother in the local market, where she is going to do the shopping. To help her when she arrives, you note down the prices of the fruit and vegetables as they are called out by the various traders.

4 While you are on a visit to a CES in Groffliers, the English Language assistant is trying to raise money for a school day-trip to London. She decides to introduce the French to the idea of jumble sales. You and the teachers are asked to help. Your job is to mark the prices on the labels as one of the teachers calls them to you.

5 Your penfriend's mother asks you to go to the shops for her, since you are to spend the day without your penfriend. Listen as she tells you each of the things that she wants. Make a note of each item and write beside it any particular thing that she says about it.

6 While on a camping holiday in France, you are at the local supermarket buying some groceries. An announcement is repeatedly made over the loudspeaker system, promoting various items. Mark beside your copy of the list the suggested best buys, the quantities you need to buy to benefit from these offers, and the price. (Note that not all the items on your list are mentioned.)

	Name of best buy	Quantity	Price
Milk			
Eggs			
Butter			
Cheese			
Cream			
Parsley			
Yoghurt			
Washing powder			
Bread			
French style sausage			

7 Your French penfriend's mother helps out at a nursery school. You go along with her one day to help and to find out what it's all about. One small group you sit with has been asked 'What is your favourite food?' You make notes of their answers to write up later in your diary.

8 In a department store in Boulogne, you hear the following announcements. You listen carefully to see if you could use any of the special offers. Jot your findings down on your copy of the grid.

	Product	Counter where available
1		
2		
3		
4		
5		

9 You are staying with your penfriend in Amiens. One day you go shopping together and, on your return, you write to your sister telling her about the trip. As you write you think back over some of the conversations you heard in the various shops. Fill in the blanks in your copy of the letter with the help of the cassette.

10 You and your exchange partner's family are discussing which restaurant to visit. For future reference, you note down who favours which one, and which one is finally agreed upon.

11 Your penfriend's father has just opened a small restaurant. He has prepared a radio advertisement mentioning decor, specialities, prices and ambience. He wants your opinion of the advertisement, so you play the tape at your leisure and make notes for yourself in English of what things he has included, what he may have omitted, and what you think of it overall.

Amiens, 29th July

Dear Kate,

Yesterday Chantal and I went shopping. Chantal's grandma in Tours has sent her some money for her birthday and she decided to buy some clothes with it. She had a few problems however. Listen! First we went to the shoeshop. Chantal wanted to buy a pair of _____ just like her friend Florence has got. The salesgirl searched high and low but _____ _____.

Next we went into a really nice boutique which had some stunning skirts in the window in really bright colours. Chantal asked for _____. Unfortunately the salesgirl said _____ _____.

It was the same story in the sports shop next door. Chantal wanted to buy a big, sloppy _____ but, of course, all they had were _____.

In the boutique down the road Chantal fancied _____ _____ but, of course, the answer was _____.

Finally, we ended up at Prisunic, where Chantal wanted _____ and, guess what! _____.

Well, I must dash now. Give my love to everyone.

Daniel

SPEAKING

1 Work in a group. You and some friends are in a café in France. You should take it in turns to play the role of the waiter. Each member of the group in turn asks for a drink and requests the bill. Don't forget that the waiter must ask 'Vous désirez, monsieur/mademoiselle?'

2 Work out these dialogues, with your partner, taking each role in turn.

In the Stationer's

Salesperson	Customer
Say hello and ask what he/she wants.	Say hello. Tell him/her that you want a pen.
Ask what colour.	Answer the question.
Say of course, sir/madam/miss.	

In the Record Shop

Salesperson	Customer
Say hello and ask what he/she wants.	Say hello and you want *Oxygène* by Jean-Michel Jarre.
Ask if he/she wants a record or a cassette.	Answer the question.

Now each of you make up your own dialogue cards and work through each one together. Swap your cards with another pair and work through theirs.

3 Work out these dialogues with your partner, taking each role in turn.

At the Clothes Shop

Salesperson	Customer
Say hello, what do you want?	Say you want a sweater.
Ask what colour.	Answer the question.
Say of course, sir/madam/miss.	

At the Shoe Shop

Salesperson	Customer
Say hello, what do you want?	Say you want a pair of slippers.
Ask what size.	Say you need size 42.
Ask what colour.	Say you'd like blue.
Say you've only got black in a 42.	Say OK, you'll take black.

Now each make up your own dialogue cards and work through them together. Swap your cards with another pair and work through theirs. Do this as many times as you can.

4 Work out this dialogue with your partner, taking each role in turn.

At the Souvenir Shop

Salesperson	Customer
Say hello and ask what he/she wants.	Say you want a scarf with the Eiffel Tower on it.
Ask what colour.	Answer the question.
Ask if it's for a present.	Say it's for your sister. Ask how much it is.
Say it's 25 francs.	Offer 30 francs.
Say here's your change.	

Now each make up your own dialogue cards and work through them together. Swap your cards with another pair and work through theirs. Do this as many times as you can.

5 You are in a grocer's shop, to buy yoghurt. Using the instructions given, talk to the shopkeeper. Your partner will play the part of the shopkeeper; when you have completed the task to your satisfaction, reverse roles. Your teacher will give you the grocer's responses.

Client(e)

Say hello.

Ask if there is any yoghurt.

Tell him/her that you prefer banana flavoured ones.

Say that you'll have strawberry instead.

Say you'll take them, thank him or her, and say goodbye.

6 You and your French friend have been shopping for gifts and you meet at the bus stop. Work with a partner and tell each other what you have bought, from where and for whom. Compare the items using the picture lists to help you. When you have worked through the dialogue once, swap roles.

Now each of you should draw two lots of pictures and discuss them. When you have finished, swap your pictures with another pair.

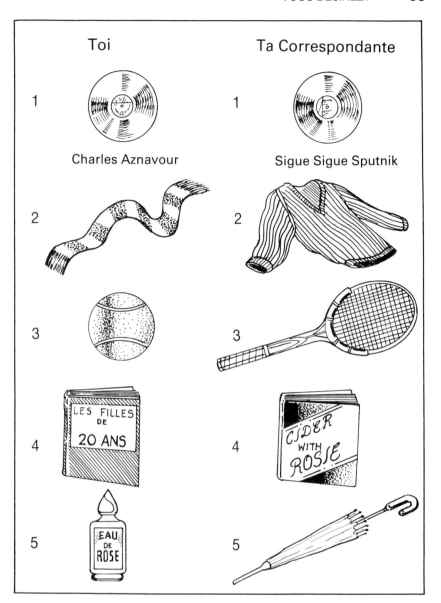

Toi | Ta Correspondante

1 Charles Aznavour — 1 Sigue Sigue Sputnik

2

3

4 LES FILLES DE 20 ANS — 4 CIDER WITH ROSIE

5 EAU DE ROSE — 5

7 You are approached in the street by a market researcher, as being a typical English visitor, and asked questions to help in preparing suitable menus at a nearby restaurant. Answer the questions, which will be asked by your partner, then swap roles.

1 Que pensez-vous de la cuisine française?
2 Que buvez-vous normalement au petit déjeuner?
3 Y a-t-il des plats anglais que vous aimeriez manger en France?
4 Préférez-vous les hors d'œuvres chauds ou froids?
5 Quel hors d'œuvre froid préférez-vous?
6 Comment aimez-vous le steak?
7 Quelles autres viandes aimez-vous?
8 Quels légumes aimez-vous?
9 Comme glace, quel parfum préférez-vous?
10 Chez vous, quand est-ce que vous mangez le fromage?

8 You are staying with your French penfriend. Today everyone is out, but a bank holiday weekend is approaching, and you have been asked to telephone various friends and relations, to ask what they have chosen to eat at a planned restaurant meal.

PIZZA

Pizza napolitaine	23 ✓
Pizza du chef	29 ✓
Pizza capricciosa	28 ✓
Pizza mozzarela	24 ✓
Pizza champignons	24 ✓
Pizza fruits de mer	30 ✓
Pizza Mont-Blanc	24 ✓
Pizza fromage	22 ✓
Pizza aquila	26 ✓
Pizza jambon	24

HORS-D'ŒUVRE

Jambon Parme - melon	50 ✓
Crevettes pescatore	30.00
Crevettes mayonnaise	25.00
Œufs mayonnaise	12.00
Salade de tomates	13.00
Salade niçoise	24.00
Salade verte	12.00
Charcuterie variée	22.00
Jambon de Parme	35.00
Escargots les 6	✓
les 12	✓
Melon au Paro	30.00
Melon nature	22.00

PATES

Chitarra boscaiola	25.00
Spaghetti alla bellanapoli	22.00
Ravioli alla panna	22.00
Spaghetti anchois	20.00
Spaghetti aquilani	20.00
Spaghetti thon	20.00
Spaghetti carbonara	21.00
Spaghetti matriciana	20.00
Lasagna al forno	30 ✓
Canelloni al forno	2f ✓
Pasta alla chitarra	22.00
Fettucine bolognese	22.00
Gnocchi maison sur commande pour 4 pers.	✓
Spaghetti bolognese	20.00
Ravioli bolognese	22.00

GRILLADES

CUISSE DE POULET	28.00
Steak grillé	28.00
Entrecôte grillée	42.00
Filet grillé	44.00
Côte d'agneau	36.00
Brochettes de viande	35.00
Brochettes de rognons	40.00

VIANDES POÊLÉES

ENTRECOTE AU POIVRE vert	50.00
Escalope milanese	38.00
Escalope marsala	40.00
Escalope veneziana	40.00
Filet pizzaiola	46.00
Bocconcini	40.00
Steak pizzaiola	34.00
Escalope du chef	42.00
Filet rossino	✓
Escalope fiorentina	42.00
Escalope genovese	42.00
Médaillon du chef	42.00
COTE DE PORC	31.00

LÉGUMES

Haricots verts	15.00
Tomates provençales	15.00
Champignons sautés	18.00

POISSONS S.A.

Rouget grillé	
Sole meunière	53.00

TOUTES NOS VIANDES SONT GARNIES SPAGHETTI OU FRITES

TOUT CHANGEMENT DE GARNITURE AU PRIX DE LA CARTE

SERVICE COMPRIS

POUR TOUT PAIEMENT PAR CHEQUE

PRESENTATION D'UNE PIECE D'IDENTITE

NOUS N'ACCEPTONS PLUS LES CHEQUES RESTAURANT LE SOIR

garni garnished, served with

Make the calls, and note the required starter, main course and dessert, in each case. Then call the restaurant, make the booking for the appropriate number of people, and give details of particular requirements for each course. You should do this working in a group, with the other members of the group playing the roles of the people you telephone, and choosing from the menu shown. The teacher, or French assistant, will play the role of the restaurant manager to whom you should report the total order of your group. Take it in turns to ask the people what they want and remember to change the order each time.

9 Your penfriend's dad is very interested in food. Having picked this page from a magazine which you sent to your penfriend, he asks you to explain about each of the restaurants mentioned. Tell him about price range, availability, times, and types of food.

COME AND DINE AT THE
The Coleshill Hotel

High Street, Coleshill, Warwickshire, B46 3BG.
We are justifiably proud of the reputation of our 'Victoria Restaurant', for the quality at affordable prices.
Relax in comfort in the 'Yeoman Bar', whilst choosing from our extensive 'A La Carte' menu or our renowned five course 'Table d'Hote' menu **at £8.50 per person.**
We also offer the 'Stowells of Chelsea' wine selection to our diners, as well as a fine range of ports, brandies, liqueurs and cigars for you to enjoy after your meal.

FOR TABLE RESERVATIONS
Please phone Coleshill (0675) 65527.

楼酒逢相慶新
New Happy Gathering
Chinese Restaurant
※ Licensed ※
43-45 Station Street   Birmingham

正宗

Enjoy authentic Cantonese Cuisine at its very best in the sophisticated atmosphere of Birmingham's most luxurious restaurant. A high standard of service and Gourmet dishes all at very moderate prices.

Telephone: 021-643 5247
Open 12noon to Midnight
Egon Ronay & AA Recommended
Facilities for Conference and Banqueting in private.

OLDE ENGLISH TEA ROOM

(The Bun & Biscuit)

32 Poplar Road, Just off High St., Kings Heath

PUT YOUR HEAVY SHOPPING DOWN

Have a break at the Bun & Biscuit
DELICIOUS!
Home Made Scones, Rock Cakes, Tarts, & Sherry Trifle

HOME COOKED

Breakfasts, Dinner and Afternoon Teas

TEL.: 021.444 0999

OPEN 9-4.30 MON.-SAT.

CAFÉ
NOW OPEN

KINGS COURT
SHOPPING PRECINCT
HIGH ST. KINGS HEATH

TEA & SANDWICHES HOT & COLD SNACKS

LUNCHTIME SPECIALS TAKE AWAY SERVICE

OMELETTE & CHIPS
LASAGNE & SALAD
PLUS MANY OTHER DISHES

ALL FRESH HOME MADE PRODUCE

GOOD FOOD AT LOW PRICES

OPEN MON-SAT 9.00-5.30

THE YEW TREE COTTAGE

43 Stoney Lane, Yardley, Birmingham B25 8RE.
(Close to Coventry Rd. & N.E.C.)
Table Reservations: 021-784 0707

"THE INDIAN RESTAURANT WITH A DIFFERENCE"
Yew Tree Cottage is the natural rendezvous for all those who delight in aromatic, authentic Indian cuisine served in an elegant atmosphere.
RECOMMENDED BY VARIOUS GOOD FOOD GUIDES
We are open 7 days a week including holidays. Business hours: 5pm-1am daily.
HAPPY HOUR SPECIAL OFFERS between 5.30pm and 8pm every evening.
Bookings are taken every evening.
We extend a warm welcome to all visitors to Birmingham.

10 You are planning to take presents home to your family. Working with a partner, who plays the role of your French penfriend, discuss what you would like to buy and why. Your penfriend asks as many questions as possible about the type of presents and the family's likes and dislikes.

11 Your exchange partner has expressed an interest in trying a typical English dish.

You

Explain in French how to prepare one of the dishes listed, but don't say the name of it.

- Apple pie
- Yorkshire pudding
- Fish and chips
- Shepherd's pie
- Another meal that you like

Partner

As your partner is telling you how to prepare the dish, write down in English what is said.

See how well your partner does, and try to guess which dish is being described.

If you have time, discuss, in French, what was said, and how it might have been improved.

Then change roles, and see if you can do better.

READING

1 Having spent a pleasant evening in town with your penfriend and his parents, you round off the day at an icecream parlour. Giving some thought to a friend of yours at home in England, you decide to make her envious, by noting in English, exactly what each of you has eaten.

GLACES

GLACE au choix (café, vanille, chocolat, pistache) ....

SORBET au choix (citron, cassis, framboise, pomme, mandarine, fruit de la passion) ....

GLACE ou SORBET CHANTILLY ....

Coupe TANGO (glace antillaise, sorbet banane, sauce chocolat chaud) ....

Coupe BRESILIENNE (glace café, liqueur de café, grain de café) ....

Coupe MEXICAINE (sorbet citron, sorbet fruit de la passion et tequila) ....

CAFE LIEGEOIS (glace café, café chaud, chantilly, grain de café) ....

POIRE BELLE-HELENE (glace vanille, poire au sirop, sauce chocolat) ....

Coupe EDEN (sorbet citron, cassis, fruit de la passion, glace antillaise, cocktail de fruits, chantilly) ..

Coupe DES BOIS (sorbet framboise, framboises fruits, sirop de framboises) ....

Coupe TWENTY (glace chocolat, pistache, chantilly, sirop de menthe, amandes) ....

Coupe SAMOURAI (sorbet fruit de la passion, litchis, sirop de groseille) ....

Coupe DIJONNAISE (glace vanille, sorbet cassis, cocktail de fruits, chantilly) ....

Coupe des TROPIQUES (sorbet mandarine, mandarine fruit, cerise confite) ....

Service à l'appréciation de la clientèle

2 Your exchange partner isn't feeling too well today, but she has been left a list of shopping to do. As you are a little nervous of making a mistake, you decide to mark down which shop to go to for each of the items. There is no nearby supermarket, so you will visit:

- La boucherie
- La boulangerie
- L'épicerie
- Le marchand de fruits et légumes

Here is your shopping list.

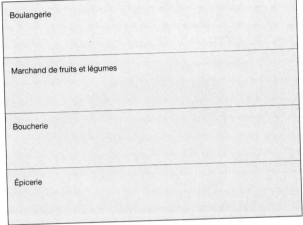

Boulangerie
Marchand de fruits et légumes
Boucherie
Épicerie

Un kilo de pommes

200 g de café instantané

500 g de farine

6 côtelettes de porc

Une bouteille de jus d'orange

2 baguettes

6 yaourts

confiture abricots

un kilo de sucre

500 g escalopes de veau

Write a separate list for each shop.

3 You receive this letter from your penfriend asking you to bring certain items with you when you go to stay with her in a few weeks' time. Make a list of what you have to get, ready for when you go shopping.

Chère amie,

comme tu dois venir bientôt j'en profite pour te demander si tu peux me ramener quelques petites choses. Si tu pouvais trouver des cartes postales de Londres parce qu'en cours d'Anglais nous faisons un texte sur ta ville et ce serait bien d'avoir des photos. Autre chose peux-tu apporter un journal Anglais c'est pour un de mes voisins il est à l'université et il essaie de lire le plus d'Anglais possible et comme tu dois t'en douter on ne trouve pas facilement de journaux dans une autre langue ici en France.

N'oublie pas non plus le gilet que j'ai laissé chez toi en avril dernier. Apart cela je crois que c'est tout. J'espère que tu penseras à tout: les photos, le journal et le gilet.

Je t'attends avec impatience.

A très bientôt

Anne.

P.S. Maman me dit de te demander de ramener du thé et si tu pouvais aussi prendre des cigares sur le bateau c'est bientôt l'anniversaire de mon père et comme il fume beaucoup il sera content.

4 You are spending a day alone while on an exchange in France, and as a special treat you decide to prepare something for the family. You come across the recipe for a dessert, *La Tarte au Riz de Tante Caroline*, which is shown on this page. Read through the recipe.

1 Write a list in English of the ingredients you will need.

2 When the first part of the cooking is going on, what are you warned may happen?

3 At what point should you add the rest of the ingredients?

4 Should your oven be hot, medium or low?

une coupe   a dish
le sucre vanillé   vanilla flavouring
la poudre   powder
attacher   to stick
éviter   to avoid
un four   an oven

une entrée!...

**LA TARTE
AUX FRUITS DE MER**

250 g de crevettes décortiquées - 150 g de champignons frais ou en boîte - 250 g de moules cuites - 10 coquilles St-Jacques en boîte ou congelées). Disposez toutes ces garnitures dans le fond de tarte, faites une béchamel épaisse, dans laquelle vous aurez ajouté le jus des fruits de mer, 100 g de crème fraîche et une boîte de concentré de tomates, versez votre sauce sur la garniture et passez à four moyen 10 à 15 minutes. C'est une entrée originale et délicieuse !!!

Conseils : Pour éviter les fuites, avant de garnir, boucher les trous de la tarte avec de la mie de pain humide. (Ces trous sont nécessaires pour assurer une parfaite cuisson de la pâte et en garantir la conservation).

TARTE FEUILLETÉE

Les Patisseries Fines

**JM
BULTHEEL**

TOURCOING

**LE SPÉCIALISTE DU
PRÊT à GARNIR**

un dessert!...

**LA TARTE AU RIZ
DE TANTE CAROLINE**

125 g de riz, 900 g de lait, un sachet de sucre vanillé, une pincée de sel, 2 œufs, 125 g de sucre poudre.

Cuire le riz dans le lait avec le sucre vanillé, mélanger de temps à autre pour éviter qu'il attache, quand le riz est parfaitement cuit, battre les œufs avec le sucre au fouet puis mélanger avec le riz chaud, déposer dans la tarte et cuire 25 minutes à four moyen.

Délicieux et nourrissant !!!

5 Fast food is one thing, but . . . you decide to find out if 'American' restaurants can offer more than hamburgers and cola. A Paris guide writes up five American restaurants. Make notes along the lines suggested by the grid, to help you decide which to visit.

	Opening hours	Price range	Food offered	Other information
Conways				
Front Page				
Joe Allen				
Mother's Earth				
Le Petit Québec				

AMERIQUE DU NORD

CONWAY'S
73, rue St-Denis (1er)
Métro : Châtelet-Les Halles
508.07.70

Service jusqu'à 1 h du matin (non stop). Fermé lundi.
Si vous voulez voir une belle Américaine, demandez Avia Conway, la patronne de ce restaurant new-yorkais tout en longueur et sur 2 niveaux (attention aux 2 marches !). Pour les douteux et les curieux, au fond se trouve la cuisine visible par tous, sans séparation avec la salle de restaurant.
Spécialités américaines évidemment et en particulier le brunch : Chantal vous expliquera, avec le sourire, que c'est un mélange entre le breakfast et le lunch, servi tard dans la matinée les samedi, dimanche et jours de fêtes. Un petit déjeuner copieux, en quelque sorte ! 40 F tout compris.

PERNOD TONIC
1 dose de PERNOD
5 doses de TONIC

Servir frais, avec un zeste de citron.

FRONTPAGE
56-58, rue St-Denis (1er)
Métro : Châtelet-Les Halles
236.98.69

Service de tous les jours jusqu'à 2 h du matin.
Ambiance rétro : un studio photo des années 30 (projecteurs et photos de stars à l'appui). Christian (le gérant) et Richard (son fils) sont là pour vous proposer leurs spécialités à la carte et carte à la « Une » ! Quelques plats mexicains (Chili con carne...) et, bien sûr, ces fameux hamburgers, symboles de la nation.
Vous mangerez américain pour environ 60 à 70 F (la carte) et 35 F si vous choisissez le menu. Alors, encocacolisez-vous !

JOE ALLEN
30, rue Pierre-Lescot (1er)
Métro : Châtelet-Les Halles
236.70.13

De midi à 1 h du matin tous les jours.
Cinéma et théâtre sont à l'affiche dans ce restaurant bâti sur un modèle new-yorkais qui a ses homologues à Los Angélès, Londres et Toronto.
Les spécialités américaines préparées par des cuisiniers français (le grand chef de N.Y. vient de temps en temps vérifier la cuisine). Ne comptez pas voir Joe Allen, the big boss, il habite New-York, mais le responsable Paul est très aimable. Compter environ 80 F.

MOTHER'S EARTH
66, rue des Lombards (1er)
Métro : Châtelet-Les Halles
236.35.57

Service jusqu'à 0 h 30. Fermé lundi midi.
Pour ceux qui ont des kilos en trop, ce resto propose un « régime-burger » un hamburger, sans pain, avec une salade spéciale.
Après s'être donné bonne conscience avec ce Burger de régime on peut, en toute tranquillité se ruer sur les irrésistibles gâteaux au chocolat et crème chantilly, dont tous raffolent !
Et pour ceux qui veulent aller au cinéma ensuite, faites parler David, l'un des serveurs, il adore ça et fait de temps en temps des critiques de films.
Pour toute personne non américaine, le resto est à éviter entre 17 et 19 h, le vendredi : Il devient le lieu de rendez-vous de tous les étudiants américains à Paris.

LE PETIT QUEBEC
101, rue de la Croix-Nivert (15e)
Métro : Félix-Faure   828.31.88

Menu à 50 F.
Super ! Ce petit restaurant québecois qui a ouvert ses portes depuis seulement le 17 octobre 81. La cuisine et l'accent de là-bas vous transportent (pour seulement 50 F) de l'autre côté de l'Atlantique. Un animateur permanent : Marcel Tanguay présente, chaque semaine, un artiste différent qui chante son pays.

Le Petit Malin – Dominique AUZIAS

le niveau level
la patronne boss (female)

l'ambiance atmosphere
le gérant manager

un régime diet
animateur/trice entertainments manager

6 You are planning to make a study of the americanisation of some Paris restaurants. As part of this study read the restaurant write-ups again and make notes about these people and the places where they work. Write about two or three sentences about each one.

Joe Allen
Chantal
Christian et Richard

Avia Conway
David
Marcel Tanguay

7 Whilst you are staying with your penfriend in France the advertising material below comes through the door. Your penfriend suggests that as it's a 'two for the price of one' offer you order some things and have one each. You read the details on the coupons to decide what you should buy.

1 Both you and your penfriend like to wash your hair every day. Which shampoo would you choose?

2 You decide to get some foundation cream. How much will two tubes cost you?

3 In order to get your skin in good condition you decide to buy a facemask. What two products are on offer?

4 Bath gel seems like a good idea. What does the product on offer claim?

5 Both you and your penfriend have rather dry skins. Which product would you choose and how much is it?

le fond de teint   foundation
vivifiant   invigorating
décontracter   to relax
remettre   to put back
la peau   skin

Le masque au concombre pour les peaux à tendance grasse

Une beauté "éclair" avec le masque au concombre. C'est un gel rafraîchissant pour matifier votre teint, le rendre plus net et plus clair.

29,80 F les 2 tubes au lieu de 59,60 F
tube de 75 ml - Réf. : 8492

Le fond de teint fluide Luminelle

Illuminez votre teint avec le fond de teint fluide Luminelle, il unifie le teint et vous donne bonne mine. Choisissez selon la carnation de votre peau l'une des 4 nuances :

27,90 F les 2 tubes au lieu de 55,80 F
Sable : Réf. 1540, Ambre : Réf. 1212, Miel : Réf. 1330 ou Cannelle : Réf. 1514

Le lait parfumé pour le corps Magnolia

Nouveau et très doux, le lait parfumé pour le corps Magnolia assouplit et satine votre peau tout en la parfumant délicatement des subtiles senteurs de l'eau de toilette Magnolia.

28,70 F les 2 flacons au lieu de 57,40 F
flacon de 200 ml - Réf. : P380

Le Riche Fluide anti-rides

Nouveau ! Le Riche Fluide anti-rides : son efficacité et la rapidité des résultats sont étonnants. En 15 jours, une seule goutte du Riche Fluide appliquée régulièrement aux couches superficielles du visage suffit pour les aider à retrouver un aspect lisse.

41,30 F les 2 flacons au lieu de 82,60 F
flacon stiligoutte de 10 ml - Réf. : V294

Le gel de bain moussant aux algues brunes et au lierre grimpant

Vivifiant comme l'air marin, le gel de bain moussant aux algues brunes et au lierre grimpant vous décontracte et vous remet en forme.

29,80 F les 2 flacons au lieu de 59,60 F
flacon de 300 ml - Réf. : C300

Le shampooing crème au germe de blé, au lait de sésame et à l'avocat...

Pour cheveux secs et abîmés :
le shampooing crème au germe de blé, au lait de sésame et à l'avocat : nourrissant et revitalisant, il aide vos cheveux à retrouver leur souplesse et leur éclat.

25,90 F les 2 tubes au lieu de 51,80 F
tube de 125 ml - Réf. : 5095

Le fluide hydratant Althéa à l'althaéa

Pour une peau souple et douce : le fluide hydratant Althéa à l'althaéa fixe l'eau dans les couches superficielles de l'épiderme et vous donne une agréable sensation de fraîcheur

31,20 F les 2 flacons au lieu de 62,40 F
flacon de 75 ml - Réf. : 0291

Le shampooing crème à l'argile, au cresson et au serpolet

Pour les cheveux gras :
le shampooing crème à l'argile, au cresson et au serpolet normalise la sécrétion sébacée qui alourdit vos cheveux et leur rend légéreté et volume.

25,90 F les 2 tubes au lieu de 51,80 F
tube de 125 ml - Réf. : 5062

Le baume embellisseur à la prêle

Des cheveux brillants et faciles à coiffer, utilisez le Baume embellisseur à la prêle pour cheveux secs après votre shampooing, le peigne glissera facilement et vos cheveux seront encore plus soyeux.

19,80 F les 2 flacons au lieu de 39,60 F
flacon de 200 ml - Réf. : V342

Le peeling végétal

Peau nette et éclatante avec le peeling végétal. En quelques minutes, votre teint devient clair, votre peau nette, débarassée des impuretés qui obstruent les pores.

41,80 F les 2 tubes au lieu de 83,60 F
tube de 50 ml - Réf. : 45G4

Le shampooing au miel d'acacia

Pour vos lavages fréquents utilisez le shampooing au miel d'acacia, très doux il rend vos cheveux brillants et soyeux.

18,80 F les 2 flacons au lieu de 37,60 F
flacon de 250 ml - Réf. : 1R04

Le shampooing crème à la capucine, à l'ortie et aux bourgeons de peuplier

Pour les cheveux à pellicules :
le shampooing crème à la capucine, à l'ortie et aux bourgeons de peuplier freine le développement de vos pellicules, grasses ou sèches et redonne à vos cheveux un aspect soigné, souple et brillant.

27,80 F les 2 tubes au lieu de 55,60 F
tube de 125 ml - Réf. : 29G5

8 This piece of advertising appears one day in your penfriend's letter box addressed to his mother. You love cartoons so you immediately start to read it. It is fascinating so you write to tell your parents all about it.

1 How is the advertisement personalised?
2 What has happened to the first advertisements your penfriend's mother received?
3 What is the name of the magazine on offer?
4 What is the old man complaining of at the end?
5 What answer does he get to his question?

You think this is a brilliant piece of advertising and you decide to find out more about the magazine advertised.

6 What subjects does the magazine cover?
7 What day does it come out?
8 What is the 'Dossier' section?
9 What is the guide section?
10 How could you take out a subscription?

ABONNEZ-VOUS AU POINT
pour en <u>savoir</u> plus chaque lundi

CHAQUE SEMAINE DANS LE POINT

LES RUBRIQUES :
nation, monde, économie, communication, société, civilisation. Pour être parfaitement informé de l'actualité nationale et internationale.

UN DOSSIER :
sur un sujet politique, économique ou social qui prépare notre avenir proche ou qui domine l'actualité. Pour mieux comprendre en toute indépendance d'opinion.

LA LETTRE CONFIDENTIELLE :
quatre pages d'informations dont on ne vous parle pas encore ailleurs, sur la vie politique, économique, française et internationale, sur les hommes qui la font. Pour être toujours en avance sur l'événement.

LE GUIDE :
une dizaine de pages qui fourmillent d'informations pratiques, de bonnes adresses, de "trucs", une sélection des meilleurs spectacles de la semaine et des meilleurs programmes télévisés. Pour la vie courante, le shopping, les loisirs.

Faites l'essai du Point avec 20% de réduction et recevez un cadeau.

Faites l'essai du Point et jugez vous-même de sa qualité et de son intérêt pendant 12 semaines. En profitant de cette offre, vous paierez Le Point **20% moins cher.**

Vous recevrez, en plus, en cadeau, cette calculette solaire format carte de crédit, réservée exclusivement aux abonnés du Point.

© C. Charillon – Paris

s'abonner à to subscribe to
être au courant to know what is going on
fourmiller to swarm, to teem
au verso on the back
la facture the bill

Pour profiter de cette offre

1 Datez, signez le bulletin-réponse au verso.
2 Glissez-le dans l'enveloppe-réponse jointe.
3 N'envoyez pas d'argent aujourd'hui. Vous paierez à réception de facture.

9 Petites faims

Having read this article, you write to an American penfriend, explaining some of the French adaptations of the McDonald idea, both in Paris, and in the USA, and asking his opinions of the latter.

s'éloigner de   to go away from
un feuilleté   flaky pastry
coller   to stick
s'embêter   to be bothered/annoyed
tremper   to soak
au fur et à mesure   bit by bit

• Petites faims

Quand la faim justifie les (petits) moyens, le trop célèbre hamburger collé à un pain rond accompagné de frites et de l'inévitable coca-cola ne fait pas encore l'unanimité de tous les Français, loin de là, on lui reproche, entre autres, son aspect « américain ».

Mais on peut s'éloigner des sentiers communs des Mac Donald et Burger King... en allant faire un tour dans les fast-food francisés que sont les « croissanteries », « croissant show », « brioches dorées », « pomme de pain »... qui proposent des produits bien français : croissants, pains au chocolat, croque-monsieur et toutes sortes de feuilletés sucrés ou salés.... la rotation rapide permet de savourer des produits toujours frais. Il existe également une formule qui réunit les deux types de fast food : c'est celle proposée par les Drug Burger du drugstore St Lazare : ouvert de 7 h (pour un croissant avant de se rendre au bureau), à 19 h 30, ce fast food propose une croissanterie, assiettes froides, mais surtout des hamburgers... provençaux ou alsaciens ! Si en France, on tente de faire du français à base d'américain, aux U.S.A., on fait la même chose.

En allant faire un tour aux U.S.A., le Petit Malin en a appris de bien bonnes sur les sandwiches. Connaissez-vous le « french dip sandwich », je vous en livre la recette qui n'a de français que le nom et l'oignon.

Ingrédient indispensable : « French bread » (en français : baguette). Le meilleur qui soit aux U.S.A., vient de San Francisco, spécialiste du French Bread.

Voilà le french dip : une soupe à l'oignon (et pour ne pas s'embêter, on l'achète en sachet au super-market du coin).

Dernière composante : une tranche de rôti (avec des restes, il n'y a qu'à réchauffer en 2 secondes au « microwave oven ».

Faire griller le pain (à défaut de french bread de San Francisco, n'importe quelle baguette fera mieux l'affaire !!). Mettre le rôti en sandwich et tremper au fur et à mesure dans l'oignon... c'est pas très élégant... mais délicious !

✎ WRITING

1 On your last day in France you fall ill and you have still not bought all the presents you want to take back. Your penfriend offers to do the shopping for you if you will make a list, in French, of what you would like. You need something for your mum, dad, grandparents, brother, sister, and best friend. Write the list, indicating something you would like to get for each person. Show who each gift is for. An example of what you might write could be 'Maman—foulard en soie'.

2 On your school's 'French Day', you are charged with writing out menus for the tables in the staff canteen. Set out, attractively in French, four typical school meals, so that they can be used on the tables.

3 Your French friends ask you to prepare a typical English dish for them to try. They will get the ingredients if you write out a list in French. Decide on a dish and write down the ingredients.

4 You have been finding home cooking in France rather difficult to get used to. On a day when your penfriend's parents are out, and due back late, you take yourself off for a feast of cheeseburgers, chips, chocolate milkshakes, and the like.

However, before going to bed, you leave a note for them—about 30 words, outlining, not the things you really ate, but some very French things which you claim to have eaten at the *Restaurant du Bouc Cornu*, as you hope this will please them.

5 You have just done your Christmas shopping with your friend. In the card you send to your French penfriend, you decide to include a letter, in French, describing your day in town and what you bought. Do not write more than about 200 words.

6 Your English friend has been invited to stay for a few weeks with a French family but is a little worried about food. She asks you to write a letter for her explaining the following:

- She is a vegetarian but can eat eggs and milk.
- She is afraid that she may be offered horse-meat, snails, frogs or rabbit to eat.
- She loves salads and omelettes.

7 After going out for a rather expensive meal with friends in England, you decide to send your penfriend's father a copy of the menu, knowing him to be a gourmet. Your accompanying letter—in French of course— tells him what you ate, and what you thought about it. Also, you recommend him to visit this restaurant the next time he is in your area.

8 You are on your school's exchange visit to Lyon, and while you are there you decide to send a card to your French penfriend Claire who lives in another part of France. You write about the food, the shops etc. Mention Lyon sausages and other things you liked or disliked, and say what you are looking forward to back home.

ARCHIE'S VICTORIAN SALOON.

SELECTION AT £7.50.

STARTERS.   Soup of the Day
               Melon
               Tomato Salad
               Country Pate

                 -o-o-o-o-o-

MAIN COURSE.   Steak
               Gammon Steak
               Mixed Grill - Lamb chop, pork chop, steak.
               Home Made Shepherds Pie.
               Faggots and Peas (Black Country Style)
               Selection from Salad Bar.

               Served with French Fries, carrots, peas.

                 -o-o-o-o-o-

DESSERTS.   Selection of Ice-creams.
               Apple Pie and cream
               Fruit Salad
               Peach Melba
               Selection from fruit bowl

                 -o-o-o-o-o-

ARCHIE'S CHILDREN'S MENU @ £3.00.

Soup or melon

                 -o-o-o-o-o-

Beefburger or sausage or Shepherds pie.

                 -o-o-o-o-o-

Ice-cream or Apple Pie.

                 -o-o-o-o-o-

Gratuities are at the discretion of our valued customers.

9 Your French friend and his parents are due to arrive in England shortly, and are planning to stay with you for the weekend. Amongst other things, you plan a visit to a restaurant with them during their stay. When you write to them, you enclose advertisements for several different kinds of restaurant. In your letter, explain what the restaurants are, and ask them to tell you which one they would prefer to visit, so that a booking can be made. Make sure you include the appropriate comments about looking forward to their visit, and what else you have planned for them.

10 Whilst in France you bought a record of *Miss Maggie*, but on your return to England you find that it is badly scratched. As you intended it as a present for your friend you decide to send it back and ask for a replacement. Write a letter, in French, to the shop, explaining the situation. Do not write more than 120 words.

MULTI-SKILL TASK

Whilst on a *gîte* holiday with your parents in France you decide, on the last evening, to go to a restaurant. You find one offering this menu and you go in.

First of all you sort out the various family preferences:

- You all enjoy tomatoes.
- Your father loves pork in any form and is also fond of chips.
- Your brother loves chops—either pork or lamb—and he too likes chips.
- Your mother likes chicken and decides to have it with pasta.
- You fancy a well-done steak and chips.

1 You call over the waiter and order. Pretend that your partner is the waiter and ask for what you want.

2 After a short while the waiter comes back. Listen to what he says.

3 Based on what he says and what you already know of your family's preferences you alter your order. Tell the waiter what you would now like.

4 The meal is really delicious and your father asks you to tell the waiter how much he enjoyed it. Pretend once again that your partner is the waiter.

5 Because the food was so good and the people so friendly you decide to leave a note in French for the next occupants of the *gîte*, recommending the restaurant and saying what you particularly enjoyed.

Au Bon Repas

Menu à 40f.

Hors d'Oeuvres

Salade de tomates
Pâté Maison

Entrées

(Plats servis avec pommes frites ou avec pâtes.)

Côtelette de porc
Escalope de porc
Escalope de veau

Bifteck
Poulet chasseur
Pot-au-feu

Desserts

Choix de fromage
Glaces (plusieurs parfums)
Tarte aux pommes

4

Logements à tout prix

1 On a rainy day during your holidays in France, you are bored. You are in the lobby of the hotel and decide to listen to what people are asking, to see if you could do the job of the receptionist. What does each of the people want?

2 You hear these announcements on the public address system of the campsite on which you are staying. Knowing that, when you get back to the tent, your mother will ask you what they were about, you make a note. There are ten announcements.

3 You are trying to book a room in a hotel. Your family have given you the following requirements:

- Less than 100 francs per night.
- Must have a toilet and shower.
- Must have a sea view.

Which, if any, of the three rooms suggested, fits them all?

Write the number of the room which fits the bill; or if none is suitable, write 'none'.

4 You arrive at a French campsite in the late afternoon. Whilst the rest of the family is pitching the tent, you go up to the camp shop for a few essentials. The campsite owner asks you to give some messages to your parents. You make a note of what he says.

5 Arriving in Lunel early one afternoon your father sends you to the tourist office to get details of where you might stay. The receptionist tells you about three hotels. You note the details in order to tell your father.

Name of Hotel	Stars	Restaurant (Yes/No)	Telephone number	Other information
Grand Hôtel Brazard				
Hôtel du Parc				
Chalet de Warren				

6 You arrive at the hotel you have booked in Chartres, only to find that there is a problem. Note down the details to give to your parents, who speak no French.

7 You are staying in a hotel in Picardy with a group from your local youth club. On the second day, the manager asks you, as one of the few members of the group who speaks French, to pass on the following complaints to the rest of the party. Make a list of the five complaints he mentions.

SPEAKING

1 With a partner, take turns to practise this conversation. When you are confident enough, practise it more, but change some of the details. For example:

- Number of nights
- Type of room
- Number of people

You	Receptionist
Bonjour monsieur/madame.	Bonjour monsieur/madame. Vous désirez?
Vous avez une chambre s'il vous plaît?	Oui, c'est pour combien de nuits?
C'est pour deux nuits seulement. Vous avez une chambre à deux lits? C'est pour mon ami(e) et moi.	Oui, monsieur/madame. Vous prenez le petit déjeuner?
Oui, ça fait combien?	Ça fait 110 francs la nuit, monsieur/madame. Vous la prenez?
Oui, merci.	

2 This section is to help you deal with making a booking at a hotel. Work with a partner, and using the diagrams here to help you, try to book the combinations of rooms given. Your partner will play the role of the hotel receptionist, and write down your requirements. See how many times you can get exactly what you wanted. Don't forget the usual greeting, politenesses, etc., as you play your part.

Now ask for different combinations, or ask extra questions, and see if you can get it right every time.

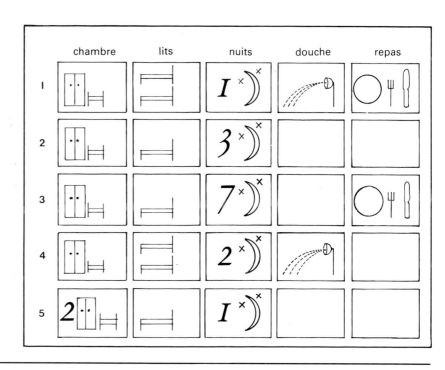

3 You go to the reception desk of the hotel where you are staying.
You want to eat out tonight. Your partner will play the part of the
receptionist.

You	Receptionist
Say hello and ask if there is a good, not too expensive restaurant nearby. .	
	Yes, *Chez Georges* is good and quite cheap.
Ask where it is.	
	Show your partner where it is on the plan, and describe how to get to it. It only takes five minutes on foot.
Say thank you and ask if you can keep the plan.	
	Say of course—eat well!

When you have done this, ask for other places on the map.
Change roles so that you both have the chance to ask the
questions.

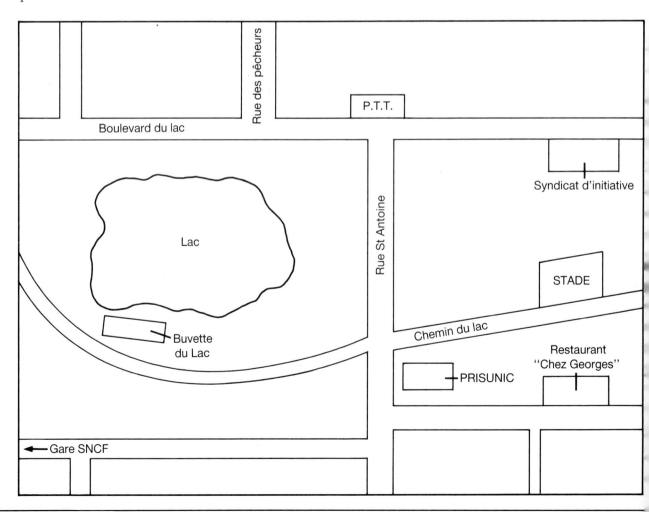

4 You ring the *Hôtel de la Plage* in Erquy to help your parents book your summer holidays, which are from the 2nd August to the 14th August. Your teacher, language assistant or partner will play the part of the receptionist.

Say hello and that you are telephoning from England to book rooms for the summer.

Answer the question you are asked.

Ask for both prices.

Say you'll book one of each.

5 You go into a hotel to book a room. Your teacher, language assistant or partner will play the part of the desk clerk.

Say you want a room.

Say you need it for two nights.

Say you are alone and ask how much it is.

Knowing that you can only afford 100 francs, answer the question you are asked.

Say that you'll take it.

6 In order to help out your friends, you are looking after their family hotel for a short while. You will receive several enquiries about rooms, facilities and prices. Here is the information about the hotel. Respond to the questions you are asked as your partner and you make them into role-plays.

10 Rooms	8 doubles and 2 singles	
Doubles	1 with shower and WC	110 francs
	4 with WC only	100 francs
	3 with shower and sea-view	130 francs
Singles	2 with shower	65 francs
Evening meals	19.00 hrs – 22.00 hrs	65 francs per person
Breakfast	7.00 hrs – 9.30 hrs	15 francs per person

7 At a campsite you are trying to explain your requirements. You have one large tent, your car and there are two people with you. You want to stay for seven nights; your mother wants to be sure that there are showers available on site. Your teacher, language assistant or partner will play the part of the campsite owner.

8 You are on holiday in England with your parents, staying in a hotel. You notice a French person at the reception desk having trouble being understood. You decide to help by acting as interpreter. The hotel receptionist needs to know the following information. Your teacher, language assistant or partner will play the part of the French person.

1 What is the name of the client?

2 Does the person want a single or a double room?

3 For how many nights?

4 Does he/she want a room with a shower/television etc, or just a simple room? (Explain that the basic room costs £15 per night, but that with the extras, it comes to £20 per night.)

5 Does the person want an English breakfast?

6 Does the person want an evening meal?

7 Has he/she got a passport?

8 Does he/she know where the car park is? (If not, explain that it is just round behind the hotel—wish the person a pleasant stay.)

READING

1 An English friend of yours who does not understand French, leaves you this document about the *Maison de la Varenne*, with this note. Can you answer his questions?

> Hi.
> Sorry to bother you, but could you possibly explain some of this paper for me?
> 1. What sort of 'ancient' thing is this?
> 2. Is there a swimming pool?
> 3. Is it really 54 people to a bedroom?
> 4. Is there a library?
> 5. Is there a games room?
> 6. What sort of lessons do they do?
> 7. What does it say about week-ends?
> Many thanks.
> Any chance of letting me have your answers today?
> Thanks.
> Biffo.

la découverte discovery
la voile sailing
la détente relaxation

LA MAISON DE LA VARENNE

– *Ancienne ferme, entourée d'herbages et d'étangs,*

– *Réserve naturelle d'oiseaux.*

A 200 M :

◊ *Piscine,*
◊ *Base de voile,*
◊ *Tennis.*

HEBERGEMENT

MAISON

OUVERTE TOUTE L'ANNEE
=====================

– *Capacité : 54 places,*
– *Chambres de 2 à 12 places,*
– *Réception,*
– *Salle à manger,*
– *Bibliothèque, TV,*
– *Douches, WC, Lavabos,*
– *Salle de classe et d'activités.*

ACCUEIL GROUPES

– *Voyages Scolaires Educatifs,*
– *Classes de découvertes,*
– *Classes de Voile,*
– *Stages Sportifs*
– *Week-end détente,*
– *Séminaires......*

2 You have decided to organise your youth club trip to France with CISL so now you must fill in the application form. Below is the information which you have collated about your party. Using this, fill in your copy of the form as completely and as accurately as you can.

Dates:

7th−18th September
Arrive 11 p.m.−Leave 7 a.m.

Composition of group:

2 married couples
15 boys under 18
17 girls under 18
 2 male staff
 1 female staff
 2 drivers (both male) Total: 41 people.

The drivers have agreed to share a room to keep down costs, but all three staff require single rooms.
You need a big room in which to meet on the 9th September. You want to book a packed lunch for the journey home on 18th September.

l'encadrement (m.) group leaders
un panier-repas packed lunch

FICHE DE RESERVATION GROUPES — CENTRE INTERNATIONAL DE SEJOUR DE LYON

DATES DU SEJOUR — ARRIVEE — DEPART
IDENTITES — ORGANISME OU AGENCE — GROUPE ET RESPONSABLE
COMPOSITION DU GROUPE — REPARTITION — AGES — BUT DU SEJOUR
RENSEIGNEMENTS SUR LE SEJOUR — CHAMBRES souhaitées — Nombre de REPAS — SALLES
CONFIRMATION DE RESERVATION — ARRHES — SIGNATURE

CISL 46 rue du Commandant Pégoud 69008 LYON −FRANCE−
Tél.16.78.76.14.22   Télex EUROL 330 949 F 185   Télétel 16(3)614.91.66

3 Your youth club group are all safely installed in their rooms in the youth hostel in Saint-Valéry-en-Caux. You are given this information sheet by the hostel warden. Write out the rules, in English, for your group, to make sure that everyone can comply with them.

l'accueil (m.) reception
plier to fold
contrôler to check
la caution returnable deposit
une effraction break-in

REGLEMENTS INTERIEUR

− Le ménage de votre chambre est à votre charge (un aspirateur est à votre disposition, demandez-le à l'accueil).

−Vous pouvez déposer votre poubelle devant votre porte tous les jours avant 10 hrs. afin qu'elle soit vidée.

−Le jour de votre départ nous vous demandons:

· · · de plier les couvertures sur les lits.

· · · de plier les draps.

· · · de fermer le chauffage.

· · · de venir chercher l'aubergiste pour contrôler et fermer la chambre et pour recouvrer votre caution.

−Vous devez garder votre clé de chambre avec vous pendant votre séjour. (La maison n'est pas responsable des vols, sans effractions opérées et évidentes dans les chambres.)

MERCI

4 You and some friends are touring France on motorbikes and camping. The campsite at Beaurainville seems to you to offer just the sort of facilities you need for a few days. One or two of your friends, however, would prefer to head further south straight away. Make a list of ten reasons why you would like to stay a few nights at Beaurainville, ready to try and convince your friends.

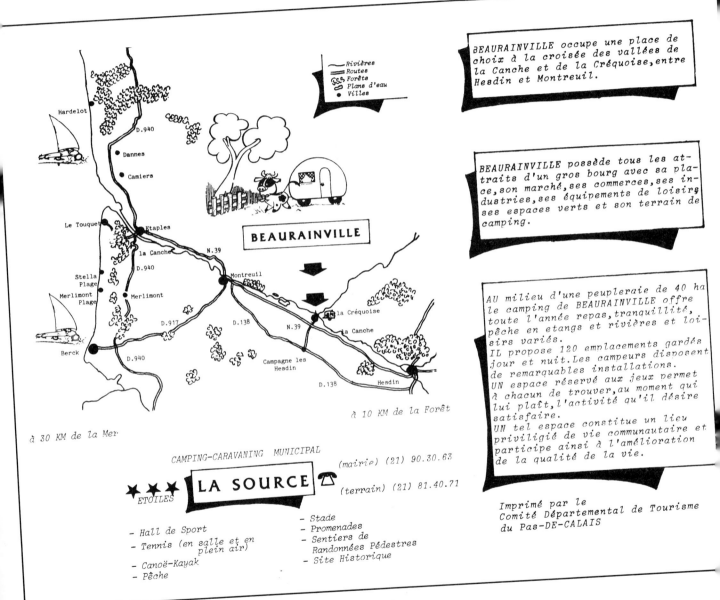

BEAURAINVILLE occupe une place de choix à la croisée des vallées de la Canche et de la Créquoise, entre Hesdin et Montreuil.

BEAURAINVILLE possède tous les attraits d'un gros bourg avec sa place, son marché, ses commerces, ses industries, ses équipements de loisirs, ses espaces verts et son terrain de camping.

AU milieu d'une peupleraie de 40 ha le camping de BEAURAINVILLE offre toute l'année repas, tranquillité, pêche en étangs et rivières et loisirs variés.
IL propose 120 emplacements gardés jour et nuit. Les campeurs disposent de remarquables installations.
UN espace réservé aux jeux permet à chacun de trouver, au moment qui lui plaît, l'activité qu'il désire satisfaire.
UN tel espace constitue un lieu priviligié de vie communautaire et participe ainsi à l'amélioration de la qualité de la vie.

Imprimé par le Comité Départemental de Tourisme du Pas-DE-CALAIS

à 30 KM de la Mer
à 10 KM de la Forêt

CAMPING-CARAVANING MUNICIPAL

★★★ **LA SOURCE** ☎
ETOILES

(mairie) (21) 90.30.63

(terrain) (21) 81.40.71

- Hall de Sport
- Tennis (en salle et en plein air)
- Canoë-Kayak
- Pêche
- Stade
- Promenades
- Sentiers de Randonnées Pédestres
- Site Historique

un attrait attraction
un bourg town
une peupleraie grove of poplar trees
un étang pond

5 You have written for information to the CISL with regard to a youth club trip you are helping to organise. You have certain criteria which must be fulfilled by the accommodation which you eventually choose. Read through the letter which you have been sent and check whether these criteria are met.

		Yes	No
1	Are all age groups accepted?		
2	Can they accommodate a group of 40+?		
3	Are there single rooms for staff?		
4	Do they cater for groups in the restaurant?		
5	Is it in the centre of town?		
6	Is there a latest time to arrive?		
7	Will they organise guided tours?		
8	Are they open in October?		
9	Do the rooms have showers?		

l'hébergement accommodation
desservi served by
les transports en commun public transport

Centre International de Séjour de Lyon

Objet : demande de documentation   Lyon, le

Madame, Monsieur,

Nous accusons réception de votre·demande de renseignements et nous vous adressons ci-joint une documentation sur notre Centre.

- Le C.I.S.L. est une centre international de séjour accueillant des personnes de tous âges (du groupe scolaire au groupe du 3ème âge), venant à Lyon dans le cadre de journées d'études, de congrès, de tourisme social, de manisfestations sportives, de stages...

- Le centre dispose d'un équipement diversifié : hébergement (89 lits), restauration (environ 400 couverts /jour), salles de réunion et cafétéria, dans un cadre agréable et d'un grand confort. L'hébergement est composé de chambres à 1, 2, 3 et 4 lits avec douche et lavabo dans les chambres, un salon télévision à chaque étage, ménage fait tous les jours. Le restaurant propose des repas en libre service et pour les groupes, des repas servis à table.

- Le C.I.S.L. accueille en priorité les groupes, les hôtes individuels sont acceptés en fonction du planning des réservations pour une période maximum de un mois.

- Le C.I.S.L. est très bien desservi par les transports en communs lyonnais qui sont fréquents et directs vers le centre de la ville (Bellecour, gare de Perrache) ou vers le centre commercial et la gare de la Part-Dieu. Situés à 10 mns du centre vill· nous n'avons pas de problèmes de parking !

- Ouvert toute l'année, un accueil vous sera réservé même très tard dans la nuit.

- Le C.I.S.L. n'assure pas de visite guidée de Lyon. Nous pourrons vous mettre en relation avec des associations touristiques lyonnaises et en particulier le service des guides conférencières de l'Office de Tourisme (nous disposons de leur documentation). Nous pourrons vous aider et vous conseiller pour passer un agréable séjour dans notre ville.

- LE SERVICE RESERVATIONS du CISL est ouvert tous les après-midi de 12 h à 19 h sauf le samedi et le dimanche, FERMETURE HEBDOMADAIRE LE MARDI APRES-MIDI.

Nous sommes à votre disposition pour vous donner d'autres informations, sur le C.I.S.L. et vous faire visiter notre équipement. Nous espérons avoir bientôt le plaisir de vous accueillir au C.I.S.L.

Dans cette attente, nous vous prions d'agréer, Madame, Monsieur, l'expression de nos sentiments les meilleurs.

46, rue Commandant-Pégoud - 69008 LYON
(à la hauteur du 101, bd des Etats-Unis)
Affilié à la F.R.M.J.C. Lyon et à l'U.C.R.I.F.
Tél. (7) 876.14.22

6 You have a class mate who wants to take part in a family to family exchange and has written off to a French organisation for details. Read through the information which she has been sent and tell her the important points. She will need to know:

1 How she will travel.

2 How much it will cost.

3 Who will be looking after her.

4 If she can travel on a group passport.

5 When she will need to send in the dossier—and if they will refund her deposit if no suitable partner is found for her.

6 How she should pay.

7 What the final dates are for the various payments to be made.

DATE:

GROUPE 1: 22 mars–5 avril 1988

GROUPE 2: 11 juillet–25 juillet 1988

Veuillez préciser un ordre de préférence.

VOYAGE:

Par avion.

COUT:

Approximativement 1700,00 FF, sauf en cas d'augmentation imprévue des tarifs avant la date du départ. Le coût comprend l'assurance-groupe obligatoire.

ENCADREMENT:

Pendant le séjour, les élèves seront encadrés par des professeurs, qui seront disponibles afin de résoudre tous les problèmes éventuels au cours du séjour.

PAPIERS D'IDENTITE:

Les candidats doivent se procurer eux-mêmes leurs papiers d'identité (passeport en cours de validité ou carte d'identité + autorisation parentale de sortie de territoire délivrée à la mairie). Vous aurez intérêt à entamer vos démarches dès que vous aurez eu confirmation de l'appariement.

REGLEMENT:

Un accompte de 300,00 FF est demandé lors du dépot du dossier (les dossiers devront avoir été envoyés avant les vacances de Noël). Si un correspondant adéquat ne peut être trouvé ou s'il n'est pas accepté, cette somme sera remboursée.

Tous les appariements devront avoir été effectués dans le courant du mois de janvier 1988.

Les règlements devront être effectués par chèque, à l'ordre de:
JUMELAGES ET RELATIONS INTERNATIONALES

et adressés à:

JUMELAGES ET RELATIONS INTERNATIONALES
Adjoint au Maire
Hôtel de Ville–B.P. 1065–Cédex 01

Puis lorsque les appariements auront été proposés aux familles et acceptés par celles-ci, versement de 50% du coût, soit 850,00 FF.

Enfin, un mois avant la date du départ, règlement du solde, soit 550,00 FF.

---

un appariement   pairing

7 Your parents have sent off for details of accommodation in a
mountain resort and have been sent this document. Answer the
questions which they put to you.

1 Are all the beds in dormitories?
2 What facilities are there on site?
3 There are six people travelling. Can they all share one room?
4 From the village, how do they get to the site?
5 Is the site accessible by car in winter?
6 What attractions does the stay offer to the winter visitor?
7 What excursions can be made from Les Houches?

— 136 lits (dont 112 en chambres et 24
en dortoir mixte),
— salle à manger pour 150 personnes,
— salle à manger et cuisine aménagée
hors sac.

— Salle de jeux,
— Salle T.V.
couleur,
— Salle de ping-
pong,
— Salle pour
veillées,

— Salle de
repassage,
— Aire de jeux
aménagée,
— Grand parking

« Les AMIS DE LA NATURE » sont une
association à but non lucratif, pour les
loisirs populaires, utilisant largement le
bénévolat.

ÉQUIPEMENT CONFORTABLE

28 chambres de 3 à 6 lits avec lavabo
(eau chaude et froide), w.c., douches,
lavabos à chaque étage.

SITUATION

**Altitude : 1 106 m, hameau des Chavants,
commune des Houches (74310)**

ACCÈS

Par la route : traverser le village. Passer devant la télécabine du PRARION et
attaquer la série de lacets qui mènent au
chalet, lequel est visible dès le début de
la montée. Accessible en hiver. Pour les
cars, chaînes obligatoires, conseillées
aux autres véhicules.

S.N.C.F. : changer à ST-GERVAIS, où
aboutissent les trains en provenance de
toute l'EUROPE, pour les HOUCHES.
Taxis ou montée à pied. En été et à pied,
demander au machiniste de s'arrêter au
viaduc de SAINTE-MARIE (30 mn à pied).

CE QUE VOUS OFFRE LE SÉJOUR AUX HOUCHES

En hiver :
Ski alpin (21 pistes)
Ski hors pistes
Ski de fond
Randonnées à peaux
de phoque ou raquettes
Village savoyard pittoresque
et animé
Patinoire naturelle
Discothèque

En été :
Randonnées pédestres aux multiples
possibilités :
Au départ du chalet :
— Col de Voza,
— Col de la Forclaz,
— Gorges de la Diosaz,
— Nid d'aigle,
— etc...

Paradis de l'escalade en haute montagne
(VERTE, GREPON, BUET, AIGUILLES
ROUGES de CHAMONIX, etc... etc...).

Excursions en SUISSE et en ITALIE (Val
d'Aoste par le tunnel du Mont-Blanc).

A noter encore que le GR 5 et le tour du
Mont-Blanc passent à proximité du Centre.

Tennis,
Pêche,
Piscine (Chamonix).

---

une aire   open space
le repassage   ironing
veiller   to stay up late
un lacet   hairpin bend
mener à   to lead to
les raquettes   snow shoes
une randonnée   ramble, hike

8 Your youth leader has received this letter in connection with a trip he is organising. As he has forgotten all the French he learned at school, he asks you to tell him what they want. Jot down the important points.

Jeunes du Monde entier Salut !

AUBERGE DE JEUNESSE   76460 SAINT-VALÉRY-EN-CAUX
(FRANCE)

B. P. 15   TÉL. (35) 97.03.98   Le premier décembre 83

Cher ami,

en réponse à votre lettre du 23 novembre dernier, nous aimerions savoir de combien personnes se compose votre groupe.

Par retour du courier, nous retourner une des deux formules de "demande de réservation" afin qu'on connaise appooximativement comment se compose votre groupe.

Par la même occasion, vous faites parvenir envôron 50% du montant total en arrhes (Deposit), ceci doit nous parvenir pour retenir votre option le plus tard le 15 janvier 83.

Recevez, Monsieur, nos salutations les plus distinguées.

M. Michel Saint-Pierre Ass. Directeur.

Pour M. Jean Berger Président.

Association déclarée (Loi du 1/7/1901) Journal Officiel de la République Française
(N° 40 NC du 6 Mai 1977 page 2512)   N° SIRET : 310 325 246-00018   Code APE : 6713

faire parvenir   to send

9 Your youth club has received this letter about a youth hostel in Normandy. As the leader speaks no French you try to give him the main details. Without translating the letter as such, make a list of the main points which it contains.

Le 13 Juin 1987

Bordesley Youth Club
Camp Hill
Stratford Road
Leamington Spa

à l'attention de Mr. Sheridan

Cher Monsieur Sheridan

Votre collègue Mr. A.R. Mars a dû vous entretenir de notre installation qui reçoit depuis de nombreuses années des groupes scolaires anglais. Aujourd'hui, nous sommes équipés de deux bâtiments de 50 lits chacun ce qui nous permet de recevoir deux groupes différents sans que cela gêne a leur séjour respectif.

J'ai l'honneur de porter à votre connaissance:

1) La période de reception qui pourrait vous être réservée serait du 1 mars au 30 avril car nous sommes maintenant complets d'une année à l'autre à partir du 1 mai jusqu'au 31 juillet avec d'autres groupes scolaires anglais.

2) Pour 1988, le prix de la pension complete serait pour votre organisation de 60Frs par jour avec un séjour gratuit par 12 eleves.

3) Les eleves devront apporter leur sac de couchage mais les chambres des professeurs seront préparées à leur arrivée avec des draps.

4) Notre bâtiment "B" (Carte-postale jointe) n'est pas encore doté du chauffage central et pour cela nous allons demander une subvention aux pouvoirs publics locaux car c'est la municipalite qui est propriétaire des locaux ici. Aussi, avant d'effectuer de nombreuses demarches administratives, nous aimerions être fixés sur vos intentions.

5) Je joins des cartes postales de notre installation ainsi que des dépliants de St-VALERY-EN-CAUX, et comme vous pouvez le constater nous béneficions d'un environnement privilegie.

Avec le plaisir de vous lire et vous remerciant par avance de votre cooperation,

Bien cordialement,

J. Berger

Jean BERGER
Président de l'Association

doté   provided with
une subvention   subsidy
les locaux   premises
effectuer une démarche   to start a process

PS: J'adresse une copie de cette lettre à Mr. Mars.
PJ: 6

WRITING

1 You are spending your summer holidays on a campsite in Brittany. Your father wants to go to the mobile shop to pick up some items, but speaks very little French. Help him by writing out a list of the things you need. Try to include at least five items and add, if possible at least one detail to each, for example:

Item	Detail
tube de dentifrice	*grand*

2 You are staying in a small hotel in Normandy with your parents. Write a postcard to your French penfriend telling her a little about the place. You could include such things as what the weather is like, what your room is like, and where the hotel is in relation to the beach.

3 Your parents want to organise a camping trip to Brittany. Write a short letter for them, to reserve a site from the 2nd to the 14th August, for one large and one small tent. You need to say that there will be four people altogether, travelling by car. Ask for details of prices, and what facilities are available on the site.

4 Your French penfriend's family are planning to spend some time in England, and have written to ask you to help them. Write back to give them the names of the best hotels in your area, and, if you can, quote some prices. You can also tell them that, at a pinch, you might be able to put them up for a few nights.

5 Write a letter to the *Hôtel des Pêcheurs* in Gerardmer, asking for details of their prices, and if they will be able to accommodate your family from the 23rd July to 6th August. Ask also if the hotel has a restaurant, and if so, ask for a sample menu to be sent to you.

6 Write a short letter to the tourist information office in Rouen, asking them to send you a list of two star hotels where you could spend one night, as you are planning a trip with a friend. Explain that your friend is disabled, and would require a hotel with the facilities for coping with wheelchairs.

7 Your youth club leader has asked you to write to the *Auberge de Jeunesse* in Saint-Valéry-en-Caux, to see if a group from the club can be accommodated there on its trip to France. You have been told to give the following information:

1 The group will be of about 40 people.
2 There will be four staff, one married couple and two single women, so they will require three separate rooms for the staff.

3 The group will arrive on Monday 6th September, and leave on Thursday, 16th September.

4 Somewhere to park the coach will be needed.

5 Packed lunches will be required on certain days.

6 There are several vegetarians in the group.

7 You need to know details of available sports facilities—the group is specially interested in sailing.

8 Your family has just spent a less than satisfactory two weeks in a hotel on the Normandy coast. It was cold and noisy and a long way from the beach (even though the brochure said it was only two minutes away). The food was very poor, as the main effort seemed to be in providing English food for tourists rather than basic French food. Finally, the showers didn't work too well and the supply of hot water was erratic to say the least. Your father has set you the task of writing a letter of complaint.

9 Write a letter to your French penfriend telling him/her about your holidays. Either use the information shown here about the place where you stayed and your diary notes about the holiday, or write about a holiday which you have really been on.

Albufeira

Algarve-Portugal

AUGUST

Flight landed six o'clock. 11
30 min. drive to Hotel.
Very pleasing.

Swam all day. 12
Restaurant in evening.
Sardines are vile!

Went to market 13
in ALBUFEIRA. Not
cheap. Lots of English people.

Went to Lisbon. 14

Another day on the 15
beach.
Disco. at night.

Still fabulous weather. 16
Am getting brown.

Home by 10 p.m. 17
Too short a holiday!

MULTI-SKILL TASK

Your parents are planning to go away on a *gîte* holiday with you and your brother. They have heard of an organisation based in France which offers such holidays at reasonable rent.

1 They ask you to write requesting a brochure.

You receive the brochure and sort out these *gîtes* as possibilities.

2 Pretend your partner is your mother and explain, in English, a little about each *gîte*. (Your partner will help you to decide which is the best one.)

3 Your parents ask you to write off to the owner of the *gîte* saying you would like to stay from the 2nd to the 16th August and telling them how many of you there are. Ask if the owner could send any further details including a plan of how to get to the accommodation.

4 About a week later you receive the following phone call from the owner.

Pretend your partner is the owner and answer the questions asked. (You can make up any details you like.)

propice favourable to

CERNEUX "Vignory"
N° G 77/14 : 2 épis. A 80 km de Paris et à 9 km de La Ferté Gaucher. Maison indépendante rénovée dans une propriété. Maison comportant deux gîtes avec entrées indépendantes. Gîte du rez-de-chaussée, terrain non clos, abri couvert, coin jeux pour les enfants. Endroit calme et reposant, très bon accueil. Vaste salle à manger/salon avec cheminée, cuisine, salle d'eau, 1 chambre (1 lit 2 pers., 1 lit 1 pers., 1 divan 2 pers., 5 adultes), W.C.

Sem. : HS 774 F BS 694 F WE 265 F
Pers. suppl. : 15 F par jour
Jours suppl. 120 F
Réservation : S.R.

 100 m 18 km 9 km 9 km 10 km
22 km 10 km 9 km 9 km 9 km

BEAUCHERY
N° G 77/15 : 2 épis. A 85 km de Paris et à 10 km de Provins. Maison indépendante dans un charmant village. Construction ancienne rénovée. Propriétaires proches. Terrain clos, jardin, garage, atelier. Chauffage central. Maison sur deux étages. Petit village propre à la détente. Salle à manger avec coin cuisine, salon, salle de bains et W.C. au rez-de-chaussée, au premier étage 3 chambres (5 lits 1 pers., 1 lit 2 pers., 7 adultes).

Sem. : HS 845 F BS 774 F
Pers. suppl. : 15 F par jour
Jours suppl. : 120 F
Réservation : S.R.

 11 km 11 km 10 km 10 km 200 m
10 km 4 km 4 km 10 km

VAUDOY-EN-BRIE
N° CH 77/04 : 3 Épis. A 63 km de Paris et à 10 km de Rozay-en-Brie. Très belle ferme dans un charmant village. Région de centre Brie, à vocation agricole. Très belle ferme aménagée avec goût et meublée agréablement. Salle commune avec cheminée et bibliothèque. Ferme calme et propice à la détente. Deux chambres au premier étage (1 lit 2 pers. et 1 lit bébé, 1 lit 2 pers., 4 adultes). Salle de bains commune aux propriétaires. Salle de petit déjeuner au r-d-c.

PRIX nuitée et petit déjeuner (par chambre)
1 pers. : 130 F
2 pers. : 143 F

Réservation : S.R. ou
Mme VANDIERENDONK
64 07 51 38

 5 km 10 km 10 km 10 km 3 km
10 km 10 km 20 km

VILLERS EN ARTHIES
N° G 95/04 : en cours de classement EC. A 75 km de Paris et à 5 km de La Roche Guyon. Corps de ferme entièrement aménagé en gîtes ruraux. Quatre gîtes mitoyens à l'étage et au rez-de-chaussée une grande salle commune. Indépendance garantie. Accueil de groupe pour de nombreuses activités. Grande exploitation agricole. Cours de cuisine et de nombreux stages sportifs possibles. Deux pièces, 1 séjour avec coin cuisine, salle d'eau, 2 lits d'1 personne. Une chambre + salle d'eau + 2 lits d'une personne, W.C., (4 personnes).

Sem. : HS 670 F BS 550 F WE 260 F
Jours suppl. : 100 F, 40 F par ½ jour.
Réservation : S.R. ou M. et Mme
VANDEPUTTE 34 78 17 73.

 sur pl. sur pl. 4 km 6 km 6 km sur pl.
6 km 15 km 4 km 4 km 12 km

Bon voyage!

 LISTENING

1 Waiting at Bordeaux St Jean station, you decide that one of the best ways to test yourself on times and numbers is to see whether you can understand the arrival and departure announcements. Can you fit times and platforms to these announcements about trains?

	Arrivées	Départs
Nice		
Paris–Austerlitz		
Arcachon		
Hendaye-Irun		
Tours		

2 You are at Bordeaux airport waiting for a friend who is to join you for the holidays. He is travelling from London. The weather has been unsettled recently and a number of delays and other problems are announced. What is the situation regarding your friend's flight and what, if anything, might you have to do?

3 Driving towards Tours late one evening you stop two passers-by to ask the way to the hotel 'Bon Séjour'. You speak to one of them and your penfriend speaks to the other. Note on your copy of the map where the hotel is. Your friend seems to have received a completely different set of instructions. Compare notes to see if you have been directed to the same place.

4 You are examining your French penfriend's mother's new car. It is one which speaks warnings and instructions to you. You play the check recording and note down the instructions etc. which the car gives, to report to your friends.

5 As part of his school project your French penfriend has to do some research on how people travel to work. While he asks various people questions you make a note of the answers, under these headings:

- Mode of Travel
- Duration of Journey
- Comment

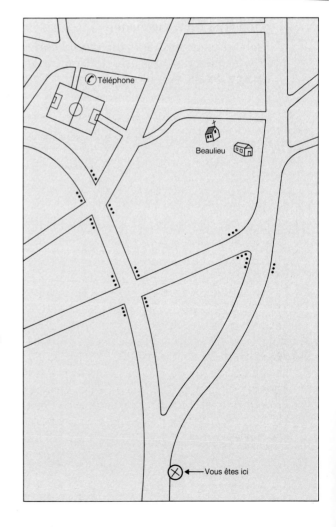

6 You are travelling from London to Paris. On the boat to Calais three people are discussing which way they prefer to make this particular journey. Thinking that this will form an interesting case study for a project you are doing, you note down the arguments for and against the following modes of travel:

- Boat-train
- Hovercraft and Train
- Aeroplane

7 You are staying with friends in Dijon but soon you are to go on holiday to St Tropez. It is the end of July and the roads will be busy. You are asked to listen to the road report and to note down which routes are the most busy and where there might be other problems.

8 On the way to St Tropez you hit a major traffic jam. You ask a policeman if there is an alternative route which will be less busy and, preferably, pleasant. Using the following questions write down the advice which he gives.

1 Which road does he tell you to take?
2 On which side of the river will you be travelling?
3 Why, apart from its being less crowded, will this be preferable?
4 How much further must you travel before changing your route?
5 What will you do at Avignon?
6 Why is Fréjus mentioned?

9 You have been staying in Nice on a school-to-school exchange. Shortly before your return the group is addressed by a French customs officer. He warns you, very firmly, about which items are prohibited on the aircraft and also about which items you may not take back to England. Make a note of these items to make sure you obey the rules.

10 You are on holiday in the Dordogne with your family. Public transport is very limited and your father is beginning to regret not having brought the car. He asks you to phone some car-hire firms to find out which cars are available, the cost involved and any other necessary details. You phone three firms all of which answer with a pre-recorded message. Note down the information which they give. The firms are Hertz, Avis and Bagnoles Boris.

11 On your way to the South of France with your family you have stopped for the day in Paris. As you return to the car a traffic policeman is about to impound it. Despite your protestations all the policeman will tell you is how to liberate your car. Write down his instructions to make sure you retrieve the vehicle as quickly as possible.

SPEAKING

1 You arrive at the youth hostel in Rouen. Using the card you are given answer the warden's questions about where you have come from and how you travelled. Your teacher, assistant or partner will play the role of the warden.

2 You are at the *Gare St Lazare* in Paris. The member of the group playing the clerk is given the timetable and the others work from the cards they are given. Take it in turns to perform the tasks shown on each card. When everyone has asked the questions on his/her card change roles.

3 One group member will be given a plan of a station and must answer the questions put by other members of the group. The others work from the cue-cards they are given. Take it in turns to ask questions and to play different roles.

4 Using the timetable and plan of the station, prepare a further ten questions which you could ask someone who was not in your group last time. Be prepared to answer someone else's questions too.

5 A French friend is planning a journey from Wolverhampton to London. He phones to ask if you have timetable details. Luckily, you do and should be able to answer his questions. Work with a partner, one of you taking the role of the French person. Your teacher will give you the questions.

InterCity

Sundays	London Euston	Sandwell & Dudley	Wolverhampton
	1000	1220	1246 ☐
	1100	1319	1345 ☐
	1200	1455B	1438 ☐
	1400		1634 ☐
	1540	1729	1740 ☐
	1640	1833	1845 ☐
	1710	1858	1910 ☐
	1740	1928	1940
	1810	2000	2012 ☐
	1840	2025	2036 ☐
	1910	2055	2107 ☐
	1940	2133	2145
	2030	2215	2227 ☐
	2140	2331	2342
	2315		0131

NOTES
B Change at Birmingham New Street.
SO Saturdays only.
SX Saturdays excepted.
Ø Hot dishes to order or restaurant car service of meals. Also buffet service.
☐ Buffet service of drinks and cold snacks.

InterCity

PRINCIPAL TRAIN SERVICES
WOLVERHAMPTON-SANDWELL & DUDLEY-LOND
30 September 1985 to 11 May 1986

Mondays to Saturdays		Wolverhampton	Sandwell & Dudley	London Euston
	MO	0552	0601	0744 ☐
	MX	0557	0606	0759 Ø MSX ☐
	SX	0627	0636	0829 Ø
		0657	0706	0859 Ø SX ☐ SC
	SX	0727	0736	0924 Ø
	SO	0727	0736	0929 ☐
	SX	0757	0806	0956 Ø
		0827	0836	1029 Ø SX ☐ SC
	SX	0849	0858	1101
		0922	0931	1132 Ø SX ☐ SC
	SO	0957	1006	1203 ☐
		1027	1036	1235 Ø SX ☐ SO
		1127	1136	1332 Ø SX ☐ SO
		1227	1236	1432 Ø SX ☐ SO
		1327	1336	1532 Ø SX ☐ SO
		1427	1436	1632 Ø SX ☐ SO
		1527	1536	1732 Ø SX ☐ SO
		1627	1636	1834 Ø SX ☐ SO
	SX	1647	1657	1901 ☐
		1727	1736	1937 ☐
		1827	1836	2029 ☐
		1927	1936	2136 ☐ SO
		2027	2036	2232 ☐
		2127	2136	2331

PRINCIPAL TRAIN SERVICES
LONDON-SANDWELL & DUDLEY-WOLVERHAMPTON
30 September 1985 to 11 May 1986

Sundays	Wolverhampton	Sandwell & Dudley	London Euston
	0757	0806	1038 ☐
	0857	0906	1134
	0957	1006	1234
	1100		1331 ☐
	1200		1431 ☐
From 10 November —	1300		1531 ☐
	1400	1352B	1633 ☐
	1500		1721 ☐
	1557	1606	1807 ☐
	1627	1636	1831 ☐
	1727	1736	1934 ☐
To 27 October —	1736	1746	1948
	1827	1836	2030 ☐
	1927	1936	2140 ☐
	2027	2036	2234 ☐
	2127	2136	2330

Mondays to Saturdays		London Euston	Sandwell & Dudley	Wolverhampton
		0010		0318
		0730	0922	0934 Ø SX ☐ SO
		0835	1022	1034 Ø SX ☐ SO
		0935	1122	1134 Ø SX ☐ SO
		1040	1231	1243 Ø SX ☐ SO
		1140	1331	1343 Ø SX ☐ SO
		1240	1435	1448 Ø SX ☐ SO
		1340	1531	1543 Ø SX ☐ SO
		1440	1631	1643 Ø SX ☐ SO
		1510	1707	1719 Ø
		1540	1725	1737 Ø
		1640	1827	1839 SX ☐ SO
	SX	1710	1855	1907 Ø
		1740	1924	1936 Ø SX ☐ SO
	SX	1810	2000	2014 ☐
		1840	2023	2036 ☐
	SX	1910	2055	2107 Ø
		1940	2133	2145 ☐
		2030	2215	2227 ☐
	SX	2140	2331	2342 ☐
	SO	2140	2331	2352 ☐
	SX	2315		0131
	SO	2325		0233

Normal return £35.
Savers £11 or £14.50

NOTES
B Change at Birmingham New Street.
MO Mondays only.
MSX Mondays and Saturdays excepted.
MX Mondays excepted.
SO Saturdays only.
SX Saturdays excepted.
Ø Hot dishes to order or restaurant car service of meals. Also buffet service.
☐ Buffet service of drinks and cold snacks.

6 You meet a group of French teenagers on the train returning from holiday in England. You ask where they have been staying, where they are going to and how they are travelling on from Paris. Some group members have cue-cards in French. Take it in turns to ask questions.

7 One partner has the timetable, the other, working from a cue-card, plays the role of a tourist and has to find out, with the help of the cue-card, the answers to such questions as:

When is the first departure for Perrache?

What is the frequency of trains at night?

Does the 25 go from the Part Dieu?

l'heure de pointe (f.)   rush hour
heures creuses (f.)   off-peak times

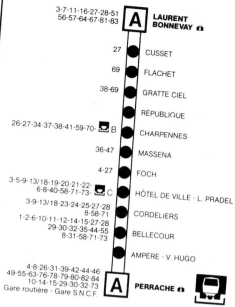

ligne A : L. Bonnevay - Perrache

MÉTRO A

LIGNE A	de Perrache	de Bonnevay
Premier départ	5.00	5.00
Dernier départ	0.18	0.02

Fréquence	heures de pointe	3 minutes
	heures creuses	5 minutes
	heures de nuit	11 minutes

ligne B : Charpennes - Jean Macé

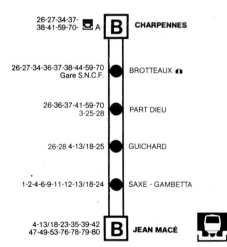

MÉTRO B

LIGNE B	de Charpennes	de Jean-Macé
Premier départ	5.00	5.00
Dernier départ	0.18	0.18

Fréquence	heures de pointe	3 minutes
	heures creuses	5 minutes
	heures de nuit	11 minutes

ligne C : Hôtel de Ville - L. Pradel Cx Rousse

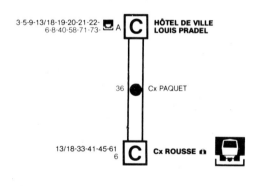

MÉTRO C

LIGNE C	d'Hôtel de Ville	de Croix-Rousse
Premier départ	4.56	5.05
Dernier départ	0.25	0.16

Fréquence	heures de pointe	3 minutes
	heures creuses	5 minutes
	heures de nuit	11 minutes

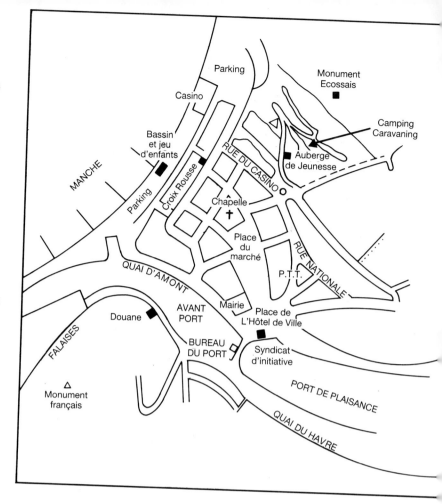

8 You are waiting for a friend in the car-park near the children's playground in St Valéry.

A string of people (the rest of the group) ask you the way to different places. Give directions and make sure that they write down your instructions. Take it in turns, within the group, to give the instructions. The 'visitors' could then report back to their group leader (teacher or assistant).

You may be asked by members of your group for directions to some of these places:

Youth hostel
Scottish memorial
Casino
Chapel
Town 'hall
Information office
French memorial
Marina
Market square
Campsite

9 You and your French penfriend have just spent four days on a 'Go Anywhere' rail card. Here are the notes you have kept in your diary. Use them to help answer your penfriend's uncle's questions about your trip. Your teacher, assistant or one of your classmates should play the role of your penfriend's uncle. Your teacher will give you the questions.

Tuesday Perpignan – train to Andorra – beautiful green countryside – camped just south of town.

Wednesday Went to bullfight pm. after shopping in morning – everything's so cheap! Caught evening train to Carcassone. Overnight in YHA.

Thursday Looked round old town (picnic lunch) – train to Beziers in evening. Stayed YHA again – this one not very good.

Friday Walked round port – went to Musée des Beaux Arts. Restaurant. Train to Perpignan.

10 On your way to Paris, you have started to write to your parents.

Use this as a guideline to answer your penfriend's questions when you arrive. Your partner should play the role of your penfriend. Your teacher will give you the questions.

> should be in Paris in about half an hour. All has gone well. The crossing was calm and the customs were no problem. The train was even early leaving Calais. It's hot on the train; I'm starving but the snacks are expensive! I've been talking to some young French guys - my French isn't too rusty!!

READING

1 As you start your journey to France, crossing from Dover to Calais on a French boat, you suddenly realise that all the signs and notices around you are going to be in French from now on. You decide to note down the signs which are on the boat and give their meaning in English as the start of a vocabulary book you intend to keep throughout your holiday.

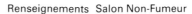

Renseignements   Salon Non-Fumeur   Privé

Pont D   Gilet de Sauvetage   Réservé aux Chauffeurs de Camions et de Cars

Boutiques Hors Taxes   Restaurant Self-Service   Contrôle des Passeports   Bureau de Change

2 By the time you have arrived in Lyon you are still writing your vocabulary book. You study some of the underground signs before using the system on your own. Once again you note them down with an explanation in English of what they tell you.

SYMBOLES MÉTRO

Taxi   Bus   Métro

Parc à voitures   Téléphone   Interdit aux chiens

en cas de chute d'une personne sur la voie

1. tirez la poignée

2. alertez le centre de contrôle

armoire de sécurité

3 You are planning a day-trip to Paris from Lyon. Study the timetable. A friend is due to meet you in the *Gare de Lyon* in Paris at 09.30 on a Saturday.

Make a note of which train will get you to Paris on time. You should note down:

1 What time it leaves the Perrache station in Lyon.

2 Where it stops.

3 If there is a buffet on the train or not.

4 What sort of train it is.

Horaire

Du 29 sept. 1985
au 31 mai 1986

SNCF

Lyon-Paris

- ● **Lyon-Perrache**
- ● Lyon-Part-Dieu
- ● Villefranche-sur-Saône
- ● Mâcon-Loché-TGV
- ● Mâcon
- ● Tournus
- ● Chalon-sur-Saône
- ● Chagny
- ● Beaune
- ● Dijon-Ville
- ● Montbard
- ● Laroche-Migennes
- ● **Paris-Gare-de-Lyon**

Cette fiche ne comporte que les horaires

1 B

Symboles

A	Arrivée	⊗	Grill-express
D	Départ	▨	Restauration à la place
⛉	Couchettes	⚲	Bar
⇌	Voiture-Lits	⛙	Vente ambulante
IC	Intercités	TGV	Train à grande vitesse

Remarque

Certains trains circulant rarement ne sont pas repris dans cette fiche.

Services offerts dans les gares

	Information	Réservation	Facilités pour handicapés	Parcotrain	Location de voitures	Location de vélos	Buffet	Change
Beaune	(80) 41.50.50	(80) 22.14.99			●		●	
Chagny	(85) 93.50.50	(85) 87.16.95	●					
Chalon-sur-Saône	(85) 93.50.50	(85) 48.09.12	●		●	●	●	
Dijon-Ville	(80) 41.50.50	(80) 43.52.56	●		●	●	●	●
Laroche-Migennes	(86) 46.50.50				●	●	●	
Lyon-Perrache	(7) 892.50.50	(7) 892.10.70	●	●	●	●	●	●
Mâcon	(85) 38.50.50	(85) 38.44.48	●		●	●	●	
Montbard	(80) 41.50.50	(80) 92.43.65	●			●		
Paris-Gare de Lyon	(1) 345.92.22	(1) 345.93.33	●	●	●	●	●	●
Villefranche-sur-Saône	(74) 65.27.16					●		

A Paris-Gare de Lyon, l'office de Tourisme de Paris assure un service d'information touristique et de réservation hôtelière.

Numéro du train	5078	5056	5060	5792	5040	5194	7100	600	602	602	7150	770	652	940	604	730	710	7152	5012
Notes à consulter	1	2	3	4	5	6	7	8	8	8	9	10	11	12	10	13	5	14
Lyon-Perrache	D 00.05	01.11	01.20	01.38	01.44	02.41		05.05	05.40		06.20	06.46						05.35
Lyon-Part-Dieu	D							05.15	05.50		06.30		07.00	07.00	07.06			05.44
Villefranche-sur-Saône	D 00.40							05.25										06.04
Mâcon-Loché	D							06.15	06.15			07.30						
Mâcon	D 01.16		02.25															06.24
Tournus	D 01.38																	06.41
Chalon-sur-Saône	D 02.19		02.57						05.53						06.17	06.57		
Chagny	D 02.32								06.04						06.35			
Beaune	D 02.43								06.14						06.49			
Dijon-Ville	A 03.08	02.57	03.16	03.34	03.27	04.23	04.37		06.35	06.56					07.25	07.29		
Montbard	A 04.55						05.20		07.30									
Laroche-Migennes	A 05.48		04.51	05.11	04.57		06.28											
Paris-Gare-de-Lyon	A 07.30	06.00	06.25	06.50	06.28			07.15	08.06	08.06		08.41	08.34	09.15	09.04	09.04	09.10	09.58

Tous les trains comportent des places assises en 1re et 2e cl. sauf indication contraire dans les notes.

Notes : * Autocar SNCF de Villefranche-sur-Saône à Mâcon-Loché. *TGV*

1. Circule les lun. sauf les 11 nov., 31 mars et 19 mai. Circule en outre les 12 nov., 02 janv., 01 avril et 20 mai. ⛉

2. Circule les lun., sam., dim. et fêtes et sauf les 02, 11 nov., 31 mars, 03, 10 et 19 mai. Circule en outre les 01, 12 nov., 26 déc., 02, 05 janv., 07 fév., 01 avril, 01, 08, 20 mai. ⛉

3. Circule toutes les nuits. Le « Côte d'Azur-Paris ». ⇌ ⇌ ⚲

4. Circule toutes les nuits. ⇌

5. Circule tous les jours.

6. Circule tous les jours sauf dim. et fêtes.

7. *TGV* Circule les lun. sauf les 11 nov., 23, 30 déc., 31 mars et 19 mai. Circule en outre les 12 nov., 01 avril et 20 mai. Sans supplément.

8. *TGV* Circule tous les jours sauf sam., dim. et fêtes et sauf les 26, 27 déc., 07 fév., 02, 09 mai. A supplément certains jours. ▨ 1re cl.

9. *TGV* Circule tous les jours sauf les 02 nov., 02 et 09 mai. A supplément certains jours. ▨ 1re cl.

10. *TGV* Circule tous les jours sauf sam., dim. et fêtes et sauf les 26, 27 déc., 02 et 09 mai. En 1re cl. uniquement. A supplément. ▨ 1re cl. ⚲

11. *TGV* Circule tous les jours sauf sam., dim. et fêtes et sauf les 26, 27 déc., 02 et 09 mai. Sans supplément. ⚲

12. *TGV* Circule tous les jours sauf les 02, 10 nov., 30 mars, 03, 10 et 18 mai. 1re cl. uniquement certains jours. A supplément certains jours. ▨ 1re cl.

13. *TGV* Circule tous les jours sauf sam. dim. et fêtes et sauf les 02 nov., 02, 03, 09, 10 mai. A supplément certains jours. ▨ 1re cl. ⚲

14. De Lyon à Dijon, circule du lun. au vend. sauf les 01 et 11 nov., 25 déc., 01 janv., 31 mars, 01, 08 et 19 mai. Prolongé jusqu'à Paris les lun. et les 12 nov., 02 janv., 01 avr. et 20 mai sauf 11 nov., 30 déc., 31 mars et 19 mai.

15. *TGV* Circule tous les jours sauf les 02, 10 nov., 30 mars, 02, 03, 09, 10 et 18 mai. A supplément certains jours. ⚲

16. Circule tous les jours sauf sam., dim. et fêtes. A certaines dates changement à Beaune A : 07.56, D : 08.05. Dijon A : 08.32. En 2e cl. uniquement jusqu'à Beaune.

17. *TGV* Circule tous les jours. A supplément certains jours. ⚲

18. Circule tous les jours sauf les dim. et sauf les 11 nov., 31 mars et 19 mai. Corail.

Nota : *TGV* : Réservation obligatoire.

4 You are in France and are planning to spend three days with another English friend who is staying nearby.

Since the weather is good and you are both in need of exercise, you think it would be a good idea to hire bicycles. You find this brochure giving information. Write to your friend, in English, suggesting the idea, saying how much it costs and describing the bicycles which are available.

vous n'emportez pas votre vélo

TRAIN + Vélo

La SNCF met à votre disposition dans 270 gares un service de location de vélos.

Il vous suffit de présenter une carte d'identité et de verser une caution de 190 F.*

Si vous présentez :
- une Carte Bleue, une Carte Bleue Visa, Eurocard, Master Card, Access,
- une carte d'abonnement à libre circulation, carte demi-tarif, carte Vermeil, carte France Vacances, carte Jeune,

vous ne payez pas cette caution.

Vous restituez le vélo à votre gare de départ ou dans une autre gare de la région (renseignez-vous auprès du personnel SNCF).

Vous payez la location en restituant le vélo.

La réservation est possible, dans la limite des disponibilités.

Deux types de bicyclettes vous sont proposés :
- des vélos, de type randonneur, à 10 vitesses, avec cadre homme ou mixte et, pour les vélos homme, guidon course et freins double poignée...
- des bicyclettes de type traditionnel : cadre mixte, guidon et selle à réglage instantané avec ou sans dérailleur.

Vous trouverez ci-après la liste des 270 gares ouvertes au service Train + Vélo.

En fonction de la durée de votre location, une tarification* dégressive vous est proposée.

vélo randonneur (m.)   touring bicycle
guidon (m.)   handlebars
selle (f.)   saddle
réglage (m.)   adjustment

	1/2 journée	journée
Vélo type traditionnel	18 F	24 F
Vélo type randonneur	28 F	33 F

	3e au 10e jour		à partir du 11e jour	
	1/2 journée	journée	1/2 journée	journée
Vélo type traditionnel	14 F	18 F	9 F	12 F
Vélo type randonneur	21 F	25 F	14 F	16 F

* Prix au 15/4/85.

SNCF Guide du train et du vélo

5 Travelling by train, you pick up a brochure about the TGV. You've
heard a lot about it and intend to make a journey on the TGV
while you are in France. Make a list of what you have to do by
way of preparation:

1 If you book before going to the station.

2 If you book at the station.

What services are available on the train?

LA RÉSERVATION TGV : OBLIGATOIRE

Dans le TGV, pour votre plus grand confort,
tous les voyageurs sont assis.
Pour qu'il n'y ait pas plus de passagers que de places assises,
la réservation est **obligatoire**.

Deux solutions sont envisageables :

1. VOUS POUVEZ ORGANISER VOTRE DÉPART AVANT VOTRE ARRIVÉE À LA GARE

Achetez alors votre billet et réservez votre place à l'avance :
- **Par correspondance** : à partir de 6 mois avant la date de votre départ.
- **Au guichet des 1500 gares et des agences de voyages agréées** assurant la réservation : dans les 2 mois qui précèdent votre départ et jusqu'à la limite du temps qui vous est nécessaire pour rejoindre la gare de départ.
- **Par téléphone en gare** : à partir de 9 jours avant votre départ. Mais vous devez alors retirer votre réservation au plus tard 30 minutes avant l'heure de départ de votre train.
Pour la restauration à la place en 1re classe, la réservation est nécessaire afin de vous assurer un service de qualité. Vous pouvez réserver votre repas en même temps que votre place, jusqu'à une heure avant le départ du TGV de sa gare d'origine.

2. VOUS N'AVEZ PAS PU ORGANISER VOTRE DÉPART AVANT VOTRE ARRIVÉE À LA GARE

POUR DÉPART IMMÉDIAT

- **Vous n'avez pas de billet**
Au guichet de la gare de départ, un vendeur SNCF vous délivre en une seule fois et jusqu'au dernier moment (quelques minutes avant votre départ) :
- votre billet,
- votre réservation TGV et le supplément éventuel (cf. page 6).
Pour permettre à un plus grand nombre de voyageurs n'ayant pas leur billet d'emprunter le premier TGV offrant des places disponibles, une procédure de "réservation rapide au guichet" a été mise en place. Elle consiste à attribuer une place dans ce premier TGV possible mais, comme la demande est tardive, elle ne permet pas le choix entre "fumeurs", "non fumeurs", "coin-fenêtre", "coin-couloir", "repas à la place".

- **Vous avez déjà votre billet ou une carte d'abonnement**
Un système de réservation rapide "libre-service" est à votre disposition.

LES SERVICES À BORD DU TGV

LA RESTAURATION

1 - LE BAR

Dans chaque rame, le bar est ouvert pendant toute la durée du trajet. Ce bar offre aux voyageurs des deux classes : • des plats simples chauds et froids • des sandwichs • des boissons chaudes et froides.

2 - LA RESTAURATION À LA PLACE EN 1re CLASSE

Un service à la place est assuré dans les voitures 1re classe réservées à la restauration de tous les TGV circulant aux heures habituelles des repas.
Ce service propose :
- le matin, un petit déjeuner,
- à midi et le soir un menu complet avec choix entre plat du jour chaud ou froid ou une grillade.
Les menus sont souvent renouvelés à l'intention des voyageurs se déplaçant fréquemment en TGV.
Réservez votre repas dans ces voitures en même temps que votre place.

3 - LA RESTAURATION EN 2e CLASSE

Un service de coffrets-repas froids, sans réservation, est proposé dans les voitures de 2e classe de certains TGV.

LES AUTRES SERVICES

Un coin boutique situé dans le bar vous propose :
- tabac • journaux et revues.

Handicapés

Une place dans une voiture de 1re classe peut être réservée pour une personne handicapée désireuse de voyager sur son fauteuil roulant. Cette personne paye le tarif de 2e classe.

Jeune Voyageur Service (JVS) [1]

Pour les enfants voyageant seuls (de 4 à moins de 14 ans) un service particulier (JVS) est mis à votre disposition dans certains TGV : une hôtesse prend en charge les enfants, de la gare de départ à la gare d'arrivée, moyennant un supplément spécifique.

[1] Les services JVS assurés dans les TGV figurent dans la brochure "Votre enfant voyage en train" disponible à votre gare ou à votre agence de voyages.

SNCF Guide du Voyageur TGV

---

rejoindre (in this context) to get to, to arrive at
retirer (in this context) to collect
moyennant at a charge of

6 During a stay with your French partner you and she are to be treated to a three-day coach holiday around Provence. Write to your family in England explaining the holiday in detail and giving an account of what you will be doing each day.

BALADE PROVENÇALE

« fifres et tambourins » nouveauté

3 JOURS DE TOULOUSE 1 180 F

1er jour : Toulouse - Sisteron
• **TOULOUSE :** Rendez-vous des participants à 7 h Gare Routière Matabiau, Quai FRAM. Départ à 7 h 15 par l'autoroute pour NIMES, (tour de ville) puis le PONT DU GARD (arrêt) ensuite, ORANGE ; visite et déjeuner. Après-midi, départ pour la Haute-Provence par VAISON LA ROMAINE (arrêt), Nyons, Serres et SISTERON (montée à la citadelle si l'horaire le permet). Dîner et logement.

2e jour : Sisteron - Arles
Le matin, par Château-Arnoux, vue sur les Rochers des Mées, MANOSQUE où naquit Jean Giono ; APT, le Pont Julien, ROUSSILLON et ses carrières d'ocre ; vue sur Gordes et arrivée à FONTAINE de VAUCLUSE. Déjeuner.
L'après-midi, par ST-RÉMY-DE-PROVENCE, les ANTIQUES (arrêt), les BAUX-de-PROVENCE (arrêt) vue sur le Moulin de Fontvieille et ARLES. Visite du cloître St-Trophime. Dîner et logement.

3e jour : Arles - Toulouse
Départ le matin pour AIGUES MORTES, la ville de St-Louis (arrêt), continuation pour FRONTIGNAN (dégustation). Puis, arrivée à SÈTE. Après déjeuner, promenade en bateau sur les canaux et reprise de l'autoroute. Retour à TOULOUSE dans la soirée.

DATES de DÉPART		Villes de départ	PRIX	Suppléments
AVRIL	19	TOULOUSE	1180 F	chambre individuelle : 160 F
MAI 1er	17			
JUIN	14	BORDEAUX LIMOGES	1180 F (+ billet SNCF)	
JUILLET	12			
AOÛT	15			
SEPTEMBRE	13			

De BORDEAUX, LIMOGES :
Départ individuel en train (horaires au choix).

• **Pour BORDEAUX, LIMOGES :**
Retour en train (horaires au choix).

carrière (f.)   quarry
dégustation (f.)   tasting

7 You are on holiday in the South of France, where your parents are shortly to join you, travelling by car. You know that your father drives like a maniac and is likely to be even worse on French roads. You send him this document, published by ASSECAR, an organisation which promotes motorway safety. In your accompanying letter you list and stress to him the six points illustrated in the leaflet.

la file de gauche (f.)   left hand lane
la bande d'arrêt d'urgence (f.)   hard shoulder

Reproduit avec l'aimable autorisation de la Gendarmerie Nationale Française

8 Before your visit to France you have heard horrific stories about the number of road accidents and the comparative danger on French roads. In order to be able to discuss the matter informedly you decide to write to a friend who works for the Automobile Association asking for facts and figures about accidents and deaths in the UK. In your letter you cite details of road accidents and deaths in France last year which you obtain from this section of the *Code de la Route*. You also give figures about the causes of road accidents. Finally, you quote the advice which is given in this section and ask if the AA publishes similar documentation. Write that part of the letter which gives information from the brochure.

9 An English friend of yours is due to arrive in Lyon shortly after you have left. As the way in which bus and metro tickets are bought and used is not all that easy to understand to start with, you decide to leave notes explaining some of the system. You should explain to your friend the following:

1 How the price of tickets varies.

2 Exactly what each ticket entitles you to.

3 What you have to do each time you get on a bus or underground train.

4 Where you can get tickets from.

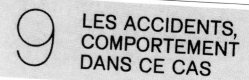

LES ACCIDENTS, COMPORTEMENT DANS CE CAS

1) NOTIONS GÉNÉRALES

Dernier bilan annuel publié :
Il y a eu en France 253.208 accidents corporels.
— 347.918 blessés.
— 12.480 tués.

Un mort sur trois avait de 15 à 24 ans.

Répartition des victimes par catégories d'usagers.

● Voitures de tourisme	
● Deux roues	53 %
● Piétons	25 %
● Poids lourds	17 %
	5 %

Répartition des accidents suivant le lieu :

● zones urbaines	
● rase campagne et petites agglomérations	67 %
	33 %

Répartition suivant l'éclairement.

● de jour	
● de nuit avec éclairage public	69 %
● de nuit sans éclairage public	20 %
● au lever du jour et à la tombée de la nuit	7 %
	4 %

2) LES PRINCIPALES CAUSES

● Vitesse excessive, non respect des limitations	
● Inobservation de la priorité et absence de précautions aux intersections	24 %
● L'alcool (voir pp. 41 et 42)	18 %
● Circulation à gauche	12 %
● Inattention, distraction, fatigue	8 %
● Changements de direction sans précautions	8 %
● Dépassements interdits ou irréguliers	6 %
● Défaillance matérielle ou humaine	5 %
	4 %

Ces chiffres montrent qu'il suffirait de respecter le Code de la route pour éviter près de 9 accidents sur 10...

3) CE QU'IL FAUT FAIRE

● Tout conducteur ou tout usager de la route impliqué dans un accident de la circulation doit s'arrêter aussitôt que possible.
● Tout usager de la route non impliqué dans un accident doit aussi s'arrêter pour porter assistance à son prochain, en veillant à ne pas être une nouvelle cause de danger.
Mais si les secours sont déjà organisés, ne nous arrêtons qui si on nous le demande, sinon nous ne serions que des curieux inutiles et dangereux pour la circulation.

bilan (m.)   figures
poids lourds (m.)   heavy vehicles
dépassement (m.)   overtaking
défaillance (f.)   failure

RESEAU

Le tarif est unique quels que soient la distance et le mode de transport utilisé (autobus - funiculaire - métro - trolleybus), exception faite de quelques lignes de grande banlieue (21, 68, 72, 73) qui ont conservé une "section", hors des limites de la Communauté Urbaine.

● Le **ticket urbain** permet d'utiliser successivement plusieurs véhicules (bus et métro) au cours d'un même déplacement. Il est valable une heure après sa 1ère oblitération (sauf en cas de blocage de circulation); il permet d'effectuer jusqu'à trois correspondances, mais **n'autorise aucun aller-retour, même partiel.**

● Dès que vous montez dans un bus ou que vous franchissez la "ligne de péage", d'une station de métro, vous devez oblitérer la "plage" du ticket marquée 1er trajet; ensuite chaque fois que vous changez de véhicule (bus ou métro) vous oblitérez une des "plages" libres, sauf de métro à métro.
Pour les lignes à "section suburbaine" il faut oblitérer, un, ou deux tickets suivant le point où vous descendez. Renseignez-vous auprès du conducteur.

● Le **ticket urbain est vendu, soit à l'unité, soit en carnet de 6 tickets** (moins cher), **par les conducteurs de bus** (monter par la porte avant) **ou aux distributeurs automatiques.**

● Le **Billet de groupe**
est un billet réservé au déplacement **collectif** d'un groupe "organisé", constitué d'au moins 10 personnes, qui est valable sur le réseau **urbain.**
Il est vendu à la Gare Routière de Perrache, au Guichet "Abonnements Lafayette", au Kiosque des Brotteaux.

● Le **Billet de tourisme**
individuel et nominatif, est essentiellement destiné aux touristes et personnes de passage à Lyon et leur donne la possibilité d'utiliser toutes les lignes du Réseau Urbain et Suburbain (Bus - Crémaillère - Funiculaires et Métro) **sans limitation du nombre de voyages.**

Sa validité est soit de **deux jours** (48 h) soit de **trois jours** (72 h), pour le valider il suffit de le composter **une seule fois** lors de l'accès dans le premier véhicule utilisé et **ce sont la date et l'heure de cette oblitération qui déterminent la durée de son utilisation.**
Il est vendu dans tous les Kiosques et Bureaux T.C.L. et certains grands Hôtels.

oblitérer   to cancel
un déplacement   journey

10 You are returning to England with your family who have been abroad for the first time. Your father wants you to explain to him the system for passing through English customs. As the only document you can find which explains this is in French you make notes for him explaining the procedure for the red and green channels. Also, write out a list for him of what duty free goods he is allowed to take into the UK.

affichette (f.) sticker
coller to stick
contrôle (m.) check
acquis acquired
en franchise duty free

BRITAIN Guide du Voyageur en Grande-Bretagne
Renseignements pratiques

NOTHING to declare

GOODS to declare

Douanes

Il existe dans la plupart des ports et des aéroports britanniques deux sorties : l'une verte et l'autre rouge. Si vous avez des marchandises à déclarer, présentez-vous au Red Channel (passage rouge) ; si vous n'avez rien à déclarer, présentez-vous au Green Channel (passage vert) où cependant des contrôles inattendus peuvent avoir lieu. Les voyageurs débarquant avec une voiture se verront proposer des affichettes rouges ou vertes à coller à bord de leur véhicule. Si le système des sorties verte et rouge ne fonctionne pas, adressez-vous aux douaniers dans le Hall des Bagages.

A déclarer au Red Channel

Boissons alcoolisées, tabacs, parfums, eau de toilette et tous autres produits dépassant la limite autorisée des produits admis en franchise (la liste des produits admis en franchise est indiquée plus loin) et tous articles prohibés ou faisant l'objet de restrictions.

A déclarer également tout ce que vous comptez laisser ou vendre en Grande-Bretagne. Si votre séjour dans ce pays dépasse six mois, vous devez déclarer tous les articles acquis à l'étranger (même s'il s'agit de cadeaux), acquis en voyage ou encore acquis au RU en franchise des droits et taxes ou acquis au Royaume Uni il y a plus de trois ans. Les douaniers vous indiqueront les tarifs applicables aux touristes et aux ressortissants nationaux.

Articles prohibés ou contrôlés

L'importation des articles suivants est interdite : la fausse monnaie, les couteaux à cran d'arrêt, les bandes dessinées d'horreur, les ouvrages, journaux, films, vidéo-cassettes et autres articles à caractère obscène. L'importation des articles suivants est interdite *sauf* sur présentation d'une licence d'importation ou sur autorisation des services administratifs chargés des réglementations des importations : les drogues contrôlées (opium, héroïne, morphine, cocaïne, cannabis, amphétamines et LSD) ; les armes à feu (y compris les pistolets à air comprimé et armes identiques) ; les munitions et les explosifs y compris les feux d'artifices ; la viande et les volailles (pas entièrement cuites) ; les appareils de radio et de téléphone (par exemple talkie-walkie et récepteurs de citizenband) ; les radio-microphones et les systèmes d'écoute ; les plantes et les bulbes de plantes, les arbres, fruits, pommes de terre et autres légumes ; les animaux et les oiseaux vivants (voir ci-dessous) ; les animaux et les oiseaux empaillés ainsi que les objets provenant d'espèces rares tels que certaines fourrures, ivoires et articles en peau de reptile.

Tous renseignements complémentaires concernant les licences d'importations peuvent être obtenus auprès de *H.M. Customs and Excise, Kent House, Upper Ground, London SE1 9PS.* Tél : 01 - 928 0533.

Animaux et oiseaux

En raison d'une exigence de quarantaine (six mois pour les animaux, 35 jours pour les oiseaux, ou si le séjour est plus court, les animaux attendront en quarantaine votre départ), il n'est pas conseillé d'amener votre animal en Grande-Bretagne pour un court séjour. La procédure permettant d'obtenir une licence d'importation après quarantaine doit être demandée au *Ministry of Agriculture, Fisheries and Food, Hook Rise South, Tolworth, Surbiton, Surrey KT6 7NF.* Tél : 01 - 337 6611.

Les peines pour importation illicite d'animaux sont sévères : amendes illimitées et – ou un an de prison. Il n'existe aucune exception à cette règle établie pour éviter les épidémies de rage.

Tous renseignements complémentaires concernant les interdictions et les restrictions d'importations peuvent être obtenus auprès des services de *H.M. Customs and Excise* à l'adresse indiquée dans le paragraphe *Articles prohibés ou faisant l'objet de restrictions.*

Rien à déclarer (Green Channel)

Les effets personnels que vous remporterez avec vous (sauf si votre séjour dépasse 6 mois auquel cas vous êtes tenu de les déclarer) ; une quantité raisonnable de pellicules et de films ; l'équipement de camping utilisé pendant votre séjour et les produits admis en franchise (la liste varie selon l'endroit où vous les avez achetés et selon que vous vivez ou non en Europe).

Produits admis en franchise *(voir ci-dessus)*	
Produits acquis soit en franchise des droits et taxes à bord d'un navire ou d'un aéronef ou en franchise des droits et taxes dans la CEE soit hors de la CEE.	Produits acquis tous droits et taxes payés dans la CEE.
Tabacs et cigares 200 cigarettes ou 100 cigarillos ou 50 cigares ou 250 grammes de tabac } le double si vous habitez en dehors de l'Europe	**Tabacs et cigares** 300 cigarettes ou 150 cigarillos ou 75 cigares ou 400 grammes de tabac
Boissons alcoolisées 1 litre de plus de 38,8° proof (22° Gay-Lussac) ou 2 litres ne dépassant pas 38,8° proof ou vin de liqueur ou vin mousseux plus 2 litres de vin de table	**Boissons alcoolisées** 1½ litres de plus de 38,8° proof (22° Gay-Lussac) ou 3 litres ne dépassant pas 38,8° proof ou vin de liqueur ou vin mousseux plus 4 litres de vin de table non-mousseux
Parfums 50 grammes (2fl oz ou 60cc)	**Parfums** 75 grammes (3fl oz ou 90cc)
Eau de toilette 250cc (9fl oz)	**Eau de toilette** 375cc (13fl oz)
Autres articles Jusqu'à une valeur de £28	**Autres articles** Jusqu'à une valeur de £120

WRITING

1 Your tickets to France have finally been sorted out. It now only remains for you to write a brief letter to your penfriend giving details of your arrival. Here is your outward schedule:

Depart London (Victoria)	10.00
Arrive Dover	11.45
Depart Dover	12.45
Arrive Calais	13.25
Depart Calais	14.00
Arrive Paris (Nord)	17.30

The most important piece of information to your penfriend is your arrival time in Paris. Ask, as well, exactly where your friend will meet you and say what you intend to wear. About 100 words should be enough for this letter.

2 A French friend is due to come and stay with you shortly. She is travelling by boat-train to London and will then have to get a bus from Victoria Coach Station to get to where you live. You send her this map showing Victoria Railway and Coach Stations and also write her a short letter explaining exactly what she must do to get to the Coach Station and onto the correct bus.

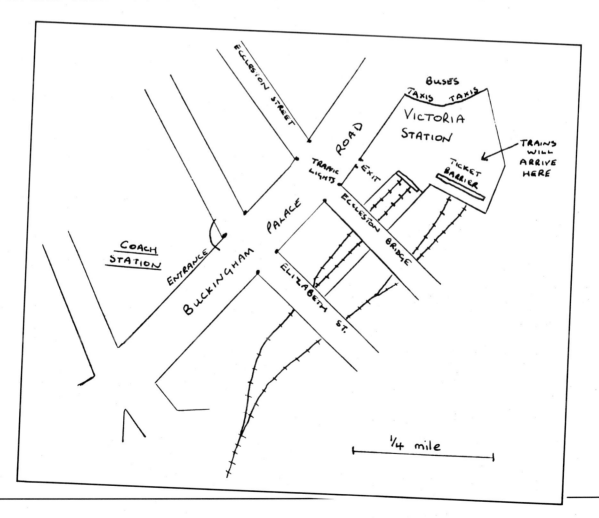

3 You are staying with your French friends just outside Nancy. Some acquaintances of your own family are planning to travel from Western France to visit you. As the house where you are staying is off the beaten track, you send them this map, and write a precise explanation of how to get there from the centre of Nancy. Don't forget the politenesses and appropriate references to their forthcoming visit.

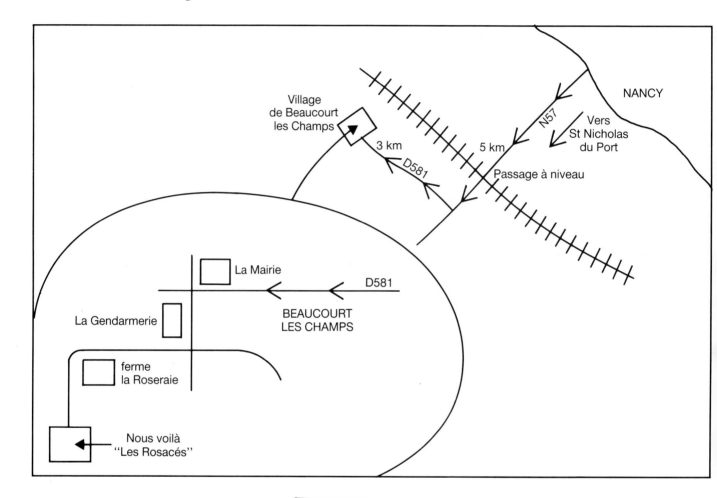

4 You are staying in France and attending your penfriend's school. In a French lesson, your class has been asked to write about a school journey in which you did not take part. The teacher agrees that it would be pointless for you to attempt this and asks you to write instead about your journey to France. Fortunately, you had written about the events of the day's journey in your diary, and are able to use this to remind you of what happened.

JULY

Thursday **17**
Week 29 · 198-167

Left home 7.30 am. Dad took me to station. Train to London crowded with businessmen. Took taxi from Paddington to Victoria (wouldn't face crowded Underground!) Journey to Newhaven uneventful. Boat trip to Dieppe long + great fun. Super lunch on boat. Weather fortunately calm! At Dieppe had to queue to go through passport control + customs. Didn't even have to open my case! Train to Paris not at all crowded so stretched out on the seat + slept. Olivier + family met me in Paris + we drove to Melun. Olivier's mum had prepared a smashing dinner + his grandparents came round to meet me. Phoned home to say I'd arrived OK.

5 One day, when your French penfriend is in school you have to go into town to find out the cost of various types of transport from Lille, where you are staying, to London as your penfriend's family is planning to visit London soon. You get the following information from the English-speaking computer at the SNCF information office.

Lille — London (via ferry Calais—Dover)—Daytime
          Return   Adult—460f.00
                   Child under 16—230f.00
                   Student under 26—300f.00

Lille — London (via ferry Dunkirk—Dover)—Night crossing
          Return   Adult—250f.00
                   Child under 16—125f.00
                   Student under 26—150f.00

Lille — London (via Hovercraft Boulogne—Dover)—Daytime
          Return   Adult—480f.00
                   Child under 16—240f.00
                   Student under 26—400f.00

You write out this information in French for the benefit of the French family.

6 You are walking back to your penfriend's flat in Amiens one afternoon when you are witness to this series of events.

You are subsequently asked by the police to write a report on exactly what you saw happen.

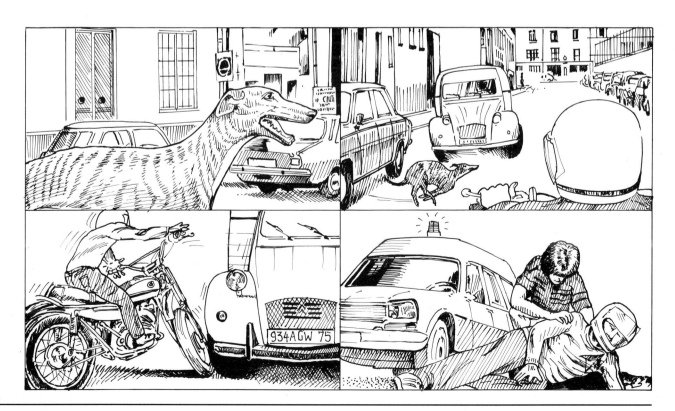

7 You are on holiday in France with your parents staying in Royan. As the car has been giving trouble you all decide to take a day excursion, by bus, into the Auvergne. However, before you go, your mother asks you to write out a note for the garage mechanic who will collect the car from the hotel, repair it and return it while you are out. Here is the note which she gives you to put into coherent French.

> — White Metro City, Reg. No. FFD 779Y — all electrics dodgy — hooter doesn't work — indicators only occasionally, — both front sidelights are broken — spare tyre has slow puncture (it's repairable — we don't need a new one) — front near side brake is seized.
>
> If it's going to cost more than 1000f.00 leave it till tomorrow — wait till I've discussed it with you. It's parked opposite hotel. Leave the keys in reception — and leave it locked!

MULTI-SKILL TASK

Whilst you are in France with your local youth club it is decided that the group will go to Paris for the day. You go along to the local railway station to make the booking.

Working with a partner:

1 Tell the booking clerk when you want to travel. Ask the times of trains to Paris in the morning and the times of trains back in the evening.

2 Listen to the booking clerk's reply and decide which train you want to take. Tell him and ask the price. Then answer his questions.

3 Listen to what the clerk now asks you to do and complete the task.

DEMANDE DE BILLET DE GROUPE

Nom de l'organisation _____

Adresse du siège social _____

Nom du Responsable du Groupe _____

Composition du Groupe

N° de Personnes au-dessus de 25 ans _____

N° de Personnes en-dessous de 25 ans _____

N° de Personnes responsables
(1 place gratuite par 15 voyageurs.) _____

Date demandée du voyage _____

Heure du départ _____

Destination _____

6

On s'amuse!

●● LISTENING

1 Your penfriend has lots of friends who are all keen to make you feel welcome. One Saturday, whilst your penfriend is out, several of them come to see you and ask you if you would like to join them in various activities. You do not like ball games and so refuse those invitations but you accept all the invitations for other activities.

Mark on your copy of the grid what was offered and whether you said yes or no.

	Activity	Yes	No
1			
2			
3			
4			
5			
6			
7			
8			
9			
10			

2 Whilst at school with your French penfriend you are collecting information about French teenagers' leisure activities for a survey your class at home is conducting. Listen whilst ten teenagers tell you what they like to do in their spare time. Make a list of their interests.

3 Whilst staying with your penfriend he and his friends are discussing the week's activities. You decide to note what is planned, in your diary.

4 You are on holiday in France with your family. One evening you decide to go to the cinema. You phone the local cinema to find out what is on. A recorded answer tells you what is showing on each of three screens. Make a note, in English, of the details.

	Title of film	Times	Any other information
Screen A	**Blues**		
Screen B	**Les Sentiers du Monde**		
Screen C	**Nuits Roses**		

5 You are staying in France with your family and one day you go to the local leisure centre. Listen to the desk clerk telling you about what activities are on offer. On your copy of the grid mark the details of the four sports given.

Sport	Days	Times	Price	Other information
Tennis				
Swimming				
Football				
Volley ball				

6 You and a friend visit a silk museum. At the entrance you ask for certain information. Make a note of what you are told in answer to the questions you ask.

1 How much is it?

2 Does it all have to be done on the same day?

3 What time do the museums close?

4 Where should one start the visit and how does one know where to go?

5 What does the ticket-seller call after you as you move off?

7 You are on a camping holiday trip with some friends and you are spending a few days near Brive-la-Gaillarde. You go into the tourist office there, in order to find out what there is to do in the town. Make a list of the various activities the receptionist suggests. She mentions six different types of place but at one there are four different activities available.

8 On holiday in France with your French penfriend you go, one morning, with her little brother aged nine and her older brother aged 18 to the sports centre. There, the hostess tells you what there is to do.

1 Where will your penfriend's little brother go?

2 Where will her older brother go?

3 What two choices of activity do you have up until 10 am?

4 How many different activities can you choose from after 10 am and what are they?

Having checked that this is a typical morning's programme you note the answers to the above questions in order to pass the details on to another friend who has asked you to let her know what is available.

9 You receive a cassette letter from a penfriend with whom you are going to stay in a few weeks' time.

1 Jot down the date and time he is expecting you in order to check with your mother who has bought your ticket.

2 Your parents are going to want to know what kinds of things are planned for your stay. Make a note of what your penfriend says you will be doing in order to tell them.

3 He has also reminded you to bring some things with you. Make a list of these so that you do not forget to pack them.

⌨ SPEAKING

1 A group game using:

J'aime . . .
Je n'aime pas . . .
Je déteste . . .   } + sports and pastimes.
Je préfère . . .
J'adore . . .

In the group, the first person starts with, for example, "J'aime le football". The second continues with "J'aime le football et la natation". The third person repeats this and adds a third activity and so on until all the group have made a contribution. This is then repeated with "Je n'aime pas . . .", and so on.

2 Working in a group prepare to put onto tape a few things about what each of you like doing and what you like watching on television. Say your name, what your favourite hobby is and say what your favourite television programme is. If you can, expand on what you say with reasons as to why you like these things. When you are ready, each member of the group should record his/her statement for other groups or the whole class to listen to.

3 **1** With your teacher, assistant or partner playing the role of the receptionist find out, at the tourist office, if there are cinemas in the town and, if so, what films are on.

> Ask if there are any cinemas in the town.
> Say thank you and ask what films are on at the moment.
> Ask if there is an afternoon performance of the Spielburg film and at what time it starts.
> Say thank you.

2 You are at the cinema buying tickets for the evening show. Your teacher, assistant or partner will play the part of the ticket-seller.

> Ask for three tickets.
> Say that you want tickets at 25 francs each.
> Ask if the ticket-seller has change for 500 francs.
> Ask at what time the film finishes.
> Say thank you.

4 In your French penfriend's home you are trying to decide how to spend the evening. Your partner will play the role of your penfriend.

You	**Your Penfriend**
Ask if there are any films on TV this evening.	
	Say there are two. One an adventure film and the other an Asterix cartoon.
	Show him/her the advertisement and ask what he/she thinks.
Say thanks and that you'll have a look.	
Say you'd like to watch the Steve McQueen film. You like adventures but not cartoons. Ask which your friend prefers.	
	Say you don't mind and that you like both and suggest you also watch *The Godfather*.
Say that's great . . . and it's nearly 20h35.	

5 You are in your French penfriend's home trying to decide how to spend the following day. Your partner will play the role of your penfriend.

You	Your Penfriend
	Ask what your penfriend would like to do tomorrow.
Say that it depends on the weather.	
	Say that you can go out if it's fine and ask if he/she would like to go on a picnic.
Say that you would like to. Ask if you will be able to go swimming.	
	Say you don't know but that it is possible.
Ask if you should bring your swimming costume.	
	Agree but ask what you should do if the weather is bad.
Say you would like to go into town.	

6 Whilst in France you are approached by a group of schoolchildren who are conducting a survey on leisure activities. When they discover that you are English they are even more determined that you should help them. You answer their questions.

  1 Quel est ton sport préféré?

  2 Quand pratiques-tu ce sport?

  3 C'est un sport d'été ou un sport d'hiver?

  4 Tu aimes le cinéma?

  5 Quel genre de film aimes-tu?

  6 Qui est ton acteur préféré?

  7 Quel passe-temps préfères-tu?

  8 Qu'est-ce que tu aimes faire le week-end?

  9 Tu regardes combien d'heures de télévision par semaine?

10 Qu'est-ce que tu aimes à la télévision?

7 With your partner imagine that you are with your youth club on an outing to France. One person will take the part of the ticket-office clerk in the leisure centre while the other buys tickets, makes reservations, asks about prices and the hire of skates. Remember to use all the appropriate politenesses. When you have practised this thoroughly swap roles and work through this again.

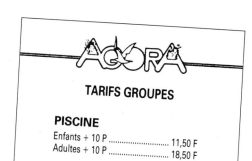

TARIFS GROUPES

PISCINE

Enfants + 10 P .... 11,50 F
Adultes + 10 P .... 18,50 F

PATINOIRE

Enfants + 10 P .... 9,00 F
Adultes + 10 P .... 11,50 F

Location de Patins: 5,00F.

8 Whilst your French penfriend is staying with you, you decide to spend some time watching films. Here are very brief summaries of what some of this week's films are about. Pick out three that you might like to watch yourself and tell your partner a little bit about them. Try to pick out at least two main points about each one.

6.0 Sherlock Holmes: Terror by Night

concluding a season of films featuring SIR ARTHUR CONAN DOYLE'S famous detective, starring **Basil Rathbone** as Sherlock Holmes **Nigel Bruce** as Dr Watson On the London to Edinburgh express the fabulous Star of Rhodesia diamond is stolen and the son of its owner murdered. Holmes, hired to safeguard the jewel, is faced with several likely suspects, among them, a cold-blooded criminal who will stop at nothing to ensure success.

May Duncan Bleek
ALAN MOWBRAY
Lestrade...............DENNIS HOEY
Vivian Vedder
RENÉE GODFREY
Lady Margaret....MARY FORBES
Train attendant...BILLY BEVAN
Professor Kilbane
FREDERIC WORLOCK
Conductor ..LEYLAND HODGSON

Cinema: Freedom

continues a major season of films new to television. Tonight starring **Jon Blake** **Candy Raymond** Ron Matheson is 22 years old, handsome and mad about cars. He is also out of work and finds that life in the 80s is increasingly divided between the haves and have nots. How is Ron to get the car of his dreams and the money and freedom to enjoy it? The answer is as clear as the keys in the gleaming Porsche . . . This vivid chase movie combines excitement with a social critique of the 80s.

Ron...........................JON BLAKE
Annie............CANDY RAYMOND
Sally ....JAD CAPELJA
Cassidy
CHARLES 'BUD' TINGWELL
Factory clerk........MAX CULLEN
Phil..................CHRIS HAYWOOD
Old farmer...................REG LYE
Employment officer
JOHN CLAYTON
Service station attendant
GREG ROWE

— Take 2: Last Day of Summer

BY IAN McEWAN

It is summer, 1970. Jenny, shy, plain and overweight, goes to live in a commune in a riverside house and befriends a 12-year-old orphan.

Jenny	Annette Badland
Tom	Graham McGrath
Pete	James Gaddas
Kate	Christina Jones
Jose	John Telfer
Sam	Steven Beard
Sharon	Karen Scargill
Linda	Saskia Reeves
Alice	Rebecca Elsworth
Mother	Denise Buckley

The October Man

JOHN MILLS
JOAN GREENWOOD

Jim Ackland is in charge of the small daughter of some friends when the bus they are on crashes. The child is killed and Jim suffers brain damage which keeps him in hospital for a year. On his release, he attempts to put his past behind him. . .

Made in black and white

Jim Ackland	John Mills
Jenny Carden	Joan Greenwood
Mr Peachey	Edward Chapman
Molly Newman	Kay Walsh
Mrs Vinton	Joyce Carey
Miss Selby	Catherine Lacey
Godby	Frederick Piper
Dr Martin	Felix Aylmer
Joyce Carden	Adrianne Allan
Harry	Patrick Holt
Wilcox	Jack Melford
Garage man	James Hayter
Little girl	Juliet Mills

SCREENPLAY ERIC AMBLER
DIRECTOR ROY BAKER

The Ladykillers

continues a season of acclaimed films introduced each week by **Barry Norman**, tonight starring **Alec Guinness** **Cecil Parker** **Herbert Lom, Peter Sellers** **Danny Green** Mrs Wilberforce is one of London's nicer landladies. A little vague perhaps, but definitely not the sort of person to have a gang of desperate criminals in her house. Unfortunately, Professor Marcus and his friends are not the musical society she supposed and their plans are anything but harmonious!

Professor ....ALEC GUINNESS
Major ....CECIL PARKER
Louis ....HERBERT LOM
Harry ....PETER SELLERS
One-Round........DANNY GREEN
Mrs Wilberforce
KATIE JOHNSON

📖 READING

1 Your English friend has shown an interest in archery while you are together in France. Answer his questions about the leaflet that he has found. (Note that it doesn't answer all of his questions—just mark 'not shown' where it doesn't tell you.)

1 Your friend is 19 years old, does he pay full price?
2 How much is one year's subscription?
3 What night is it on?
4 When does it start?
5 Where do you go to find out more?

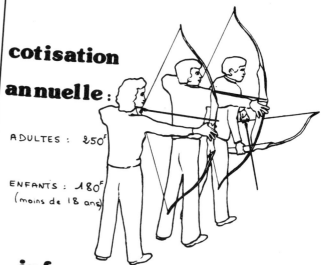

nouveau **TIR A L'ARC**

« **LES ARCHERS VAUDAIS** »

cotisation annuelle :

ADULTES : 250ᶠ

ENFANTS : 180ᶠ
(moins de 18 ans)

informations . inscriptions

GYMNASE CROIZAT 81, AVENUE ROGER SALENGRO À VAULX EN VELIN

à partir du 4 octobre le vendredi : 17h30 . 19h30

cotisation (f.)   subscription

SAMEDI 15 MARS 20H30
IL SERA ENCORE TEMPS DE FAIRE
LE BON CHOIX EN VENANT VOIR

MICHEL   LAGUEYRIE

DANS SON DERNIER SPECTACLE

VOYEUR

SON PROGRAMME

rire.. sourire..
esprit..humour..
rêve..tendresse

CENTRE CULTUREL COMMUNAL
"CHARLIE"
CHAPLIN
Place de la Nation
69120 VAULX-EN-VELIN

Renseignements - Réservations
78.79.25.28

TARIFS :
Entrée .... 60 F
Réduit .... 50 F
Adhérent .... 40 F

(Métro Bonnevay - Bus 52 - 56 - 57
- Arrêt Grand Vire - Hôtel de Ville)

2 You are trying to decide what to do on a free weekend in Vaulx-en-Velin. You see this advertisement. Answer the questions to find out if it is what you want.

1 What is the day, date and time of the show?
2 Is the piece said to be funny or serious?
3 How much will it cost you as a person of school age?
4 If membership of the club costs 20f.00 and you went to three shows would it be worth your while joining?
5 Which buses will get you there and at which stop should you get off?

adhérent (m.)   member

3 You have arrived to stay with your penfriend in France. He/she shows you in his/her diary all the things which have been planned for your visit. Make similar notes, in English, in your diary.

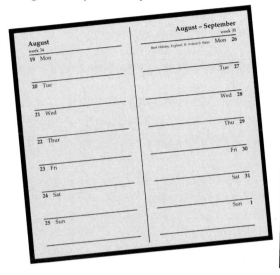

AOUT ———— lundi 19 ————

———— mardi 20 ————

———— mercredi 21 ————
Arrivée de
Michèle 9H30
à l'aéroport

———— jeudi 22 ————
Promenade en   Piscine avec
Ville avec   les cousins
Jean-Pierre   15 H 30

———— vendredi 23 ————
Promenade   Cinema
en vélo avec   21H
des copains

———— samedi 24 ————
Sortie à
Paris avec
Papa et Maman

———— dimanche 25 ————

———— lundi 26 ____ **AOUT**
Visite au château
Apporter pique-nique

———— mardi 27 ————
Promenade en   Cinéma
Vélo   21H

———— mercredi 28 ————
Patins à
roulettes
avec Marie-France 10H30

———— jeudi 29 ————
Retour de
Michèle
avec l'avion de 20H

———— vendredi 30 ————

———— samedi 31 ————

———— dimanche 1 ____ Septembre

4 You are in France during the period of the World Cup (football) and do not want to miss your favourite teams. Look at this leaflet which shows you how to overcome this problem.

1 How will the matches be shown?
2 How much will you pay to see the World Cup matches?
3 What 'extra' will you receive with your admission?
4 Write down the days, dates and times of all the matches involving England, Scotland and Ireland.
5 Will you be able to get a meal here?

31 MAI - 29 JUIN MUNDIAL

Samedi 31 mai	19 h 55	Italie-Bulgarie
Dimanche 1er juin	19 h 55	Brésil-Espagne
Mercredi 4 juin	9 h 15 20 h 00	Portugal-Angleterre (R) Allemagne-Uruguay
Jeudi 5 juin	10 h 00 19 h 55	Ecosse-Danemark (R) France-U.R.S.S.
Vendredi 6 juin	10 h 00 10 h 15 19 h 55 22 h 00	Bulgarie-Corée (R) Italie-Argentine (R) Hongrie-Canada Brésil-Algérie (R)
Samedi 7 juin	10 h 30 20 h 00 22 h 00	Maroc-Angleterre (R) Mexique-Paraguay Espagne-Irlande (dif)
Dimanche 8 juin	10 h 00 22 h 00 23 h 55	Pologne-Portugal (R) Belgique-Irlande (dif) Uruguay-Danemark
Mardi 10 juin	14 h 55 19 h 55 22 h 00	France-Hongrie (R) Bulgarie-Argentine Italie-Corée (dif)
Mercredi 11	10 h 00 20 h 00	Maroc-Portugal (dif) Belgique-Paraguay
Jeudi 12 juin	14 h 45 19 h 55	Belgique-Paraguay (R) Brésil-Irlande
Vendredi 13 juin	14 h 45 20 h 00 22 h 00	Mexique-Irak (R) Allemagne-Danemark Uruguay-Ecosse (dif)

(R) : rediffusion
(dif) : différé

Du 26 mai au 29 juin, téles-portez-vous bien en suivant tous les matches de tennis de Roland Garros et tous les matches de foot du Mundial de Mexico sur le grand écran du Vidéo-Club de l'AGORA.

Le Vidéo-Club de l'AGORA :

une nouvelle façon de vivre les grands événements sportifs !

VIDÉO-CLUB AGORA

Entrée visiteurs : **10 F** jusqu'au 15 juin
15 F du 15 juin au 15 septembre

Cette entrée donne droit à une consommation gratuite.

———— L'AGORA c'est aussi ————

- Piscine de compétition 25 m x 20 m
- Piscine à vagues avec toboggan
- Bains bouillonnants
- Saunas - Musculation
- Patinoire
- Bowling 8 pistes - Bar
- Fast-food

AGORA : Esplanade Parmentier
(face à la mer)
Tél. 21.09.01.81

5 Your friend's mother has been sent to work in France and will be taking the family with her. While she is there, your friend wants to keep up her dance classes. Look at this leaflet which she has been sent and answer her questions.

1 What kind of dancing is covered?
2 What day will it be on?
3 When will it start?
4 Will lessons be organised during the school holidays?
5 What age range will be catered for?

VILLE DE VAULX·EN·VELIN

Service des Loisirs de l'Enfant

| *de Septembre 85 à Juin 86* |

- **Type d'activité** : Danse contemporaine

- **Adresse et téléphone du centre** : Groupe Scolaire F.G. LORCA, rue Robert DESNOS
  Tel. 880-72-82
- **Jours et horaires de fonctionnement**
  MERCREDI de 15 H.45 à 17 H.45
- **Dates de fonctionnement**
  du MERCREDI 11 SEPTEMBRE au 25 JUIN (35 jours)

  Des stages seront <u>peut-être</u> organisés pendant les congés scolaires

- **Activités Prévues**   et   **Age des enfants**
  Danse - Expression
  Apprentissage du rythme,
  de l'équilibre   14-15 ans
  Mime
  Relaxation
  Préparation d'un spectacle
            Avec Louisette MORVAN

- **Renseignements** : Hôtel de Ville - Service Enfance 2° étage.

HOTEL DE VILLE. PLACE DE LA NATION. 69120 VAULX· EN· VELIN· TEL.(7) 880-88-53-

---

2ᵉᵐᵉ SALON DE LA CARTE POSTALE DU VIEUX PAPIER ET DE LA BANDE DESSINEE
12/13 AVRIL
GYMNASE TOLA VOLOGE
VENISSIEUX

RENSEIGNEMENTS 72.50.09.16

ENTREE 10 F avec remise de la carte numérotée du Salon
gratuit pour les - de 12 ans
OUVERTURE : 9 - 19h SANS INTERRUPTION
Gymnase TOLA VOLOGE ; (quartier Moulin à Vent)
FLECHAGE A PARTIR DE LA ROUTE DE VIENNE
ST JEAN DE DIEU OU
RUE FRANCIS DE PRESSENSE

---

6 You see this leaflet in the tourist office of the town where you are spending a holiday. Your friend asks you some questions about it.

1 What is it about?
2 What sort of things can be seen there?
3 How much will it cost?
4 Is it open at lunch time?
5 How can we get more information about it?

7 You are a cinema buff. You have picked up this leaflet about Ciné-Villeneuve. You would like to see a lot of the films on offer as some are real classics of comedy. You decide to see if it is worth your while joining the club as you are in France for only a month.

  1 If you are still at school how much will it cost to see ten films?

  2 How much would you save on each film compared with simply paying the normal youth admission price?

  3 Is the Asterix film just for youngsters?

  4 If you decided to take your penfriend's younger sister to see the film *Au Méliès*, how much would it cost?

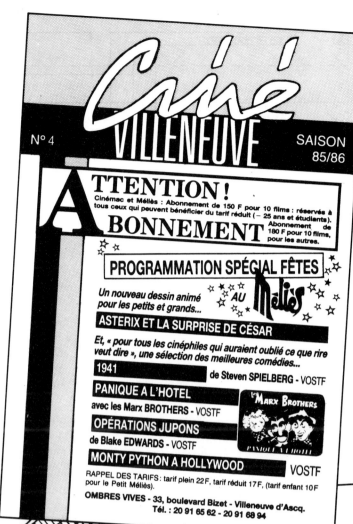

Ciné VILLENEUVE

N° 4   SAISON 85/86

ATTENTION !

Cinémac et Méliès : Abonnement de 150 F pour 10 films : réservés à tous ceux qui peuvent bénéficier du tarif réduit (− 25 ans et étudiants). Abonnement de 180 F pour 10 films, pour les autres.

ABONNEMENT

☆☆☆

PROGRAMMATION SPÉCIAL FÊTES ☆☆☆

Un nouveau dessin animé pour les petits et grands... *AU Méliès*

ASTERIX ET LA SURPRISE DE CÉSAR

Et, « pour tous les cinéphiles qui auraient oublié ce que rire veut dire », une sélection des meilleures comédies...

1941   de Steven SPIELBERG - VOSTF

PANIQUE A L'HOTEL

avec les Marx BROTHERS - VOSTF

OPÉRATIONS JUPONS

de Blake EDWARDS - VOSTF

MONTY PYTHON A HOLLYWOOD   VOSTF

RAPPEL DES TARIFS : tarif plein 22 F, tarif réduit 17 F, (tarif enfant 10 F pour le Petit Méliès).

OMBRES VIVES - 33, boulevard Bizet - Villeneuve d'Ascq. Tél. : 20 91 65 62 - 20 91 68 94

8 Your tennis club is interested in combining its favourite pastime with a holiday in France. As the club's resident French speaker, you are asked to make sense of this publicity leaflet which has been sent to the club. Answer the committee's questions.

  1 How many people can we take?

  2 Do they give lessons?

  3 Will they accept beginners?

  4 What other attractions are there for us?

  5 How much tuition will we receive?

  6 What is the price of a double room and of a dormitory?

  7 Are meals included in the price?

  8 Do all the rooms have showers?

  9 Can we take wives/ husbands and children who don't want to play and how much will it cost for them?

  10 Is there anything for the younger children to do?

un stage   course (of lessons)

STAGES de TENNIS

GROUPES DE 8 PERSONNES MAXIMUM

INITIATION OU PERFECTIONNEMENT

AU PROGRAMME :
– 10 h d'entraînement avec moniteur.
– 10 h d'entraînement libre.
– 4 h de bilan théorique.

LE SEJOUR : Dans un cadre agréable, au bord du Rhône dans un parc verdoyant, avec mini-golf et piscine. A 2 km au sud de Valence.

TARIFS (en pension, complète par personne, balles fournies)
– Chambre simple ** .... **1 490,00 F**
– Chambre double ** .... **1 340,00 F**
– Chambre collective .... **1 200,00 F**

  ** chambres avec cabinet toilette, WC, douche.

centre de l'épervière

26000 VALENCE Tél. 75-43-63-01

POUR LA PERSONNE ACCOMPAGNANT LE STAGIAIRE SANS ACTIVITE

TARIFS (en pension complète)
– Chambre simple .... **860,00 F**
– Chambre double .... **720,00 F**
– Chambre collective .. **580,00 F**

NOUVEAUTE

LES VACANCES 6/11 ANS

Pour les enfants qui accompagnent leurs parents à un stage de TENNIS. Ils pourront pratiquer du Lundi au Vendredi, de 9 h à 11 h 30 et de 13 h 30 à 17 h :
– Jeux de plein air,
– Travaux manuels,
– Promenade *,
– Piscine *,
– Sports *.
* Certificat médical nécessaire.
– Repas pris avec les parents.
– Chambre avec annexe pour les enfants * (maximum 2).   **700,00 F**

TARIF (en pension complète) ....

* **exemple** : 1 parent participant au stage, accompagné de son enfant (participant aux activités 6/11 ans) se verra appliquer les tarifs suivants : 1 340,00 F + 700,00 F soit 2 040,00 F.

9 You receive the following letter from your penfriend with whom you are going to stay. She gives you details of the things she has planned for your visit. Make a note of them, in English, in your diary and put in any relevant details.

July week 28		July week 29
7 Mon		Bank Holiday, N. Ireland Mon 14
8 Tue		Tue 15
9 Wed		Wed 16
10 Thu		Thu 17
11 Fri		Fri 18
12 Sat		Sat 19
13 Sun		Sun 20

Morestel le 23 Juin 1985

Chère Brigid,

Je suis très heureuse de t'accueillir dans ma famille pendant la semaine du 12 au 19 Juillet.

J'espère que ce séjour te permettra de mieux connaître mon pays et te donneras envie d'y revenir et de parler la langue.

Aussi ai-je déjà préparé un programme d'activités pour la semaine, car étant en vacances à ce moment là, je pourrai te consacrer tout mon temps.

Nous viendrons te chercher le samedi à l'aéroport.

Le Dimanche nous irons manger chez ma grand-mère paternelle à midi. Il y aura aussi mon cousin et ma cousine qui ont 16 ans et 18 ans. Nous repartirons en fin d'après-midi, vers 18h00 car il y a toujours un bon film le dimanche soir à la télévision.

Lundi après-midi nous irons au cinéma voir le film "La Boum". Il parle des jeunes de 15-16 ans et de leurs problèmes amoureux avec leurs petit-(ou petite-) amis.

Mardi matin nous irons visiter le château de Morestel. Au départ je pensais y aller le lundi mais il n'y a pas de visite ce jour-là.

Mercredi matin nous pourrons aller à la piscine et je pense même que nous y retournerons le vendredi après-midi. Il serait donc utile que tu amènes ton maillot de bain.

Le jeudi après-midi nous irons à la patinoire dès l'ouverture, c'est à dire à 14h00. Une de mes amies viendra avec nous. Si tu as des patins à glace tu peux les apporter ou sinon il n'y aura aucun problème pour en louer sur place.

J'espère que ce programme te plaira et si jamais tu veux faire d'autres choses tu pourras toujours me le dire à ton arrivée.

Je t'embrasse en attendant avec impatience ta venue.

Sylvie

10 You are staying in France in a *gîte* with your parents. Your mother decides that she wants to go to the cinema and collects the brochure below from the local cinema. When you get back to the *gîte* from a morning's swimming you find your mother has gone out and left you this note.

I'd like to go and see this film – I've always liked Agatha Christie. See if you can work out what it's all about.

You read the brochure and jot down the details ready to tell your mother when she gets back.

AGATHA

Wally Stanton . . . . . . **Dustin Hoffman**
Agatha Christie . . . **Vanessa Redgrave**
Archie Christie . . . . . **Timothy Dalton**
Evelyn . . . . **Helen Morse**
William Collins . . . . **Tony Britton**
Kenward . . . . **Timothy West**

SCÉNARIO
DE KATHLEEN TYNAN,
ARTHUR HOPCRAFT

D'APRÈS UNE HISTOIRE
DE KATHLEEN TYNAN

IMAGES DE VITTORIO STORARO

MUSIQUE DE JOHNY MANDEL

Nancy Neele . . . . **Celia Gregory**
Lord Brackenbury . . . . . . **Alan Badel**
John Foster . . . . **Paul Brooke**
Charlotte Fischer . . **Carolyn Pickles**
Pettelson . . . . **Robert Longden**
Oncle Jones . . . . . . **Donald Nithsdale**

LE SUJET

En Angleterre en 1926. Un épisode mystérieux de la vie de la célèbre romancière Agatha Christie.

LE SCÉNARIO

Décembre 1926 à Londres. Le journaliste américain Wally Stanton assiste à une réception donnée en l'honneur d'Agatha Christie, qui vient de connaître la consécration avec son roman « Le Meurtre de Roger Ackroyd ». Mais derrière ce succès littéraire, se cache, pour la romancière, une grave crise sentimentale. Celle-ci atteint son apogée lorsque son mari, le colonel Archie Christie, lui annonce, à l'issue d'un déjeuner, son intention de divorcer pour pouvoir se remarier avec sa secrétaire, Nancy Neele. Agatha s'oppo-

Wally Stanton (Dustin Hoffman) et Agatha (Vanessa Redgrave)

sant résolument au divorce, le colonel quitte leur cottage, refusant du même coup, à Stanton, d'interviewer son épouse.

NOTE CRITIQUE

Policier. *Il y a beaucoup de charme dans cette aventure de la jeune Agatha Christie. Un couple d'acteurs merveilleux sert admirablement l'intrigue et fait du film un divertissement subtil et émouvant.*

Plus tard dans la nuit, Agatha a un accident de voiture, près des Bershire Downs...

Appréciation
Office catholique : pour adultes et adolescents

la romancière novelist
assister à to attend
atteindre to reach

11 You are with a group of friends on a fishing trip in St Valéry-sur-Somme. You receive this leaflet at your hotel and decide that the information contained in it should be passed on to your friends. Make notes on the most important points in the leaflet.

DÉPARTEMENT
DE LA SOMME

ARRONDISSEMENT
D'ABBEVILLE

**MAIRIE
DE
SAINT-VALÉRY-SUR-SOMME**

Téléphone N° (22) 27.52.16

PÊCHEURS AU RACCROC !

Si vous pouvez pratiquer votre sport préféré, n'oubliez surtout pas que c'est par pure <u>tolérance</u> de la part de l'Administration.

En conséquence, dans votre intérêt, respectez impérativement les consignes suivantes :

- Ne circulez pas en voiture sur les ouvrages publics, digues en particulier.

- Une priorité absolue est accordée à la navigation de commerce, de pêche ou de plaisance. En conséquence, vous ne devez pas jeter votre ligne à l'approche d'un navire ou d'une embarcation.

- En cas d'accident, votre responsabilité civile peut être engagée.

- Ne laissez pas de déchets sur place. <u>Utilisez les poubelles.</u>

Si vous prenez plaisir à venir pêcher en Baie de Somme, et si vous voulez le faire encore longtemps, faites preuve de civisme.

Merci !

Le MAIRE,

digue (f.)   sea front
ouvrages publics (m.)   public works
déchets (m.)   rubbish

WRITING

1 Your French penfriend is spending a week with you. Mark down in his diary what you intend to do on each of the six days. Choose different things for each day and also note down the places where you will go for each activity. One day has already been done for you.

```
┌─────────────────────────────────────┐
│ SAMEDI                              │
├─────────────────────────────────────┤
│                                     │
│   Football  Stade                   │
│                                     │
└─────────────────────────────────────┘
```

2 You are expecting your French penfriend to phone you one evening but, unexpectedly, you have to go out. He is coming to stay with you next week and you are planning a camping trip. Prepare a list, in French, of ten camping items that he needs to bring so that your father, who speaks some French, can read it out over the phone.

3 You have nearly finished a very busy week's holiday in Normandy. Amongst other things you have visited the castle at Dieppe, the Joan of Arc museum at Rouen, the car museum at Clères and the cheese factory at Royville. You have also been to hypermarkets, eaten out, been swimming, played tennis and you have even played *boules*. When you get home the horrifying task of talking to your class, in French, awaits you so you make notes, in French, in your diary about what you have done.

4 1 Your French friend is a film enthusiast. She has asked you if there are many cinemas in your town and if any of them show more than one film at a time. Using the information shown here for Birmingham cinemas, write two to three sentences, as part of a letter, saying how many cinemas there are and how many show more than one film.

2 As part of the same letter you send your friend this cutting stating which films will be showing at the Metropole during her stay. This time, say what the cutting is and suggest that you go to the cinema once during her stay. Say which film you prefer but ask her to choose the one she would like to see.

LOCAL CINEMAS

ABC, Bristol Road, (3 screens) Tel: 440 1904.

Capitol, Alum Rock, (3 screens) Tel: 327 0528.

Classic, Quinton, (4 screens) Tel: 422 2562/2252.

Futurist, John Bright St., (2 screens) Tel: 643 0292.

Kings, Kings Square, W. Bromwich (3 screens). Tel: 553 0192.

Metropole Hotel, N.E.C. Tel: 780 4242.

Midlands Arts Centre, Cannon Hill Park. Tel: 440 3838.

Odeon, Queensway Film Centre Tel: 643 2418. (3 screens).

Odeon, Sutton Coldfield, (3 screens) Tel: 354 2714.

Solihull, High Street Tel: 705 0398.

Tivoli, Station Street, (2 screens) Tel: 643 1556.

Triangle, Holt Street, Aston Tel: 359 4192.

Warwick, Westley Road, Acocks Green. Tel: 706 0766.

THE METROPOLE

NEC. Tel: 021-780 4242.
Until 26 Sept: **A View To A Kill** (PG).

Moore as 007, up against **Christopher Walken** and **Grace Jones** and a bid to corner the world's silicon chips market by sinking part of America.

Fri. 27/Sat. 28: **A Passage To India** (PG). First in a **David Lean** week of films is his Oscar winning recent adaptation of the Forster classic with **Judy Davis.**

Sun. 29/Mon. 30: **Lawrence Of Arabia** (PG). Brilliant biopic with **Peter O'Toole** and **Omar Sharif.** A classic.

Tue. 1 Oct: **The Bridge Over The River Kwai** (PG). Archetypal stiff-upper lip British resolve war-film and tremendous stuff. Jack Hawkins, Alec Guinness.

Thu. 3: **Dr Zhivago** (PG). **Sharif** and **Christie** in romance amid the Russian revolution.

Fri. 4: **Mask** (15).

5 While visiting your French friend's school the Ciné-Club asks you to write, in French, a brief account of a recent English or American film. Choose a film and write an account for the Club in about 100–120 words, in French, of what the film is about.

6 Your penfriend's sister is visiting your town and is interested in knowing what cultural activities are available in your area. Find the information and write to tell her what is on offer.

7 It is the school holidays. You decide to write to your French penfriend telling him/her how you are spending your time. You could write about sport, outings, holiday courses, or anything else connected with free-time.

8 Write a letter to the tourist office in St Malo, asking for details of leisure activities for young people in the town. You are particularly interested in sports activities available for people travelling alone.

9 You are writing to your French penfriend to tell him about a film or TV or radio programme that you have enjoyed. Give him some details and say why you enjoyed it.

10 You are on an exchange visit to France. Whilst at your partner's school you are asked to contribute to the school magazine. Pupils have expressed an interest in knowing about a typical English sport. See if you can write a short article about cricket or golf or, indeed, any game that you have played or which interests you.

MULTI-SKILL TASK

You are staying with a penfriend and when you get home one evening you find that his younger brother has taken this phone message for you.

1 You phone back to agree to the suggestion and sort out details. Pretend that your partner is the Jean-Louis you phone. Then swap roles.

 2 Jean-Louis tells you that his sister has seen the film and puts her on the line to tell you about it.

> Jean-Louis a téléphoné. Il veut t'emmener au cinéma voir "Arsenic et vieilles Dentelles". Peux-tu lui téléphoner quand tu rentreras? C'est pour vous mettre d'accord sur l'heure du rendez-vous, etc.

la dentelle lace

3 At the cinema you pick up the following information about the film you are to see.

4 You enjoy the film so much and are so enthusiastic about it that your penfriend suggests that you write a short review for the *carnets du cinéma* section of his school magazine. You agree and

- make some notes in French to help you
- write a short article.

arsenic et vieilles dentelles

(ARSENIC AND OLD LACE)

Réal: Franck CAPRA (USA,1944)/NB/ 118'/
Sc: Julius J. EPSTEIN et Philip G. EPSTEIN/
d'après la pièce de Joseph KESSERLING/ Ph:
Sol POLITO/ Mus: Max STEINER/ Int: GARY GRANT,
RAYMOND MASSET, PETER LORRE, JOSEPHINE HULL,
JEAN ADAIR, PRISCILLA LANE,...

Les deux exquises vieilles dames qui, par gen-
tillesse, empoisonnent les messieurs seuls
qu'elles enterrent ensuite dans leur jardin se
moquent de la démocratie américaine, bien que
leur neveu se prenne pour Théodore Roosevelt.
Cette adaptation d'un grand succès de BROADWAY
est certainement l'une des meilleures comédies
macabres jamais portées à l'écran. Gary GRANT
à son sommet. A hurler de rire en plusieurs
moments.

enterrer to bury
un écran screen
hurler to yell, to shout

7

Conseils de classe

LISTENING

1 You are spending some time, on exchange, in a French school. One day, you are told of certain timetable changes. Listen to the changes and write them down on your existing timetable.

2 Several people at your penfriend's school have asked you to find penpals for them. You already have some details about them but decide that you need to have a note of their likes and dislikes with regard to school. Make a note of what they say in order to transfer the information to the notes they have already given you.

Name	Likes	Dislikes
Sylvie		
Bernard		
Didier		
Annette		
Béatrice		
Patrick		
Jacques		
Robert		
Nathalie		
Christiane		

3 Before you listen to the tape, write which subjects you study at school in the left-hand column of your grid. You will hear a French person asking you about school subjects. Mark on your grid the answers to her questions. If you do not study the subject she mentions write it in the right-hand column. All your answers should be in English.

I study	I like it	I don't like it	I do not study

4 Listen to this tape sent by pupils from your link school in France. Make notes of the details given on the grid to help your classmates choose someone to write to.

Name	Age	Class	Best subjects	Worst subjects
Marie-Claude				
Henri				
Alain				
Philippe				
Nadine				
Nicole				
Marie-Louise				
Claudine				
Jean-Claude				
Nathalie				

5 On a visit to your exchange school in France, you are shown round the building. You have been given a plan of the school, but none of the names of the rooms are written in. As you follow the guided tour you jot down what each room is for on your plan.

6 You are on an exchange visit to France and are spending two days at school. Listen while a teacher gives you your timetable and fill in the details on the blank provided.

7 During a history lesson at your link school where you are spending a term, you are being asked to write an essay on what it was like to be a child at school in Victorian times in Britain. Your teacher draws your attention to a series of points that she wishes you to include in your essay. Listen and note down in English, the points she makes.

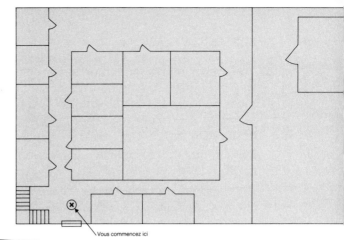

Vous commencez ici

	Lundi	Mardi	Mercredi	Jeudi	Vendredi
8 à 9					
9 à 10					
10 à 11					
11 à 12					
14 à 15					
15 à 16					
16 à 17					

SPEAKING

1 Working with a partner, look at this timetable taken from a *classe de 3ᵉ* (4th year in an English school). Take turns at playing the role of the French pupil, as your partner asks questions about your school week. Use these questions and add extra ones if you can.

1 Tu commences à quelle heure d'habitude?

2 Combien de cours d'anglais as-tu par semaine?

3 Quelle est ta matière préférée?

4 Y a-t-il une leçon que tu n'aimes pas du tout?

5 Combien de langues étrangères étudies-tu?

6 Combien de jours par semaine as-tu des cours de maths?

7 Combien de temps dure chaque cours?

8 Tu as cours le samedi?

9 A quelle heure finis-tu le mercredi?

10 A quelle heure finis-tu le jeudi?

	LUNDI	MARDI	MERCREDI	JEUDI	VENDREDI
8 à 9	Math	Musique	Géographie	Piscine	Allemand
9 à 10	Histoire	Français	Dessin	Piscine	Math
10 à 11	Anglais	Allemand	Sciences	Français	Français
11 à 12	Français	Math	Naturelles	Allemand	Anglais
14 à 15	Sciences	Anglais		Travaux	Dessin
15 à 16	Physiques	Géographie		Manuels	
16 à 17		Gymnastique		Histoire	

2 You are spending some time in a French school as part of your stay in France. Today you unfortunately missed your bus and must try to find your classmates. You pop in to the school secretary . . . . Your teacher, assistant or partner can play the role of the secretary.

Explain that you have arrived late and that you don't know where to go.

Say that you are with the *classe de 2ᵉ*.

Answer the question.

Repeat the instructions to show that you have understood, and thank her.

3 As part of a trip to France you have gone to spend a day at a French school. You agree to be interviewed by the spokesperson of a group of pupils who want to know about life in England. Answer the questions as fully as possible. Your partner should be the person asking the questions. Afterwards swap roles.

1 Quel âge as-tu?

2 Donc tu es dans quelle classe au collège?

3 Tu fais combien de cours par jour?

4 Tu as des cours libres?

5 Tu finis à quelle heure le soir?

6 Tu fais du sport au collège?

7 Tu portes un uniforme?
Décris-le-nous!

8 Tu fais combien de devoirs le soir?

9 Tu étudies combien de langues étrangères?
Lesquelles?

10 Est-ce que tu as certains cours qui sont obligatoires?

4 Working with a partner, find out the names of two school subjects they enjoy and two they dislike. Find out the reasons for this. Now swap roles.

5 Conduct a survey in your class to find out which subjects studied are the most popular. Each pupil can nominate two subjects. You could record the results as a bar chart with names of subjects (in French of course) along the bottom and numbers up the side.

6 Working in a group, each person takes it in turn to describe a school subject without mentioning the name of the subject or referring to the teacher concerned. Other members of the group have to guess in French what the subject is. The first person to guess each time gets a point and then has to describe the next subject. You could set a limit of say ten subjects and see who is the winner.

7 You are spending a few weeks in France on exchange. While at school you are asked to talk about school life in England. You could mention things like times of starting and finishing, which lessons you do, out-of-school activities, organisation of the school, and, perhaps, the disciplinary system!

Be prepared to answer questions from other members of your group on what you say. When you feel more confident you could perhaps do the talk for the whole class who could ask you questions.

8 Your partner will take the part of a French pupil who wants to know more about life in your school. Answer his/her questions and then exchange roles and try to ask for similar information about French schools. (It would be helpful to have discussed this first either with a French person or your teacher, or at least to have done a little research on French school systems.)

French role: Est-ce que vous allez au collège le mercredi?
Portez-vous un uniforme?
Les cours commencent à quelle heure et finissent à quelle heure?
Est-ce que vous mangez à la cantine?
A quel âge commence-t-on au collège?
On doit rester au collège jusqu'à quel âge?

Respond to your partner's queries.

READING

1 Your friend in France is not feeling too well, and has decided to spend a day with you instead of going to school. As his father is busy, fill in his *Justification d'Absences* form for him.

These are the details his father calls to you.

"On est à Corbas, Jean-Michele a mal à la tête. C'est le 21 mars aujourd'hui. Je pense qu'il peut retourner en classe demain."

A_____ le _____	A_____ le _____
Absence depuis	M ou Mlle_____
le ____ à__h__	élève de_____, a été absent (e) depuis le ____
Motif _____	à____h____ pour le motif suivant _____
Retour le ____ à__h	
VISA DU SERVICE / SIGNATURE DES ABSENCES / DES PARENTS	Il ou elle rentrera le _____ à__h__
	Signature des parents

2 Your penfriend's younger sister comes home from school with this Maths problem to solve, but the family are too busy to help her. Can you help? Work out the problems for her, and write down your answers—in English if you prefer.

Problème . CM1.

Une ménagère va au marché. Elle achète 2,850 kg d'oranges ; 0,620 kg de laitue ; 1,195 kg de bananes ; 1,325 kg de pommes et 1,760 kg d'endives. Son panier pèse 0,580 kg. Quelle masse portera-t-elle pour rentrer chez elle ?
Les oranges lui ont coûté 12,60 F ; la laitue 5,80 F. Les bananes 11,45 F ; les pommes 12,15 F. Combien a-t-elle dépensé ?
Combien lui reste-t-il si elle est partie avec 100 F ?

3 Whilst looking at the notice-board in your penfriend's school, this poster catches your eye. Make notes about it in English so that you can discuss it with your penfriend. You will need to note:

- what the exhibition is about
- what is on show
- the time and dates

4 On arriving at a French school where you will spend a week, you are given the timetable below.

Study it carefully and mark down the days and times when you will be studying these subjects:

Maths
French
Biology
English
Sport

Since you do not speak Spanish at all, you have been excused this lesson. When need you not come to school?

Les Carroz

EXPOSITION ARTISANALE

à la Salle de la Chapelle
du 26 décembre
au 1er janvier
de 10 h à 12 h et 16 h à 19 h

Tissages

Bougies

Cuir

Avec la participation d'artisans

EMPLOI DU TEMPS D'UNE CLASSE DE 3ème

	LUNDI	MARDI	MERCREDI	JEUDI	VENDREDI
8 à 9		FRANGAIS	FRANGAIS	ANGLAIS	MATHEMATIQUES
9 à 10	HISTOIRE	SCIENCES PHYSIQUES	ANGLAIS	FRANGAIS	ESPAGNOL
10 à 11	ESPAGNOL	TRAVAUX MANUELS	MATHEMATIQUES	GEOGRAPHIE	ANGLAIS / RECREATION
11 à 12	MATHEMATIQUES		DESSIN	MATHEMATIQUES	HISTOIRE
14 à 15	FRANGAIS	EDUCATION PHYSIQUE ET SPORTIVE		ESPAGNOL	EDUCATION PHYSIQUE ET SPORTIVE
15 à 16	ANGLAIS	EDUCATION PHYSIQUE ET SPORTIVE		FRANGAIS	SCIENCES NATURELLES
16 à 17		MUSIQUE		ANGLAIS	

5 Your class has received this letter from your link school in France. The French children involved are doing a project about your school and want some information. Your teacher asks you to make a list of what they want, so that the staff can start getting the information together.

LEP Agricole
Contamine sur Arve
Bonneville 74130

Contamine le 2 novembre.

Bonjour les Anglais,
Avec l'aide de notre professeur d'Anglais, Madame Biffiger, nous travaillons sur un journal intitulé "La vie des Anglais à l'école". Nous espérons ainsi, grâce à votre aide compléter notre journal.
Dans votre prochaine lettre pouvez vous nous joindre un plan de votre collège une photo de l'entrée de votre établissement, une de votre classe ainsi qu'une photo de votre laboratoire. Pouvez vous nous faire passer une copie de votre emploi du temps et une liste des activités qui sont proposées dans votre école. A propos de sport, serait-il possible d'avoir une photo de vous pratiquant un sport.
Nous serions aussi intéressés par un enregistrement d'une assemblée car en France nous n'avons pas ce genre de réunion et ce serait très intéressant pour nous. Pour notre journal nous avons aussi besoin d'une photo de vous en classe.
Nous vous remercions par avance. Tous ces documents nous serons utiles pour mieux vous connaître et compléter notre journal.
Merci à tous au revoir.
La classe de Madame Biffiger.

6 You are spending a few weeks in France and attending school with your penfriend. A lot of the people in the class are collecting and swapping football cards, so you decide to make a collection.

Read the back of this card and write down where to get more, and what you have to buy in order to get them.

How much will the album cost?

Will you have to buy anything else before you can buy the album?

coller   to stick

NICE

JEAN-PHILIPPE ROHR

FOOTBALL 86 PANINI 239

offert par BUITONI

Tu peux coller cette image dans l'album Football 86, édité par les Editions PANINI (prix maximum conseillé 3 F).
Cet album est en vente chez les marchands de journaux indépendamment de toute obligation d'achat de produits BUITONI.

FIGURINE PANINI

7 Whilst you are staying with your penfriend, her little sister leaves an exercise book in your room. You look at the first page and realise that it is not a normal school book.

1 What is its purpose?

2 Where should it be?

3 Who seems to write in the book?

4 What has your penfriend's parent signed?

8 You are spending a term at a school in the Massif Central. A new swimming pool has recently opened in the town and one day you are given this letter to take home. Read it carefully, and make notes about:

- what event it concerns
- the times and dates
- what things to avoid
- what things you are advised to take.

épinards (m.) spinach

Guillemette Lachenal
née le 20, 3, 74

cours moyen
1e année

Cahier de correspondance

Ce cahier sert de liaison entre les parents et l'école. Il doit rester dans le cartable

---

L'étude commence lundi 12 septembre
Votre enfant y restera - t - il ?
~~oui~~ ou ~~non~~
tous les jours - ~~occasionnellement~~

signature

Parents,

Votre enfant va suivre cette année des cours de natation sous la responsabilité du professeur de gymnastique et/ou d'un maître nageur- sauveteur à la piscine de l'Étoile d'Alaï.

Début des séances : mardi 4 octobre.

Pour les élèves de 3e de 13h45 à 14h25. Pour les élèves de 2e de 14h30 à 15h10. Soit 40mn de cours effectif.

Température de l'eau 25º Température de l'air ambiant 27º Le but premier de cet enseignement est d'apprendre aux élèves à se sentir à l'aise dans le milieu aquatique: sauter, plonger, savoir respirer, nager sur et sous l'eau.

La piscine est obligatoire sauf avis médical contraire.

Le transport se fait par autocar spécial: départ du collège à 13h20 pour le 1er groupe.

Conseils Le jour de la piscine, prendre un repas léger et digeste. Éviter absolument les fritures, les épinards, le chou, le chocolat.

Apporter un goûter à prendre après le bain.

Prévoir un maillot, 2 serviettes normales plutôt qu'un drap de bain et un bonnet en caoutchouc (marqués au nom de l'élève)

le proviseur

Visa des parents

9 As part of a project you are doing on school life in France, you
have written to your penfriend asking him to explain as fully as
possible about his school. Here is his reply. Write notes about it in
English for incorporation into the project—*don't* spend time
translating it.

une dissertation essay
un contrôle check
une colle detention

Lyon, le 15 janvier

Cher Peter,

J'espère que tu vas bien. Quel temps fait-il
à Birmingham ? Ici il fait très froid et il neige.
Comme tu me l'as demandé, je vais te parler de mon
école. Cette année, je suis entrée au lycée Malraux,
en classe de seconde. Si je ne redouble pas, je
passerai le baccalauréat dans deux ans. En
seconde, on doit étudier le français, les maths,
une langue vivante (j'ai choisi l'anglais bien
sûr !), l'histoire-géo, la physique, la chimie et
les sciences naturelles. Et nous avons aussi deux
heures de sport par semaine. Et puis nous
avons aussi des options : moi, j'ai choisi l'allemand
et l'espagnol car j'aime beaucoup les langues.
          Le matin j'ai mon premier cours à 8h et
je finis souvent à 5h. Sauf mercredi et samedi,
je n'y vais que le matin. Le midi, nous avons
deux heures pour manger. Moi, je mange à la
cantine. Et le soir, en rentrant chez moi, j'ai
toujours beaucoup de devoirs à faire; exercices
de maths, traduction en anglais, dissertation de
français... Et des leçons à apprendre aussi.
          Nous avons souvent des contrôles en classe
et si tu ne sais rien, tu es un 0 sur le
carnet de correspondance et même une colle
quelquefois. Quand les parents voient le
carnet, ils peuvent devenir très en colère.
Heureusement pour moi, j'ai beaucoup de
bonnes notes et même quelques 20/20. Je pense
que la moyenne du deuxième trimestre sera
bonne. Quand ta moyenne est correcte, tu
as un encouragement des professeurs et quand
elle est très bonne, tu as leurs félicitations.
Il faut maintenant que je te quitte : j'ai
une dissertation à faire en français pour la
semaine prochaine. Si je veux avoir la moyenne,
je dois bien la préparer.
Parle-moi de ton école aussi dans ta
prochaine lettre.

          À bientôt
          Amitiés

✎ WRITING

1 You have been asked, while on exchange in France, to give details about school life in England. As part of this exercise, you write out your timetable in French.

2 You have received this letter from your penfriend, Cédric. As he has made the effort to write in English, you feel that you must reply in French. Tell him a little about yourself and what you like at school.

3 Write a letter to your French penfriend, asking for information about the school set-up in France. Explain that you need this information for a project that you are doing at school. You will need to know about such things as:

- times
- which subjects are compulsory
- sporting activities
- foreign languages studied
- school uniform
- school meals.

4 You have already been on exchange to France, and your partner is soon to return to England. You realise that he will be obliged to go to school with you—and risk the perils of school dinners! As you already know that his family eat very well, you write to warn him of what to expect in the school canteen—maybe you could give him a typical day's choice. (Don't worry too much, school dinners have the same reputation everywhere!)

5 The school where you are on exchange in France operates a termly magazine. During your stay, you are asked to contribute 150 words to it in the form of an article about the life of a sixteen year old in Britain. You should mention that for some, this is the age of transition from school to work, which, of course, has many complex implications.

Dohein Cedric,
112, Rue jean meraton
Wandignie - Hamage
59870
MARCHIENNES

Dear Gregory

Thank you for your last letter.
Speak in school:
in math, I am very good;
in English, I am good;
in French, I am good too;
I am 6 sur 25
Now the weather is good enough
I go in england with the school
at Kanterberry
The next year, I go in 4e.

. Please, give me your photo

Good Bye

Write soon

Your friend Cedric

MULTI-SKILL TASK

Your school is doing an exchange with a school near Tours. One day the person with whom you are staying is unwell and, since there is an outing that afternoon, you decide to go into school on your own. (The tape should be paused at the appropriate points.)

1 When you get to school the *proviseur* calls you and gives you some information.

He also asks you to do something.

Working with a partner do what you were asked to do.

2 He now gives you a paper and also some instructions.

Groupe d'Élèves Anglais.

Visite au Château de Salmarony

Départ du Car　　Devant le CES à 1h30.

Arrivée aux ruines du Château　　2h. Visite des ruines avec explication de M. Roche (prof. d'histoire)

Suivie de　descente dans le village (à pied).

Visite　au musée de l'Artisanat. On verra un souffleur de verre et un sculpteur en bois.

Rendez-vous　devant la Mairie du village à 4h30. Le car viendra nous chercher là.

Retour au CES.　　5h.

---

l'artisanat　craft

3 You now receive a further task.

You make some notes in English in order to carry out your task and using the information given here do what the *proviseur* asked.

There are 29 English pupils in school. 27 will go on the trip. One will be a little late as she goes home with her penfriend for lunch so could the bus wait an extra ten minutes for her?

8

Circuit touristique

 LISTENING

1 You are camping with friends near St Malo in Brittany and on the day after your arrival you go into the local tourist office in order to find out a bit about what there is to see in the town. Make notes, using the headings below, about what you are told so that you can relay the information to your friends.

	Where to go	What is interesting
1		
2		
3		
4		
5		

2 Having been to see the Bayeux tapestry you hear this announcement over the loudspeaker as you are leaving.

  1 Who is responsible for this advertisement?

  2 What special event is happening each evening at the cathedral?

  3 During which months is this on?

  4 What time would you need to go if you wanted to hear information in English?

  5 What have they done to help you appreciate the architecture of the cathedral?

3 Your French friends have done a survey, on tape, about tourism, in which several people have been asked questions about holidays. You feel that the survey is interesting as it shows what French people look for in a holiday. You decide to note the answers under the following headings:

- Where do you go on holiday?
- How do you travel there?
- How long do you go for?
- Why do you like it there?

4 You receive this cassette letter from your penfriend whose family is coming to stay soon. She asks you for certain information. Make a note in English of what each person wants so that you can send them some details.

	Who made the request?	What do they want?
1		
2		
3		
4		

5 You are in Paris with a party from your school. A group of you want to go for a trip on the Seine on a *Bateau Mouche*.

    1 You have asked for a trip at 1 pm but this is not possible. Why not?

    2 You ask for an alternative and are told . . . . .

    3 Only one trip will allow you to have lunch on the boat. Which one is this?

    4 How much is the trip?

    5 How much will your school-friends each pay if they take lunch?

6 Whilst touring in the Vendée with some friends, you stop at an antique shop in the village of Sallertaine. You have heard that there is plenty to see there and so you ask the shopkeeper for some details. Listen to what you are told and make notes about the four places mentioned.

    ● Where are you told to go?
    ● Give two or more facts about the place.

7 Your penfriend lives in Clermont-Ferrand and one day she sends you a cassette letter describing the town and what there is to see. Make some notes so that you can tell your family about the place.

8 You are on an exchange in Lyon and, one day, whilst your penfriend is busy elsewhere, you are wondering what to do. Your penfriend's mother makes some suggestions about what you might go to see in the town. Make some notes about what she suggests so that you can visit as much as possible.

9 You are visiting Haute-Savoie as one of the older pupils on a school trip. One free afternoon you happen to find a little museum and decide to visit it. You soon realise that this would be an ideal place to bring a group of the younger pupils. However, you decide that you will have to write a short account, in English, of the information the guide is giving as they are unlikely to understand it. You go round twice taking notes in order to write the account. Make your notes under the following headings:

    ● The origins and contents of the museum.
    ● The education of peasant children.
    ● The peasants' summer.

SPEAKING

1 Using the plan provided and working with a partner, take it in turns to ask each other questions about how to get from one place to another. Begin at the railway station and then start each time from the last place at which you arrived.

> For example: Pour aller au château s'il vous plaît?
> Il faut prendre la première rue à gauche, etc.

1 Ask each other for directions to all of the places shown.

2 Draw two plans. On one, mark ten places of interest and under the other simply list the places. Give your partner the plan with the list and let him/her ask you for directions. Following the directions you give (according to the plan with the places marked on it) your partner draws in where he/she thinks the places are. You should then compare the two plans.

3 Now your partner invents the plans and you ask for directions.

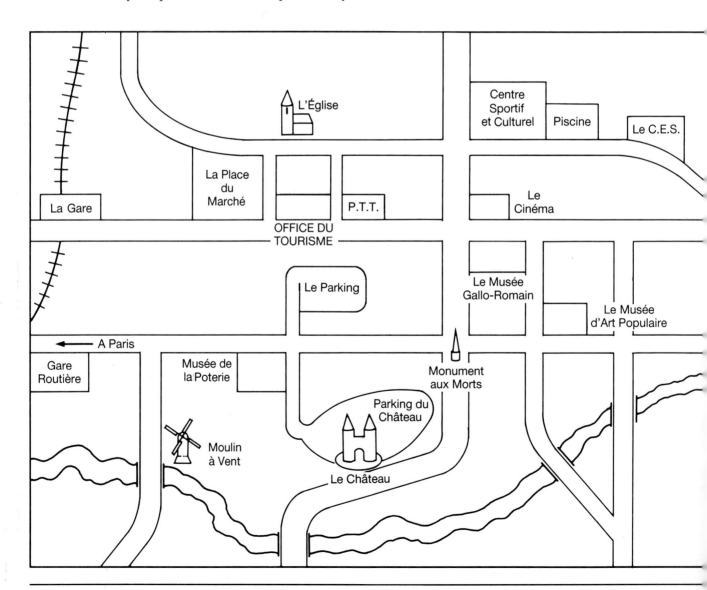

2 Whilst on holiday in France with friends, you go into the tourist office of a small town. You want to know what there is to see in the area. Work with a partner who will play the receptionist in the tourist office.

1 Ask if there are any public toilets nearby.

2 Ask if there is a castle.

3 Ask where it is.

4 Ask when it is open and how much it costs.

5 Ask if there are any museums in the town.

6 Ask which museums he/she would recommend.

7 Ask if you can park your car near to the Roman History museum.

8 Ask if the shops in the town are open on a Monday.

9 Ask if they have any brochures about the area.

10 Ask if the *Syndicat* is open every day.

3 Your penfriend's family are all coming to stay with you in the summer. Naturally, they are anxious to know about where you live and ask you the following questions. Your partner will ask you the questions and you answer. Then swap roles. (You should answer these questions about your own town.)

1 Elle est près de la mer, ta ville?

2 Est-ce qu'il y a un terrain de golf?

3 Y a-t-il des monuments historiques à visiter?

4 Est-ce qu'on peut facilement aller à Londres?

5 Y a-t-il des 'pubs' pittoresques à visiter?

6 Est-ce qu'il y a beaucoup de magasins?

4 You have just arrived in Rouen and want to visit those monuments which are to do with Joan of Arc. You go to the information office in the station. If you can, work through this with the French assistant or with your teacher. If not, work with your partner.

1 Say you have just arrived in Rouen and want to visit the Joan of Arc church.

2 Repeat the instructions to show that you have understood and ask if there is a museum as well.

3 Say thank you and that you must hurry. It is already 17h00.

5 You are stopped in the street by a man whose arms are dripping with cheap bangles and necklaces. You do not want to buy any but he is very insistent. Again work preferably with your teacher or the assistant.

1 Say you have no money and that you are going home tomorrow . . . and thanks.

2 Say you are not interested and thanks!

3 Say that is too expensive and that you don't want any . . . and *goodbye*!

6 You are on a visit to Paris and you decide to go out and see the sights. Work with your teacher, the assistant or a partner.

At the métro station
1 Ask for a ticket to the Trocadéro.
2 Say you will buy a carnet instead.
3 Ask how much it costs.
4 Say you will buy two.

At the Eiffel Tower
1 Ask how much it costs to go up.
2 Say you will go up to the second storey.
3 Ask if there is a lift.
4 Ask if there is a restaurant on the second floor.

At the Ile de la Cité
1 Ask where Notre Dame is.
2 Ask if it is far away.
3 Ask if it is possible to see the bell.
4 Ask how much it costs.

At the entrance to the Bateaux Mouches
1 Ask how much the trip costs.
2 Ask when the next trip is.
3 Ask for three tickets—two adults and one child.
4 Ask where to wait for the next boat.

7 You are working during the holiday in your local tourist office when a French visitor to the town comes in. He speaks no English and wants to know all about the place. Working with a partner, take it in turns to pretend to be the visitor and ask and answer the following questions. If you like, draw a rough sketch of the town or town centre first to help you.

1 Le bureau de poste est où s'il vous plaît?
2 Où est-ce que je peux acheter des cartes postales?
3 Y a-t-il un château à visiter dans les environs?
4 Y a-t-il des musées à visiter?
5 Quel musée recommandez-vous?
6 C'est loin?
7 Y a-t-il un terrain de camping près d'ici ou une auberge de jeunesse?
8 Y a-t-il d'autres sites historiques à visiter?
9 Y a-t-il une bonne sélection de magasins dans les environs?
10 Nous avons une journée de libre—que recommandez-vous?

8 You are on a school visit to Normandy and you go on a day-trip to the Mont-St-Michel. You have read a little about the place and are fascinated by it. On the way, you manage to sit next to the guide and ask him some questions.

(It would be best if you could work on this dialogue with your teacher or French assistant. Otherwise work with your partner.)

1 You ask when an abbey was first built there.
2 Why did they build an abbey in such a place?
3 You ask how you get to it.
4 Find out if it is possible to sail right round the rock.
5 Can one walk around the rock on the sand?
6 Find out why.
7 Find out how long you will spend there.
8 Find out if there is anything else to see on the mount apart from the abbey.

9 Find out if a lot of people visit the mount.

10 You have heard that there are a lot of souvenir shops. Say you think this is a pity as it must spoil the historic atmosphere of the place.

9 Cards 1 and 2 show the details of a recent day-trip made to Paris.

1 Working with a partner take a card each and compare the visits you made to Paris. You could start like this:

You: Je suis arrivé à la Gare du Nord.
Your partner: Moi, je suis arrivé à la Gare de Lyon.
You: J'y suis arrivé à 10h00.
Your partner: Moi, j'y suis arrivé à 9h00.
You: Puis, j'ai marché jusqu'au Sacré-Coeur.
Your partner: Moi, j'ai pris le métro jusqu'à Notre Dame.
You: Et puis, j'ai marché jusqu'au Moulin Rouge.
Your partner: Et moi, j'ai marché jusqu' à la Place de la Concorde.
And so on.

2 You could make up your own cards about any visit you have made, in France or elsewhere.

3 Using one of the cards as a guideline talk about the day's events, saying where you went and how and what you did.

10 You have been asked to help with a group of French pupils who are on exchange at your school with pupils in the 2nd and 3rd year. One afternoon you all go to visit a nearby castle. Before the pupils wander round the castle, where the guides speak only English, you are asked to tell them a little bit about the place in French. You have jotted down the following details from a preliminary visit you made. Pretend your partner is your audience and give him/her the information in French.

1 The castle was built in the 12th century by Sir Gervase de la Roche whose grandfather arrived with William the Conqueror and who received the land from the king.

2 It is supposed to be haunted by a lady in white who lived there during the 15th century. She was engaged to a soldier who died in the wars in France and she was so unhappy that she committed suicide. Her ghost appears on the tower.

3 During the civil war, the soldiers of Oliver Cromwell tried to destroy the castle but it was very solid and much of it still remains.

4 There is an exhibition of waxwork figures in the great hall which show what life was like in the 12th century.

5 There is a tea-room in the old kitchens where you can get something to eat and drink quite cheaply.

11 Now imagine that you are going to take a group of French people to a place of interest in your own locality. You could find out some details about the place and then describe it to your partner. (If you do not mention the name of the place, see if he/she can guess where you are talking about. You could also do this as a group or as a whole class.)

📖 READING

1 When staying with French friends near Sedan you express an interest in visiting the castle. Your friends show you this brochure.

  1 What kind of castle is it and how old is it?

  2 You note that there is a bar. What else will you see?

  3 It is now early September. If you visit the castle before Sept 9th, at what times will it be open?

  4 If you visit the castle after Sept 9th, at what times is it open?

  5 What day should you avoid after Sept 9th?

  6 A group from your school is coming to Sedan at half-term at the beginning of November. If they are interested in visiting the castle then, what will you tell them?

CHATEAU FORT DE SEDAN

LE PLUS ÉTENDU D'EUROPE
1000 ANS D'HISTOIRE

  — **Visite archéologique**
  — **Musée**
  — **Expositions**
  — **Bar**

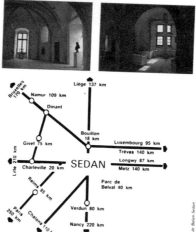

HORAIRES	
du 24 mars au 8 sept. 10 h 00 - 17 h 30 tous les jours	du 9 sept. au 27 oct. 13 h 30 - 17 h 30 sauf lundis
et sur rendez-vous Tél. (24) 29.03.28	

Imp. de Balan-Sedan

OFFICE DE TOURISME — 08202 SEDAN

2 On a visit to Touraine with your school you see this poster advertising the *château* at Ussé, in the tourist office in Tours. The picture looks interesting so you look for details and make a note to tell your teacher about it.

  1 What can you see at the castle?

  2 What are the opening times?

  3 It is only the beginning of March. How can your school party visit the castle?

  4 With which fairy story is the castle connected?

USSÉ

Château de la Belle au bois dormant

Tapisseries, collection d'armes, appartements royaux, jardins en terrasse.
Nouvelles salles ouvertes au public.

Visite (extérieur et intérieur)
du 15 mars au 1er octobre : de 9 h. à 12 h. et de 14 h. à 19 h.
du 1er octobre au 1er novembre : fermeture à 18 heures.
Le château est fermé du 1er novembre au 15 mars.

Tous renseignements :
Château d'Ussé - Rigny-Ussé, 37420 Avoine - tél. : 93-14-05

En hiver, ouverture pour groupes sur demande 48 heures à l'avance.

3 On a sight-seeing trip to Lyon you want to visit all sorts of places. Try to decide which signs or notices you would follow for each place you want to visit or activity you want to do.

  1 You want to go to the swimming pool, which building would you go into?

| BIBLIOTHÈQUE | PISCINE | MUSÉE | BOULODROME |

  2 You decide to visit the puppet museum. The guide you read gives you details of how to get to four different museums. Which details must you follow?

| MUSÉE GALLO ROMAIN | MUSÉE DES BEAUX-ARTS |

| MUSÉE DE LA MARIONNETTE | MUSÉE HISTORIQUE DES TISSUS |

  3 You decide to visit a pancake restaurant you have heard of. You see several restaurants and cafés, which one would you go into?

| CRÊPERIE | BUVETTE | BRASSERIE | CAFÉ-BAR |

  4 You have bought a postcard to send home. Where would you be likely to be able to buy a stamp and post your letter right away?

| BUREAU de RENSEIGNEMENTS | BUREAU de POSTE |

| BUREAU de TOURISME | BUREAU des OBJETS TROUVÉS |

  5 You decide to hire a bike to visit the surrounding area. Which place should you go to?

| LOCATION ET VENTE | LOCATION DE VOITURES |

| VENTE DE VÉLOS | LOCATION DE VÉLOS |

  6 You are riding the bike you hired in the countryside and you are looking for a suitable track to ride along. Which sign should you follow?

| CHEMIN PRIVÉ | ALLÉE PIÉTONS | PISTE CYCLABLE | ROUTE DE PROMENADE |

  7 You decide to visit a friend who is staying in a youth hostel. Which sign should you follow?

| CAMPING DE MIRIBEL | AUBERGE DU LAC |

| AUBERGE DE JEUNESSE | HÔTEL LEJEUNE |

8 You decide you want further information on the tourist attractions. Which building should you look for?

SYNDICAT D'INITIATIVE	GENDARMERIE

SOCIÉTÉ GÉNÉRALE	GARE ROUTIÈRE

9 You wish to visit the cathedral on the hill in Lyon. Which sign should you follow?

THÉÂTRE ROMAIN DE FOURVIÈRE	NOTRE-DAME DE FOURVIÈRE

MAISON DES CANUTS	AMPHITHÉÂTRE ROMAIN

10 You have heard that the town hall in Lyon has some splendid reception rooms. You hope to visit them. Which sign should you follow?

COMMISSARIAT	JARDIN PUBLIC

MARCHÉ AUX PUCES	MAIRIE

4 You are visiting Pau in the company of a Swedish friend who does not speak much French. You get this information from the tourist office and explain to your friend what is available.

Working with a partner explain, in English, what there is to see in Pau. Your partner plays the role of your Swedish friend and makes notes about what you say, in English. Swap roles halfway through so that each of you has a turn. You could write your answers down instead.

1 What is there in particular to see at the castle?

2 When can you visit it and how much does it cost?

3 Which museum would be most likely to interest your friend and why?

4 When can you visit it and how much does it cost?

5 What is there in the *Musée des Beaux-Arts* and when can you visit it?

6 Why is the *Boulevard des Pyrénées* worth a visit?

7 The *Parlement de Navarre* had a stormy history. What is now in the building which used to house it?

8 Why is the *Tour de la Monnaie* so called and what used to take place on the *Place de la Monnaie*?

Visite de la ville

● monuments et musées

- **LE CHATEAU** où naquit Henri IV le 13 décembre 1553 fut créé au XIIe siècle par les vicomtes de Béarn, agrandi et embelli par les rois de Navarre au XVe siècle et les rois de France au XVIe siècle. Magnifique collection de tapisseries.

Heures d'ouverture : Eté : 9h-11h 45, 14h-17h 45 - Hiver : 9h 30-11h 45, 14h-16h 45.

Prix d'entrée : 6 F pour adultes - Gratuit pour enfants - Tél. (59) 27.35.29.

- **LE MUSEE BEARNAIS** : Situé au 3e étage du château est consacré aux Traditions et Arts populaires en Béarn. Exposition temporaire durant l'été. Prix d'entrée : 2 F.

- **LE MUSEE DES BEAUX-ARTS** : Premier musée à acquérir une œuvre de Degas, il abrite une fantastique collection de tableaux et une section sculpture intéressante. Rue Mathieu-Lalanne - Entrée gratuite - Fermé le mardi - Tél. 27.33.02.

- **LE MUSEE BERNADOTTE** : Belle maison béarnaise du XVIIIe siècle, où naquit en 1763 Jean-Baptiste Bernadotte. En 1951, elle fut transformée en musée. De nombreux documents (peintures, gravures, médailles) évoquent le jeune lieutenant, le maréchal de France et le roi de Suède et de Norvège. Rue Tran - Entrée gratuite - Fermé le lundi - Tél. 27.48.42.

- **LE BOULEVARD DES PYRENEES** : Créé à la fin du XIXe siècle par Henri Faisans alors maire de la ville, il relie le château au parc Beaumont. De là, on peut admirer, au-delà de la vallée du Gave de Pau et des côteaux, 150 km de la chaîne des Pyrénées.

- **LE PARLEMENT DE NAVARRE** : Créé en 1620, par Louis XIII, cœur d'une résistance acharnée aux ordres de Louis XVI au XVIIIe siècle, il abrite actuellement le Conseil Général des Pyrénées-Atlantiques.

- **LA TOUR DE LA MONNAIE** : Ce bâtiment où autrefois était frappée la monnaie se situe sur la place de la Monnaie, ancien centre important de la vie paloise ; cette place servait de champ clos aux duels judiciaires.

la chaîne mountain range
frapper to strike (coins)

5 Your penfriend lives in Honfleur in Normandy. He writes you this letter telling you what there is to see in his town. Jot down some details in English to tell your father about where you will be staying.

Honfleur le 5 juin.

Cher Mark,

J'attends avec impatience ton arrivée à Honfleur. Tu sais il y a tant à voir dans cette ville, qu'on va passer la moitié de notre temps à faire les touristes.

D'abord, bien sûr, il y a le port avec le Vieux Bassin car Honfleur est un port de pêche, de commerce et de plaisance.

Il y a aussi, beaucoup de vieux bâtiments comme l'Eglise Ste-Catherine qui date de la fin du XVe siècle construite toute en bois. Il y a également le clocher qui, lui, est séparé de l'église et dont l'intérieur reste à voir. Mais il ne faut pas oublier les vieilles maisons qui se trouvent dans le secteur sauvegardé.

Le musée le plus intéressant est le musée d'Art Populaire Normand. C'est une visite guidée de 3/4 d'heure et ça vaut vraiment le coup.

Il y a aussi de très belles promenades à effectuer aux environs de la ville. Tu vas t'amuser, je t'assure, toi qui aimes l'histoire et tout ce qui est pittoresque.

Alors à bientôt.

Franck.

un port de plaisance pleasure port, marina
un clocher bell tower

6 Shortly before Christmas you are staying with your penfriend in Paris. The whole city is decorated for the festive season and is really a sight worth seeing. You write to your family telling them all about what you have seen. Use the information in the brochure to help you. Be sure to mention the special activities for old people and children and the concerts available.

LA FORET ENCHANTEE

sur le Champ de Mars
(côté École Militaire)

du 19 décembre au 2 janvier

Tous les jours de 14 h. à 18 h.

Promenade à bord de petits trains dans un décor féerique scintillant de mille lumières composé de près de 800 sapins et de sculptures géantes.

Manèges de chevaux de bois

sous le chapiteau central

à 14 h. 30 et 16 h.

du 19 au 23 décembre : **LES FORBANS**
du 24 au 28 décembre : **LES CHARLOTS**
du 29 décembre au 2 janvier : **KAREN CHERYL**

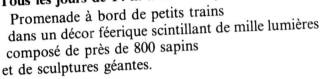

EUROPE 1

Organisées par la Mairie de Paris et l'Office municipal des fêtes de la ville de Paris toutes ces animations sont gratuites.

concours de dessins d'enfants

Un concours de dessins sur le thème de Noël à Paris est organisé pour les enfants des écoles primaires et maternelles publiques et privées.

Les enfants nés entre 1972 et 1980 devront déposer leur dessin (dimensions 24 x 32) dans les boîtes aux lettres installées dans le hall des mairies d'arrondissement du 3 décembre au 3 janvier, après avoir mentionné leur nom, prénom, adresse, date de naissance et école fréquentée.

Les résultats seront affichés dans chaque mairie le 14 janvier 1985.

les Lauréats seront reçus et récompensés à l'Hôtel de Ville par M. Jacques CHIRAC

LA CRECHE MERVEILLEUSE

Présentée sur le parvis de l'Hôtel de Ville (4ᵉ) du 7 décembre au 6 janvier de 11 h. à 19 h. (entrée : 10 F au bénéfice de l'UNICEF)

pour les personnes âgées...

SPECTACLES DE FIN D'ANNEE ORGANISES PAR LE BUREAU D'AIDE SOCIALE DE PARIS

A l'occasion des fêtes de fin d'année, le Bureau d'Aide Sociale de Paris propose aux Parisiens âgés une grande variété de spectacles durant les mois de décembre et janvier. Les personnes âgées de tous les arrondissements sont invitées à y assister gratuitement.

Renseignements: Bureau d'Aide Sociale de votre mairie

EXPOSITIONS
dans les musées de la ville de Paris

MUSÉE D'ART MODERNE
11, av. du Président-Wilson
75016 PARIS - Tél. : 723.61.27
Jean Hélion
Quatre-vingts peintures, quatre-vingts dessins.
Lucien Clergue
Trente ans de photographies.
Helmut Newton
Vingt ans de photos de mode.
Ces photographies qui ébranlèrent le monde
New York, ailleurs et autrement
Proposée par Claude Gintz.
5/5 - Figuration libre - France / U.S.A
Par Otto Hahn et Hervé Perdriolles.

MUSÉE DES ENFANTS
La Fête des Morts au Mexique

MUSÉE CARNAVALET
23, rue de Sévigné
75003 PARIS - Tél. : 272.21.13
Petits métiers et types parisiens vers 1900
Photographie d'Atget, Vert et Géniaux.
Henri Cartier-Bresson et Paris
Cent-vingts photos à découvrir.

MUSÉE DE LA MODE ET DU COSTUME
10, av. Pierre 1er de Serbie
75016 PARIS - Tél. : 720.85.46
De la mode et des lettres

MUSÉE DU PETIT PALAIS
Av. Winston-Churchill
75008 PARIS - Tél. : 265.12.73
*Symboles et réalités,
la peinture allemande 1848-1905*

PAVILLON DES ARTS
101, rue Rambuteau
75001 PARIS - Tél. : 233.82.50
Les collections de photographies contemporaines de la Bibliothèque Nationale

MUSÉE RENAN-SCHEFFER
16, rue Chaptal - 75009 PARIS
Tél. : 874.95.38
Michel Delaborde
« Correspondances imaginaires, voyages d'images ».

FESTIVAL D'ART SACRE

• **Mercredi 5 Décembre à 20 h 30**
Église Saint-Louis-en-l'Ile
F.-Bernard MÂCHE : Muwatalli
Philippe HERSANT : Khayâl
Esther LAMANDIER

• **Vendredi 7 Décembre à 20 h 30**
Église Saint-Louis-en-l'Ile
Édith CANAT DE CHIZY :
« Livre d'Heures »
M. JAUBERT : psaumes
F. LISZT : « Via Crucis »
ENSEMBLE INSTRUMENTAL
ENSEMBLE VOCAL

• **Dimanche 9 Décembre à 10 h**
Église des Billettes
LES PETITS CHANTEURS DE PARIS
J.S. BACH - G. FAURÉ -
F. MENDELSSOHN -
G.B. PERGOLÈSE - H. PURCELL

• **Lundi 10 Décembre à 20 h 30**
Théatre Musical de Paris - Châtelet
G.F. HAENDEL : Le Messie
LONDON CHORAL SOCIETY
ENSEMBLE ORCHESTRAL DE PARIS

• **Samedi 15 Décembre**
Église Saint-Germain-des-Prés
J.S. BACH
Pièces liturgiques du Père André GOUZES

• **Lundi 24 Décembre à 22 h 30**
Église Saint-Roch
Au cours de la veillée de NOEL et de la MESSE DE MINUIT
H. SCHUTZ, J. GRIMBERT
H. DU MONT, G. GABRIELLI
CHŒUR NATIONAL
SOLISTES ET ENSEMBLE INSTRUMENTAL

Renseignements : 277.18.83

ILLUMINATIONS DES QUARTIERS

La Mairie de Paris apporte son concours, comme chaque année, à près de 50 Associations de commerçants afin d'illuminer du 13 décembre au 7 janvier les rues les plus fréquentées de notre ville.

un concours competition
la crèche manger scene

7 You are camping with your family near Avranches in Normandy.
In the tourist office you pick up this brochure. It certainly seems to
have something for everyone and the three visits are suggested for
a single day.

Your mother is interested by the *Musée du Granit* and asks the
following questions:

1 Shall we see how they quarry it and the kinds of tools they use?

2 Shall we see what they use the granite for?

3 How much does it cost?

Le Parc Animalier
de ST-SYMPHORIEN-DES-MONTS

Merveille de la Nature
Parc authentique dessiné
au XVIIIème siècle

sur 50 ha un vrai contact
avec la nature, sa faune, sa flore

— Réserve d'animaux sauvages Européens
— Plaine des Bisons, des Yacks et des Buffles
— Le Bois des Loups · L'Etang des Flamants Roses
  et des Cygnes
— Les Espèces en voie de disparition
  (les rarissimes Anes du Poitou)
— Les animaux familiers, amis des enfants

EXCLUSIF **EXPOSITION
ECOLOGIQUE
de Plein-Air,**
21 tableaux de l'évolution de l'Homme
et de la Nature à travers les siècles

AIRE de Jeux d'Enfants
PIQUE-NIQUE aménagé
SALON de THÉ – CRÊPERIE
MAGASIN   ☎ (33) **49.02.41**

Le Musée du Granit
de ST-MICHEL-DE-MONTJOIE

Dans un vaste parc ombragé vous découvrirez les usages
de la pierre dans l'habitat, l'agriculture, l'artisanat, etc...
Vous connaitrez les façons de l'extraire, la travailler,
l'outillage ancien et moderne...
Vous serez impressionnés par les collections d'objets et
d'ouvrages sculptés ou polis.   ☎ **(33) 59.84.94**

CULTURE et PLAISIR pour les enfants,
TRADITION et SURPRISE pour les aînés
DÉCOUVERTE pleine d'enseignement
en visitant le 1er musée du granit créé
en Europe.

Tarif : adultes 8 F
        enfants 6 F

prix par groupe

☎ **(33)
59.84.94
59.91.08**

Your father loves nature and is interested by the *Parc Animalier*. He wants to know:

1 How long has the park been there?

2 What animals shall we see?

3 Can we get anything to eat there or should we take a picnic?

Your little sister is captivated by the idea of *Le Village Enchanté*. She wants to know:

1 What is there to see?

2 What is there for children to do?

3 Why is it called 'enchanted'?

Which visit do you think you would enjoy most and why?

Le Village Enchanté
de BELLEFONTAINE

Parc naturel aménagé à vocation éducative, culturelle et artistique.

- La vallée des **contes de fées.**

- Les villages du monde avec le village typique Bas-Normand.

- Le parc de loisirs (poneys, petit train, jeux)

- Les expositions vente d'artisanat régional

- L'**Auberge paysanne** dans un cadre rustique, cuisine typique. (accueil de groupes)

- Le village de **gîtes** ruraux (hébergement en toutes saisons)

☎ (33) 59.01.93

l'outillage tools
extraire to extract
un ouvrage piece of work
une fée fairy

8 You are going to stay with your penfriend at Apremont in the Vendée. He sends you this brochure about the town. Make some notes about what there is to see and do, so that you can explain to your parents a bit about the town.

Dans un écrin de verdure et de fraîcheur, à quelques minutes de la Côte Vendéenne, vous découvrez APREMONT, Commune rurale d'origine gallo-romaine, étymologie latine : ASPER-MONS, montagne âpre, sauvage, qui nous offre la particularité de son relief très varié harmonieusement souligné par les méandres de la VIE.

Les amoureux de la nature trouveront dans ce décor inhabituel en cette région de VENDÉE, un charme nouveau et un plaisir renouvelé par la diversité du site.

Un barrage formant un lac de 166 ha de 8 km de long.

Un Club Nautique dynamique initie les jeunes au plaisir de la VOILE et de la Planche à VOILE.

Il peut accueillir ses jeunes sur une aire de camping naturelle à Gourgeau.

Une Plage de sable en pente douce plantée d'arbustes donnent un ombrage léger et reposant. Les enfants peuvent s'y ébattre agréablement grâce aux équipements placés pour eux.

Un Bar de nombreuses tables de pique-nique à l'ombre des chênes permettent de s'y restaurer face au lac.

Les Pêcheurs peuvent s'adonner à leur plaisir favori tant sur le lac que sur la rivière, où abondent gardons, perches, brochets, sandres, carpes.

Le Château ouvrage du début du XVIème siècle, dû à l'initiative de l'Amiral de France Philippe Chabot de Brion.

Du sommet de la tour EST le visiteur découvre le BOURG pittoresque d'APREMONT ; La Charpente d'étage et de toiture est une réalisation remarquable.

Une Allée Cavalière, vaste galerie souterraine permettant à 4 chevaux d'y accéder de flanc jusqu'à la rivière qui bordait la tour Ouest à cette époque n'a que d'égale celle du Château d'Amboise.

La Salle Panoramique, on accède rapidement au sommet (80 mètres) sur le Château d'eau, pour y découvrir un panorama unique par temps clair jusqu'à la côte St-GILLES-CROIX-DE-VIE et même NOIRMOUTIER.

Un Camping-Caravaning, privé très bien équipé vous accueille dans un site reposant.
— Sentiers pédestres et cyclotouristes,
— Terrain de moto-cross.

Nombreuses fêtes organisées pendant la saison :

FÊTES FOLKLORIQUES
FEU D'ARTIFICE
MOTO-CROSS
EXPOSITIONS ARTISTIQUES

un barrage   dam

9 Your aunt and uncle are planning an autumn break in Brittany. Some French friends, Pierre and Marie Lenoir, have sent them details of what looks like an interesting week in Quiberon, organised by V.R.M., a club to which they belong. Your uncle brings the information to you and asks you some questions.

1 Will we have to pay for membership of V.R.M?

2 Does it say what the hotel is like?

3 Pierre says in his letter that the price includes almost everything. What is actually included?

4 What are we going to see on the excursions?

5 Will we have a courier?

VISAGES & REALITES DU MONDE **VVD**

VACANCES
VOYAGES
DÉCOUVERTES

En collaboration avec

11, Avenue de la Libération 42000 StEtienne Tel.77.34.18.46

La **BRETAGNE**

**LA COTE SAUVAGE,
BELLE-ILE-EN-MER,
QUIBERON,
CARNAC ...**

VACANCES
VOYAGES
DÉCOUVERTES
Bât.i La Taillée 42390 VILLARS
Tél.: (77) 74-13-69 —

**DU 16 AU 22-09-86
2.360 F/PERS.**

```
        La BRETAGNE nous la connaissons bien et Jacques notre
guide plus encore ! C'est à QUIBERON, face à la mer, à deux pas
du centre ville et de la criée aux poissons, que nous avons
réservé pour vous un hotel avec ascenseur de bon confort et à
l'ambiance très familiale.

        Notre forfait séjour à QUIBERON, avec les excursions
comprises et les visites. Vous n'avez rien à débourser durant
votre voyage. Alors laissez vous guider !

Excursion journée : - BELLE ILE EN MER - avec promenade en bateau
                      tour de l'île et déjeuner.

Excursions 1/2 journée : - Le château de JOSSELIN
                         - L'ORIENT avec visite de la base de sous-
                           marins.(carte d'identité obligatoire)
                         -La presqu'île de Quiberon et la côte
                          sauvage
                         - VANNES et les alignements de CARNAC
                         - Le golfe du MORBIHAN (excursion bateau à
                           l'île AUX MOINES facultative)

Le tarif comprend: - le transport - le séjour en pension complète
- la boisson - les excursions mentionnées - les assurances - le
guide V.R.M

Le tarif ne comprend pas : - l'adhésion V.R.M 50 F/Pers. - l'excur-
sion bateau à l'ILE AUX MOINES -
```

comprendre to include
la presqu'île peninsula
l'alignement line (of rocks etc.)

10 Whilst visiting Lyon you decide to have a look at some of the museums the town has to offer. The brochure is very detailed so you skim through it, pausing to read certain parts in more detail.

LES MUSÉES DE LYON

MUSÉE DES BEAUX-ARTS :

Le Musée des Beaux-Arts est installé dans le Palais Saint-Pierre, ancien monastère construit par Royer de la Valfrenière au temps de Louis XIV.

Il a su harmonieusement accorder des aménagements modernes à un cadre ancien et ses 90 salles proposent une grande variété d'aspects. Il offre les plus larges possibilités à la délectation des amateurs aussi bien qu'au travail des chercheurs. Des visites dirigées sont régulièrement organisées. Des expositions temporaires sont fréquemment présentées. Les collections se répartissent en plusieurs sections : Sculpture, Peinture, Peinture lyonnaise, Objets d'Art, Art Oriental. Elles permettent ainsi d'étudier l'évolution des arts plastiques sous toutes leurs formes, dans tous les temps et dans tous les pays, grâce à de nombreuses œuvres bien choisies, dont quelques-unes sont universellement célèbres. Les collections de peinture des XIXe et XXe siècles sont particulièrement abondantes et riches en chefs-d'œuvre.

Palais Saint-Pierre, place des Terreaux (1er). - Tél. (7) 828.07.66 - Métro, Bus 3, 6, 13/18.

MUSÉE HISTORIQUE DES TISSUS :

Ce Musée, propriété de la Chambre de Commerce de Lyon, est installé dans l'ancien Hôtel Villeroy. Construit par Bertaut de la Vaure en 1730, le bâtiment doit son nom au Duc François-Anne de Villeroy, Gouverneur du lyonnais, qui, en 1734, en fit le siège du gouvernement de la Province du lyonnais.

Une aile récemment ajoutée à l'ancien bâtiment a permis l'ouverture de 12 nouvelles salles réservées pour la plupart aux collections orientales (tapis, tissus, et broderies). La section des tissus européens présente un choix de tissus italiens et espagnols qui donne une idée des principaux décors employés dans ces deux pays depuis le XIVe siècle jusqu'au XVIIIe siècle.

Les tissus français constituent le fonds le plus important des collections. Ils sont représentés par quelques-unes des plus belles étoffes tissées à Lyon du XVIIe siècle à nos jours, et de nombreuses pièces en réserve.

Une importante section a été consacrée également au tissu dans l'art religieux.

Une bibliothèque, accessble au public aux heures d'ouverture du Musée, contient environ 10 000 volumes sur les Beaux-Arts (peinture, sculpture, architecture, arts décoratifs). Elle est fermée le samedi et le dimanche et durant tout le mois d'août.

34, rue de la Charité (2e) - Tél. (7) 837.03.92 - Bus 8, 44.

MUSÉE DES ARTS DÉCORATIFS :

Aménagé dans l'ancien hôtel Lacroix-Laval, construit par Soufflot en 1739, ce Musée renferme une riche collection de meubles, objets d'art, bronzes, pendules, faïences, porcelaines, orfèvrerie, tapisseries, principalement des XVIIe et XVIIIe siècles, riche de 205 pièces d'une qualité exceptionnelle.

30, rue de la Charité (2e) - Tél. (7) 837.15.05 - Bus 8, 44.

MAISON DES CANUTS :

Exposition de tissus anciens : lampas, damas brochés, brocarts, velours aux fers et au sabre, impression sur chaîne.

Vieux métier à main en activité, dit à la Jacquard, tissant des brochés pour ameublement. Métier mécanique traditionnel avec mécanique Verdol.

10/12, rue d'Ivry (4e) - Tél. (7) 828.62.04 - Métro, Bus 6, 33, 41.

MUSÉE GALLO-ROMAIN :

Dans ce Musée, où sont rassemblées diverses collections autrefois dispersées, ou peut admirer une série épigraphique de premier ordre dont les pièces maîtresses sont le calendrier gaulois de Coligny, la dédicace de l'amphithéâtre, l'inscription sur bronze dite Table Claudienne, des épitaphes permettant de suivre l'évolution des mœurs au cours de l'Antiquité. A côté de ces inscriptions un peu austères, on remarquera un char gaulois de l'époque du fer, une statuaire abondante, de nombreux objets de la vie quotidienne, des mosaïques vastes et luxueuses qui permettent de restituer le cadre de vie des anciens habitants de Lugdunum.

On accordera une attention particulière à l'édifice qui contient ces collections, et qui, construit pour les recevoir, établit une heureuse harmonie entre les pièces anciennes et l'écrin moderne dans lequel elles sont présentées.

17, rue Cléberg (5e) - Tél. (7) 825.94.68 - Funiculaire.

MUSÉE DE LA MARIONNETTE :

Il est juxtaposé au Musée Historique en l'Hôtel de Gadagne. Autour des Marionnettes Lyonnaises de Laurent Mourguet, créateur de Guignol et de ses successeurs, les Josserand, sont présentées des Marionnettes à gaine des théâtres parisiens (Théâtre Paul Jeanne et des Buttes-Chaumont) ainsi que de divers pays étrangers (Angleterre, Hollande, Russie). Des personnages de Bruxelles, de Liège, de Venise et d'Amiens illustrent le genre de marionnettes à tringle, tandis que des ensembles aux mécanismes ingénieux provenant du Nord de la France ou des théâtres forains représentent le type de marionnettes à fils.

Le Musée expose, aussi, une importante série de Marionnettes à tige et d'ombres de Turquie ou d'Extrême-Orient (Cambodge, Java et Siam).

Place du Petit-Collège (5e) - Tél. (7) 842.03.61 - Bus 2, 3, 44.

MUSÉE GUIMET D'HISTOIRE NATURELLE :

La GRANDE SALLE, renferme, au centre, les représentants de grands animaux disparus ou vivants : Baleine, Mammouth, Rhytine, Cerf Géant, Éléphants. A sa périphérie, on remarque : La section des "Oiseaux-mouches", et le résultat de quelques fouilles du Museum, l'exceptionnelle section de Minéralogie.

La salle d'EGYPTOLOGIE.

La galerie RÉGION LYONNAISE, présente l'histoire géologique de la région, la faune actuelle avec surtout une remarquable collection des Oiseaux de la Dombes.

La galerie PROTECTION DE LA NATURE montre les mécanismes naturels du monde vivant, leurs équilibres et les dangers des ruptures d'équilibre.

La section PALEONTOLOGIE présente quelques tableaux modernisés de l'évolution des grands groupes animaux.

L'immense galerie de zoologie, suit tous les groupes animaux, invertébrés et vertébrés, dans une présentation rénovée, la moins statique possible.

La nouvelle section ETHNOGRAPHIE brosse un panorama particulièrement attachant de toutes les civilisations humaines.

Les AQUARIUMS introduisent la vie des mers tropicales et des fleuves du monde dans un musée moderne.

28, boulevard des Belges (6e) - Tél. (7) 893.22.44 - Bus 27, 36.

INSTITUT LUMIÈRE :

Exposition permanente de photos pour la promotion de l'art photographique.

25, rue du Premier Film (8e) - Tél. (7) 800.86.68 - Bus 9, 1, 24.

MUSÉE DE LA RÉSISTANCE :

5, rue Boileau (6e) - Tél. (7) 893.27.83 - Bus 27, 36.

MUSÉE DE L'IMPRIMERIE ET DE LA BANQUE :

Installé dans un hôtel du XVe siècle, qui abrita au XVIIe siècle la Maison de la Ville de Lyon, ce musée veut être un instrument didactique d'enseignement et de culture aussi bien sur le plan technique que sur le plan esthétique.

Imprimerie : Manuscrits, Incunables, Bible de Gutenberg. Presses des XVe, XVIIe, XVIIIe, XIXe et XXe siècles. Caractères d'imprimerie du XVe siècle. Collection de bois gravés et de cuivres gravés. Les supports graphiques : Papyrus, feuilles de palmier, tablettes de cire, parchemin, 2 200 estampes.

Banques : Puissance financière de Lyon au XVIe siècle. Les banques de crédit au XIXe siècle.

13, rue de la Poulaillerie (2e) - Tél. (7) 837.65.98 - Métro, Bus 3, 13/18.

MUSÉE AFRICAIN :

Musée privé, appartenant à la Société des Missions Africaines. Le Musée Africain se veut témoin de la culture des peuples de l'ex - A.O.F.

150, cours Gambetta (7e) - Tél. (7) 858.45.70 - Bus 1, 24.

AUTOUR DE LYON

MUSÉE FRANÇAIS DE L'AUTOMOBILE (Henri Malartre) :

Le château de Rochetaillée-sur-Saône abrite une rétrospective d'automobiles anciennes (1890 - 1970), de la voiture à vapeur 1890 jusqu'aux prestigieux modèles de course Talbot, Ferrari, Gordini, etc., et les prototypes 2 CV Citroën 1936, J.-P. Wimille 1948. La Mercedes d'Hitler. On trouve aussi une importante collection de cycles depuis 1918 et de motocycles (1898 - 1954).

Rochetaillée-sur-Saône - Tél. (7) 822.18.80 - Bus 40.

MAISON AMPÈRE - MUSÉE DE L'ÉLECTRICITÉ :

A Poleymieux-au-Mont d'Or, dans la maison où l'illustre physicien passa sa jeunesse et forma son génie.

Poleymieux - Tél. (7) 891.90.77.

MUSÉE CLAUDE BERNARD :

Musée installé dans la demeure du savant. Tout à côté, maison natale du créateur de la médecine expérimentale où avaient été primitivement rassemblés tous les souvenirs de Claude Bernard.

Saint-Julien-en-Beaujolais - Tél. (74) 67.51.44.

1 In which two museums would you find information about Lyon's silk industry?

2 Lyon is well known for its puppets. Guignol is the best known. Where could you see these puppets and who was the creator of Guignol?

3 As well as puppets from different parts of France, what other puppets are on show in the puppet museum?

4 What could you see at the *Institut Lumière*?

5 What could you see at the *Musée Français de l'Automobile* as well as cars?

6 Which museum is to be found outside Lyon at Polymieux-au-Mont-d'Or and in whose former home is it housed?

7 Who built the former *Hôtel Lacroix-Laval* and which museum does it now house?

8 Which is the only private museum listed and to whom does it belong?

9 Which museum would you most like to visit and why? Give as many details as you can.

WRITING

1 You are on holiday in France with your family and you are going to the nearest tourist office to find out what is on offer in the area. To help you remember what to ask for jot down a list of things the family is interested in, in French, so that you will not be lost for words when you get there.

Mum enjoys castles and shops. Dad likes to play golf and likes films. You want to go swimming and to see a football match. Your brother likes museums.

2 Your penfriend's family are hoping to visit your town and your penfriend has written asking you what facilities and things of interest there are in and around the town. Write a list, in French, to send to her.

3 Your French penfriend has sent you this postcard while he is on holiday in the Loire Valley.

Jean has made the effort to write in English so, when you send him a postcard during your holiday in Cornwall, you make the effort to write in French. You are staying in a hotel near the beach but the weather is awful.

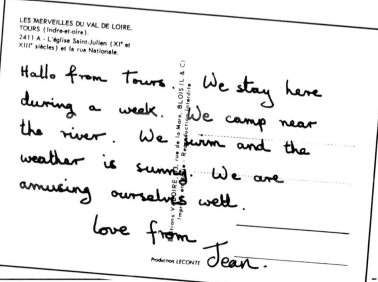

LES MERVEILLES DU VAL DE LOIRE.
TOURS (Indre-et-oire).
2411 A - L'église Saint-Julien (XI⁰ et XIII⁰ siècles) et la rue Nationale.

Hallo from Tours. We stay here during a week. We camp near the river. We swim and the weather is sunny. We are amusing ourselves well.

love from

Jean.

Production LECONTE

4 On holiday in Paris with your grandparents you are lucky enough to be bought a meal in the restaurant at the Eiffel Tower. You decide that you must send your French penfriend a card while you are there so you write a brief note, in French, saying what you are doing, where you are, what you can see, and that Paris is fantastic.

5 You are staying with friends in Paris. While they are out and you are at home alone, a family friend, Daniel Tybin, phones. As the others are not there he asks you to give them a message. He will arrive at the *Gare de Lyon* on Friday and will be staying for a week. He is coming for the celebrations on the 14th July and wants to take your friends to a restaurant on the *Champs Elysées* on the evening of the 14th. Your friends must phone him in Nice.

Write this message as briefly as possible.

6 Your French friend is shortly due to come and stay with you for about ten days. All the organisation of travel and meeting places has been arranged but your friend does not know much about what you actually plan to do. This is the ending of her last letter.

Write back to her outlining some of the places of interest in your area and saying when you plan to visit them.

> donc tout est organisé. Je sais qu'il y a beaucoup d'endroits intéressants à visiter dans la région. Est-ce que tu as déjà prévu un programme d'activités ? Si tu peux donne-moi une idée des visites qu'on va faire.
>
> En attendant de te voir très bientôt
> ton amie

7 Before you leave England to spend time with your French partner, she writes to you saying that, during your stay, you can either go to Paris together for a couple of days or to the Loire Valley and she asks you to choose which.

Since you have not visited Paris properly you would prefer to go there. Write back to your friend saying this and also mentioning the things you would particularly like to see and do.

8 Does your town produce any publicity material for French-speaking tourists? As a group you could make such a brochure using pictures of local views and with a text you have written. Your local tourist office might even be interested in having a copy.

⦿⦿ ▭ MULTI-SKILL TASK

Whilst on a visit to York, you meet French tourists in a café. They seem a bit confused and ask your help. Using the following information try to help them as best you can. Pretend your partner is one of the tourists and tell him/her the answers. (The tape should be paused at the appropriate points.)

Now do what was asked of you at the end.

Stonegate

A number of York's streets have names ending in 'gate', the Vikings' word for 'street'. But Stonegate existed long before the Vikings came: it was the 'Via Praetoria' to the main gate of the old Roman fortress.

Stonegate is kept free of all traffic so that its rich medley of medieval and Georgian architecture may be enjoyed in peace and at leisure. An ancient thoroughfare has become the most delightful of shopping streets.

The Minster

York uses the old word for its Minster, meaning a centre of Christian teaching or ministering. It is, of course, also a cathedral, containing the Archbishop's 'cathedra' or throne. The first minster was 7th century: the present minster is 7th century: the present

one is the fourth on the site.

It is the largest medieval structure in the United Kingdom. Its grandeur and its surpassing beauty attract visitors to it from all over the world. Archbishop de Grey began the great building about 1220. Stage by stage the work proceeded until finally, in 1472, the Minster was complete.

Among the Minster's many treasures are its 128 windows of stained glass, dating from the 12th to the present century.

Admission to the Minster is free.

The Walls

York's first walls were Roman. Substantial fragments of these still remain but it is the medieval walls, carefully maintained and restored, which now encircle the old city, almost three miles round.

The earth ramparts on which they stand were raised by the Romans and

the Anglo-Danish kings of York. The Normans strengthened them. They are now planted extensively with daffodils. Open daily till dusk.

The Bars

Gateways let you in but they can also 'bar' your way and often, in York's turbulent past, that was the thing which counted most.

Bootham Bar is the defensive bastion for the north road. On the road south is Micklegate Bar, illustrated above, traditionally the monarch's entrance, where traitors' heads were displayed.

Monk Bar has kept a portcullis in working order, while Walmgate Bar is the only town gate in England to have preserved its barbican: a funnel-like approach, forcing attackers to bunch together.

Treasurer's House

The house was built on the site of the Roman Legionary Fortress and was the residence for Treasurers of the Minster until 1547.

It then had a succession of private owners and in 1720 was divided into Gray's Court, with its fine courtyard, and the present Treasurer's House. In 1930 it was left to the National Trust, together with a fine collection of period furnishings. Open Spring to Autumn. Admission charges.

Projet 56

MULTI-SKILL TASKS

1 You will be going to France to stay with your penfriend for a month in the summer. Here is what he writes in one of his letters. He encloses this sheet of information as well.

You are delighted. Working with a partner you do as Thierry asked. You make up as many questions and answers as you can and then swap roles.

Alors, maman nous a inscrits à Projet 56. J'espère que cela te plaira! J'ai un copain qui y est allé l'année dernière — il a dit que c'était drôlement bien. Peux-tu me téléphoner pour me dire ce que tu en penses? Quelles activités t'intéressent le plus?

A bientôt

Thierry

PROJET 56

VACANCES DE JEUNES DANS LE MAGNIFIQUE MORBIHAN

13-16 ans

PRIX: 2.980 FRANCS

ACTIVITEES PROPOSEES
Équitation
Randonnées en vélo
Ski nautique
Planche à voile
Plongée sous-marine
Natation

PROJET 56, avec la vie en commun, permettra aux jeunes de vivre leurs vacances de façon autonome et responsable, tout en profitant de la mer et de la campagne sauvag et magnifique et de diverses activités passionnantes.

IMPORTANT
Chaque jeune apportera son vélo en bon état. Exceptionnellement PROJET 56 pourr louer un vélo.

CONTACTER Marie ou Pierre
972-36-54
975-41-57

DATES DE SEJOUR
04 juillet au 31 juillet
04 août au 31 août

PROJET 56 – Association Loi 1901 – 39 avenue de la République, 56100 VANNES.

2 A few days later Thierry sends you a copy of the letter his mother
has received. You make a note (in English) about what you will
need to take with you for the holiday.

You are a bit worried about the bike and so phone Thierry to ask
what you should do.

Work with your partner and sort out the problem.

(Partner says he can borrow brother's bike or else hire one. Ask
which he would prefer to do.)

You also give Thierry details of when you will arrive in Paris.

PROJET 56

Vannes le 30 mai

Madame,

Nous vous remercions de la demande d'inscription de Thierry Lesol et Paul
Harrison.

Les jeunes gens doivent se présenter le 4 août à 9H. précises à nos bureaux de
Vannes. De là le groupe sera transporté en car sur les lieux de vacances.

Chaque jeune doit apporter un vélo en bon état ainsi que des vêtements de sport
(short, chaussures de tennis ou de basket, maillot de bain) et des bottes
solides pour faire de l'équitation.

L'équipement spécialisé pour faire du ski nautique, de la planche à voile et de
la plongée sous-marine sera emprunté sur place, ainsi qu'une bombe pour ceux qui
font du cheval.

Le groupe sera hébergé en châlets rustiques avec 8 personnes par châlet. Chaque
jeune doit apporter un sac de couchage, des articles de toilette et des
serviettes. Le groupe sera lui-même responsable de la sécurité et de la
propreté du châlet.

Prière de trouver ci-jointe une fiche médicale à remplir pour le jeune ainsi
qu'une autorisation de sortie du territoire à cause de la sortie prévue à
Jersey.

Votre enfant DOIT être assuré (responsabilité civile, individuelle, accident,
rapatriement, voyage-séjour) par une assurance valable en pays étranger.

Nous vous remercions des arrhes que vous avez versées et vous rappelons que le
montant de 1980 francs par personne doit être versé avant le 1er juillet.

Tout courrier pour les jeunes doit être addressé à

Camp de Bois Sauvages,
Kervignac
56794 MORBIHAN.

Avec l'assurance de nos sentiments distingués,

Marie et Pierre Soulhex

PROJET 56 - Association Loi 1901 - 39 ave de le République, 56100 VANNES.

3 On the evening you arrive at *Projet 56* Thierry does not feel well. He goes to bed early whilst you go to the briefing session held by the group leader.

•• Listen carefully to what you are told and make notes (in English or French) ready to tell Thierry.

You go back to the chalet and as Thierry is awake you tell him, in French, what you were told. (Pretend your partner is Thierry.)

•• Listen to what Thierry then says.

You do as Thierry asks.

4 One day, after an afternoon's swimming you return to the changing area to find that your bag, containing several personal items, is missing. You go to report this matter to the police.

   1 Pretend that your partner is the policeman/woman and explain how and when the loss occurred and what you have lost. Use this picture of the contents of your bag to help you. Your partner will ask you some questions.

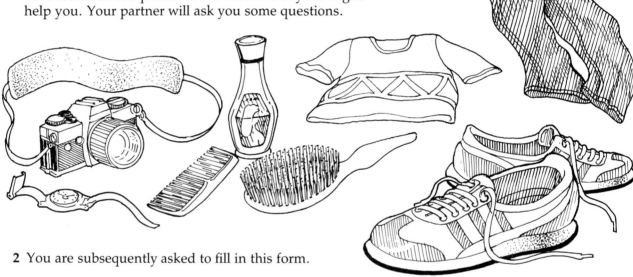

   2 You are subsequently asked to fill in this form.

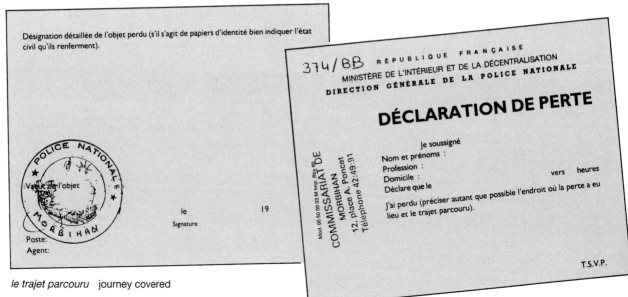

le trajet parcouru journey covered

5 Today the entire group from *Projet 56* is going to visit Concarneau. One of the French teenagers with whom you are sharing a chalet has been there before.

1 Listen carefully whilst he tells you about it.

2 Pretend that your partner is the French teenager and find out some more details about the visit, for example: how long it will take to get there, is it near the sea and any other questions you can think of based on what you have been told. (Your partner can make up the answers.)
Now swap roles.

3 On arrival you get further details about Concarneau. Whilst you are actually on the visit you buy a postcard to send to another penfriend in the South of France. Write a short message, in French, about your visit and address the card. (You can make up the address if you like or give a real one.)

** CONCARNEAU

18 225 h. (les Concarnois)

Carte Michelin n° 58 pli 15 ou 230 plis 32, 33 – Lieu de séjour p. 14.

Troisième port de pêche de France pour le poisson frais débarqué, en deuxième position si l'on ajoute le grand marché du thon congelé réparti dans des ports africains avant de parvenir en France. Concarneau possède en outre deux usines de conserves de poissons, une **criée** (ventes aux enchères très pittoresques) et deux fabriques de boîtes métalliques. Il offre, avec le spectacle de la vie maritime, l'attrait original de sa Ville Close, enserrée dans des remparts de granit. Du pont du Moros, ② du plan, on a une très jolie **vue d'ensemble★** de Concarneau, de son arrière-port et de la baie (p. 76).

La **Fête des Filets Bleus★** *(voir p. 226)*, instaurée en 1905 pour venir en aide aux pêcheurs de sardines et à leurs familles, a pris un caractère folklorique avec de joyeux groupes costumés, des danses et des défilés.

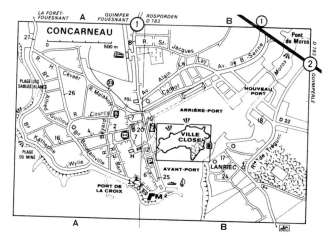

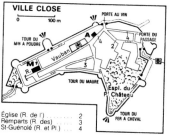

Gare (Av. de la)	A 8
Guéguin (Av. Pierre)	B 10
Le-Lay (Av. Alain)	B
Berthou (R. Joseph)	A 2
Courbet (R. Amiral)	A 4
Croix (Quai de la)	A 5
Dr.-P.-Nicolas (Av. du)	B 6
Écoles (R. des)	A 7
Jaurès (Pl. Jean)	B 12
Libération (R. de la)	A 16
Maudit-Duplessis (R.)	B 17
Moros (R. du)	B 18
Morvan (R. Gén.)	A 20
Pasteur (R.)	B 24
Pénéroff (Quai)	B 25
Renan (R. Ernest)	A 26
Sables-Blancs (R. des)	A 27

VILLE CLOSE

Église (R. de l')	2
Remparts (R. des)	3
St-Guénolé (R. et Pl.)	4

** VILLE CLOSE *visite : 2 h*

Ses ruelles étroites occupent un îlot de forme irrégulière, long de 350 m et large de 100, relié à la terre par deux petits ponts que sépare un ouvrage fortifié. D'épais remparts, élevés au 14e s. et complétés au 17e s., en font le tour. Par les deux petits ponts, puis une porte on arrive à une cour intérieure fortifiée. Beau puits.

Le tour des remparts. – *Suivre les plaques indicatrices. Pour la 1re partie de la visite, monter les marches à gauche et prendre le chemin de ronde. Par les meurtrières, vue sur l'arrière-port, sa flotte de pêche et la tour du Moulin à poudre.*
Pour la 2e partie de la visite, revenir au point de départ et redescendre les marches. Après avoir contourné l'esplanade du Petit-Château donnant sur le port de plaisance, on domine la passe qui relie les deux ports. Près d'une grosse tour, tourner à gauche, descendre une rampe et passer sous les remparts. Rentrer dans la ville par la porte du Passage. A l'angle de l'Hospice, la rue St-Guénolé mène à la place du même nom.

Exposition d'œuvres en coquillages (A). – Tableaux, bouquets, personnages, vitraux sont composés à partir de coquillages et de crustacés. L'ingéniosité du créateur s'exprime aussi bien dans un paysage de la Ville Close battue par les vagues noir-bleu des « moules » que dans un chat blanc hérissé ou un majestueux vaisseau Louis XV aux voiles en « nacres » de la région.

De la place St-Guénolé, une courte ruelle à droite conduit à la **porte au Vin**, ouverte dans les remparts ; en la franchissant, on aura une vue caractéristique sur les chalutiers amarrés dans le port et sur la criée. La rue Vauban ramène à la sortie de la Ville Close.

★ Musée de la Pêche (M¹). – Il occupe les bâtiments de l'ancien arsenal qui servit ensuite de caserne puis d'école de pêche. Des panneaux explicatifs, maquettes, photos, dioramas, y évoquent l'histoire de Concarneau, l'évolution de son port, les pêches traditionnelles (baleine, morue, sardine, thon, hareng), les chalutiers, la conserverie, la construction navale, les appareils de navigation. Dans un immense hall consacré aux pêches lointaines, on peut voir une baleinière des Açores et d'autres embarcations : cotre, misainier, doris, etc., un canon lance-harpons, un crabe géant japonais, un cœlacanthe... Des poissons vivants, des tortues évoluent dans 40 aquariums.

AUTRES CURIOSITÉS

Les ports. – Par l'avenue P.-Guéguin et le quai Carnot, jeter un coup d'œil sur l'arrière-port et le nouveau port où se tient la grosse flotte : on y verra les chalutiers et cargos à quai, avec une chance d'assister au déchargement de crustacés ou de poissons. L'avenue du Docteur-P.-Nicolas longe l'avant-port animé par les bateaux de plaisance. L'embarcadère pour les excursions est en bout de ce quai, sur la digue, à gauche. A gauche du quai de la Croix s'élève le laboratoire maritime du Collège de France dont on peut visiter le **marinarium (B M²)**, exposition consacrée au milieu marin ; aquariums, dioramas, présentations audiovisuelles se succèdent.
Après avoir dépassé l'ancien marché aux poissons où se faisait la criée, la chapelle N.-D.-de-Bon-Secours (15e s.) et un petit phare, on longe le port de la Croix (boulevard Bougainville) que protège une jetée. Jolie vue en arrière sur la pointe du Cabellou et, en avant, sur la pointe de Beg-Meil. On aperçoit, au large, les îles de Glénan.

Les plages (A). – Le boulevard Katherine-Wylie, tracé en corniche, longe la plage du Miné et offre de belles vues sur la baie de la Forêt et la pointe de Beg-Meil, puis le boulevard Alfred-Guillou donne sur les plages des Petits et des Grands Sables Blancs.

---

tracts from the Michelin Tourist Guide 'Bretagne' are reproduced with the permission of Michelin.© Michelin et Cie.

6 Whilst at *Projet 56* you are involved in the accident depicted here.

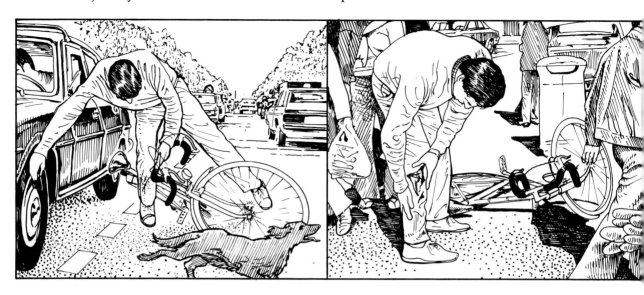

1 You go to see the doctor. Give her your personal details and say what happened. Tell her about your injuries and answer any questions she may ask you.

Your partner will play the part of the doctor.

> *Partner's Instructions*
>
> You must find out:
> - partner's name and home address
> - where he/she is staying
> - what happened
> - how he/she feels
> - where it hurts
> - whether insured or not
> - if he/she is taking any medication.

2 Listen while the doctor then gives you some instructions.

Repeat these, in French, to the doctor to make sure you have understood.

3 On returning to the camp you have to complete an accident form.

```
P56/A/1
                          PROJET 56

                       FICHE D'ACCIDENT



NOM _____    PRÉNOM _____

SEXE _____    AGE _____

DOMICILE PERMANENT _____

_____

_____ TÉL: ___

LIEU ET DATE DE NAISSANCE _____

_____

DATE ET HEURE DE L'ACCIDENT _____

_____

COMMENT L'ACCIDENT S'EST-IL PRODUIT? _____

_____

_____

INTERVENTION MÉDICALE _____
```

7 One day the leader of *Projet 56* asks you if you would be prepared
to take part in an evaluation exercise about what people like most
and least about *Projet 56*.

1 There are four of you carrying this out and the first job is to sit
down together and work out what questions you will ask, for
example: what activity was most enjoyed, least enjoyed, what
you would add etc. You also need to sort out the grid on which
the answers will be recorded. Each of you will ask twelve
people. In a group of four devise your questionnaire. You need
to ask about ten questions.

2 You now ask nine people your questions and record their
answers.

3 Three people are not able to speak to you personally as they had to leave early. However, they each left you a brief note giving their impressions of the holiday. You record their views on your grid. (NB: They had not seen the questionnaire before writing the notes.)

> C'était très bien. J'ai beaucoup apprécié les randonnées en vélo. Ça c'était super. Par contre je n'ai pas trop aimé la planche à voile, ça me faisait peur. La nourriture? ça allait, pas trop mauvais mais pas trop bon non plus!

> Projet 56? Super! La vie en commun avec de bons camarades j'adore ça. J'ai tout aimé, même la soupe qu'on nous servait si souvent. A l'année prochaine alors!

> Ça allait mais je ne recommencerai pas. C'était trop organisé pour moi. Moi j'ai besoin de liberté personnelle et c'est ce qu'on n'avait pas au Projet 56. Les activités? oui ça allait mais ce genre de vacances c'est pas pour moi.

4 You now have to write up your findings e.g. Eight out of twelve
enjoyed cycling best of all, etc.

8 A group of you have decided to hold a party on your last evening,
a Friday, at *Projet 56*. You have collected a contribution from
everyone and set out to buy food and
arrange entertainment.

1 You have seen a handbill put out by a local
teenager.

●● 2 You decide to get in touch. Listen to the
message on his answering machine. You
make a note of costs to tell the others.

3 You then leave an appropriate message on
the tape.

4 Your friends decide that the charge is
reasonable so you scribble a quick note to
put through the DJ's door confirming that
you would like to book him.

DISCO?   BOUM?   SURPRISE PARTIE?

Yann Treloyec.

A votre service.

Musique pour tous les goûts
Des valses à Punk Rock

Prix très abordables

Téléphonez le 23-72-19 à Hennebont

ou adressez-vous au

19 ave des Ecoles, Hennebont

5 Working with a partner decide quickly, in French, what you would need to buy and what shops you will need to go to. You could record this discussion. Make your shopping list, in French.

6 In a group of four or six take it in turns to play the roles of shopkeepers or shoppers and buy the items you and your partners decided on. (Try to sort out all the necessary arrangements, for example designating roles, in French as well.) Remember to record prices or any charges, in French.

9 One of the last activities in *Projet 56* is a treasure hunt. For this you are working in pairs and you are paired with a German boy whose French is not very good and whose English is non-existent. Therefore, you have to do all the listening to instructions and reading of clues.

1 You are all gathered in the games room where the leader gives you the initial instructions. Listen carefully and make any notes you need (in English or in French). You then explain to the German boy what you have to do. Explain in French as it is your only common language.

2 As you follow the trail you find the following clues. Mark your path on your copy of the plan.

- Allez dire bonjour à M. le Maire.
- Dépêchez-vous pour joindre le clocher au lointain.
- Sous le pont il y a des gens qui pêchent.
- Vous avez soif après votre voyage en train?
- Vous aimez les jeux d'enfants?
- Vous avez besoin d'un timbre ou d'un mandat?
- Allez vers le sud-est pour trouver le siège d'un seigneur d'autrefois.
- Ici vous pouvez acheter tout ce que vous voulez; mais seulement un jour par semaine. Aujourd'hui vous avez besoin de fromage.

3 Here someone tells you where to go to find the final clue and what you must ask.

4 You do as you were told and receive more information.

5 Explain to your partner what 'prize' you have won.

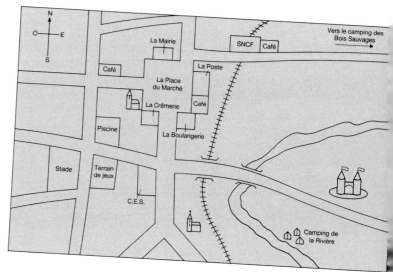

10 The time has come to leave *Projet 56*.

  1 You go round saying goodbye to everyone and asking them where they are going next. Don't forget to promise to write etc.

  2 When you get back to Paris your penfriend's parents naturally want to know all about your experiences. Answer their questions. (The tape should be paused at appropriate points.)

  3 You decide to write about your experiences as a piece of work for your French coursework folder. During the holiday you made the following notes in your diary. Use them to help you write your essay.

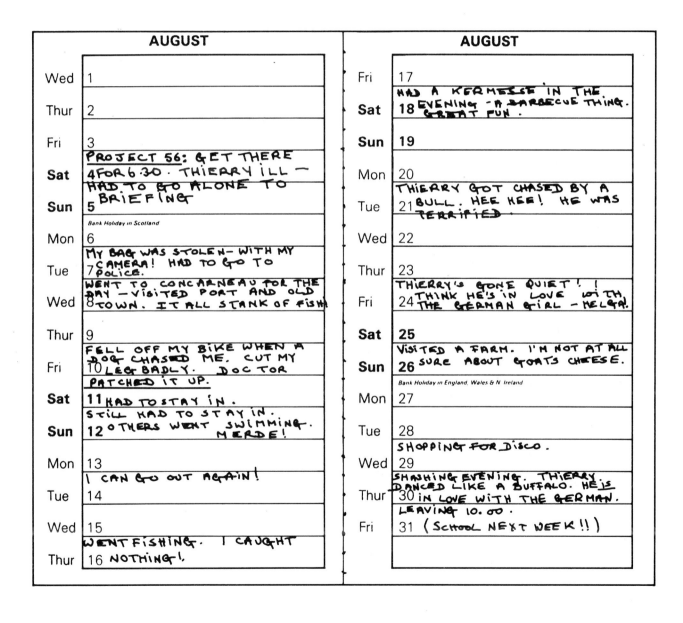

	AUGUST			AUGUST
Wed	1	Fri	17	
Thur	2	Sat	18	HAD A KERMESSE IN THE EVENING – A BARBECUE THING. GREAT FUN.
Fri	3	Sun	19	
Sat	4 PROJECT 56: GET THERE FOR 6.30. THIERRY ILL – HAD TO GO ALONE TO BRIEFING	Mon	20	
Sun	5	Tue	21 THIERRY GOT CHASED BY A BULL. HEE HEE! HE WAS TERRIFIED.
Mon	6 *Bank Holiday in Scotland*	Wed	22	
Tue	7 MY BAG WAS STOLEN – WITH MY CAMERA! HAD TO GO TO POLICE.	Thur	23	
Wed	8 WENT TO CONCARNEAU FOR THE DAY – VISITED PORT AND OLD TOWN. IT ALL STANK OF FISH!	Fri	24 THIERRY'S GONE QUIET! I THINK HE'S IN LOVE WITH THE GERMAN GIRL – HELGA.
Thur	9	Sat	25	
Fri	10 FELL OFF MY BIKE WHEN A DOG CHASED ME. CUT MY LEG BADLY. DOCTOR PATCHED IT UP.	Sun	26 VISITED A FARM. I'M NOT AT ALL SURE ABOUT GOATS CHEESE.
Sat	11 HAD TO STAY IN.	Mon	27 *Bank Holiday in England, Wales & N Ireland*
Sun	12 STILL HAD TO STAY IN. OTHERS WENT SWIMMING. MERDE!	Tue	28	
Mon	13	Wed	29 SHOPPING FOR DISCO.
Tue	14 I CAN GO OUT AGAIN!	Thur	30 SMASHING EVENING. THIERRY DANCED LIKE A BUFFALO. HE IS IN LOVE WITH THE GERMAN.
Wed	15	Fri	31 LEAVING 10.00. (SCHOOL NEXT WEEK!!)
Thur	16 WENT FISHING. I CAUGHT NOTHING!			

10

On se dépanne

 LISTENING

1 You are in the centre of her home town with your penfriend, who has several small jobs that she has to get done. As she asks the person in each place how much the job costs and how long it will take, she asks you to write this down for her, so that she can return to each in the right order. Here is the list she has given you. Mark down prices and when to call back on your copy of the list.

		Price	When ready
Clé – minute	Faire copier la clé de la porte d'entrée		
Talon – minute	Faire réparer les chaussures de papa		
Pressing	Faire nettoyer la jupe à maman		
Photographe	Faire faire les photos		
Coiffeur	Mise en plis pour moi		

2 You have had terrible toothache during your stay in France. At last you have been able to see the dentist, and he has given you a temporary filling. He explains to you what you must and must not do between now and going home, and what to do when you get home. Your penfriend repeats his advice, while you make notes of what you have to do.

3 At the launderette, you find that, unfortunately, instructions explaining how to use the various machines have been removed. A lady kindly explains the routine to you, and as another English friend of yours is intending to use the launderette later, you note down what she tells you.

4 Your visit has been fraught with minor health problems, and you have had to visit the doctor on three occasions. The doctor and then your penfriend explain what you must do, while you note down their instructions.

And that is not all! Two other things happen for which you seek advice from the chemist rather than from the doctor. Again, your penfriend repeats the advice, and you make notes.

5 You need to change some traveller's cheques one afternoon, and although the banks are open, several are reluctant to change them. This becomes rather annoying, so at each bank you make a note of why they can't help, and what they tell you to do next. The purpose of this is twofold. Firstly for issuing letters of complaint later (if you get round to it once you've cooled down!) and secondly so that you don't lose track of what you're doing!

Bank	Reason	Advice
Société Générale		
BNP		
Crédit Lyonnais		
Crédit Agricole		
Bureau de Change SNCF		

6 While your penfriend and the family are out, you listen to the radio, and tune in to a 'swap-shop' type programme. Some of the things on offer seem quite attractive, so you decide to make notes, in case anyone in the family is interested. Fill in your copy of the grid, so that you have the information to discuss later.

Item for sale/exchange	Phone number	Item wanted/cost
1		
2		
3		
4		

7 You are thinking of hiring bicycles for a day, or maybe a few days. You make enquiries at the *Locations de Vélos SNCF*, and make notes under the following headings to report back to your friends:

- types of bike available
- cost per hour/day/week
- opening hours of office
- insurance details
- care of bikes required

8 On holiday in Lyon, you would like to go to see some of the events in the Music Festival. You enquire at the *Syndicat d'Initiative* as to where you can buy tickets, and are given this document.

You don't understand it so you ask again for the document to be explained to you. The answers you get should enable you to decode it, so that you know where tickets may be obtained.

---

(1) = P = Progrès
R = Rabut
B = Bouvier

ETE A FOURVIERE

Mois de Juillet

Dates	Manifestations		Renseignements – Locations
1.2.4. Juillet	SISYPHE (danse), Cie Hugo VERRECHIA............	21 H 00	Lieu : Odéon de Fourvière Rens : 78.39.20.04 Loc. : Fnac, R, B. (1)
08/07	Le PAYS du SOURIRE (opérette) avec José TODARO.....................	21 H 00	Collectivités et par corresp. : 78.58.18.60 (de 9H à 13H) 78.31.39.93 Loc. : P, R, B. (1)
09/07	TALK TALK (rock).....................	21 H 00	Loc. : Music Land, P. (1)
22/07	Alan STIVELL (folk).....................	21 H 00	
24/07	Rhoda SCOTT (jazz).....................	21 H 00	Collectivités et par corresp. : 78.58.18.60 (de 9H à 13H) 78.31.39.93 Loc. : P, R, B. (1)
25/07	VALSES de VIENNE avec le Budapest Symphonie Orchestra...........	21 H 00	
10/07	KID CREOLE AND THE COCONUTS....................	21 H 00	Rens. + Loc. : P, R, B. (1)
14/07	Concert ROSSINI Dir. : Claire GIBAULT Orchestre Opéra de Lyon.....................	18 H 30	Concert gratuit

Date	LYON MUSIC FESTIVAL		Renseignements – Location
16/07	KASSAU – CARMEL – MALAVOI....................		
17/07	Otis RUSH – Doctor JOHN – John MAYALL : Nuit du Blues.....	21 h 30	Rens. : 78.58.15.59
18/07	Lloyd COLE and the Commotions – Flestones Immaculate Fool.	21 h 30	Loc. : P, R, B, ML, TM
19/07	INDOCHINE....................	21 h 30	Cerra
20/07	RENAUD....................	21 h 30	

9 Driving into a French town late one afternoon, after having been on the road since early morning, you stop to ask a traffic-warden where best to park in order to find a cheap hotel. The warden is only too happy to help and gives you a plan of the town. The map only shows the car-parks, but the warden is chatty and as well as explaining how to get to two of these, she tells you about various places of interest you will see on the way. You mark these on your copy of the map.

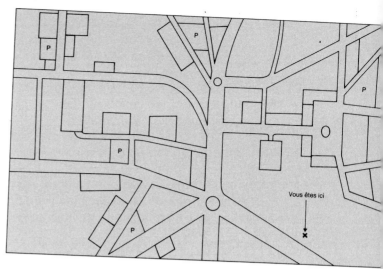

Vous êtes ici

10 At your penfriend's house alone one day, you smell gas. Already pleased with yourself at having found the *Gaz de France* number in the telephone book, you decide to be ultra-careful, and write down the instructions which the person who answers the phone gives to you.

🗨 SPEAKING

1 This is a pair or group-work exercise, set either in a post office or in a café-tabac. You will need a supply of French coins.

One pupil has a supply of stamps, and uses the price list below. This pupil plays the part of the employee. Other pupils each have a list of stamps to be purchased.

Lettre	2f.50
Carte Postale	2f.00
Lettre, Angleterre	3f.00
Lettre, Espagne	3f.00

You need to buy stamps, as shown on your list, at the post office/café-tabac. Ask the prices, and then ask for the number and type of stamps that you require. (Don't forget the appropriate politenesses, and to count out your money and check your change.)

2 This group exercise is set in a bank. One pupil is the bank clerk and holds all the French money; the others are customers and need to change varying amounts of English money.

The exchange rate, preferably found from a current newspaper, should be either 'marked up', or, at least, known to the bank clerk.

Customers should:

- find out what the current exchange rate is
- say how much English money they wish to change into francs
- find out if they can change coins
- count and check aloud all money which changes hands, as the transaction takes place.

3 One member of the group plays the role of the bank clerk and the others act as tourists who are short of change and go into the bank to ask for change for a 100 franc note. Make sure that the bank clerk counts out the coins, and that the person receiving them checks the money aloud.

4 One member of the group is to take the role of the doctor. This person holds the 'Carte du Médecin' which shows illnesses and relevant treatments. The other group members have cards showing their symptoms, how long they have been suffering, and what perhaps has caused the problem.

Patients should:

- say what's wrong with them
- tell the doctor how long this has been going on for
- answer the doctor's questions.

The doctor should:

- ask the patient his/her nationality, and find out how long he/ she has been in France
- ask what's wrong, and find out how long the patient has been ill
- find out the reasons
- recommend treatment and send the patient to the chemist's.

5 This time, one member of the group is the chemist, and holds the 'Carte du Pharmacien', which gives details of maladies and relevant medication.

Other group members should explain their illness, ask for the item prescribed by the doctor, and pay as appropriate.

6 Your French friend is intrigued about the pocket money which you receive weekly. Working with a partner answer these questions. Then reverse roles, so that you play the part of the French person.

1 Tu as combien d'argent de poche par semaine?

2 Qui te le donne?

3 Tu dois travailler pour l'avoir?

4 Tu le dépenses comment?

5 Tu fais des économies?

6 Tu dois t'acheter des vêtements avec?

7 Que fais-tu si tu veux sortir—aller au cinéma par exemple?

8 Et pour les cadeaux d'anniversaires, et à Noël, et tout ça?

7 You are staying with a French family for three weeks. After two weeks you run out of money. Not wanting to ask the family, you call the French exchange organiser to ask for a loan. Your teacher, French assistant or partner could play the part of the organiser. Your teacher will give you details of the questions to be asked. Be prepared to be questioned on:

- how much you had
- what you've spent it on
- how much you need, and what for
- how you're going to pay it back.

8 You are spending a week camping in Normandy. One night your companion becomes alarmingly ill. He is thoroughly sick, can't take water, and obviously has a fever. Your teacher, the assistant or your partner will play the role of your doctor.

When the doctor comes you must be prepared to answer questions on:

- details of your friend's illness
- his general state of health
- your activities in recent days — including diet
- your plans for the rest of the holiday.

9 After playing tennis with your French friend, you return to the changing rooms to find that your bag has been stolen. For insurance purposes, you must report the theft to the police.

At the police station, using the picture of your bag and its contents to help you, be prepared to:

- say exactly when and where you first noticed that the bag was missing
- list the contents of the bag, and describe individual items as requested
- give reference numbers and details of any documents taken
- give or estimate the value—in francs—of particular items.

Your partner can pretend to be the police officer and can help you, if needed, by asking questions.

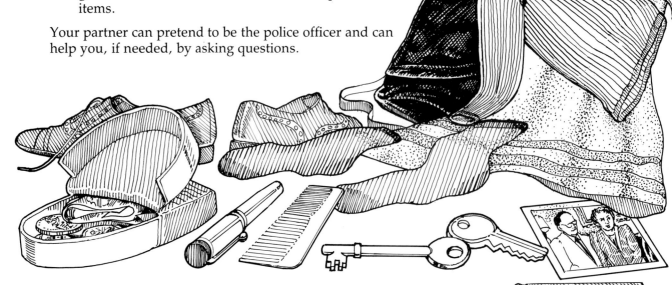

10 On the *métro* in Lyon, you take a photo of one of the trains as it comes into the station. You are immediately pounced on by a security officer, who insists angrily that you are not allowed to take photographs. Your teacher, the assistant or your partner can play the role of the security officer. Answer his questions, as he proceeds to interrogate you about what you are doing in France, what you are doing in Lyon, who you are, and why you are taking photographs.

You will also need to explain why you have no identification with you . . .

11 You are staying with your French penfriend's family. In a few days' time, it will be his mother's birthday. She will be 45! You are very fond of her. She is kind hearted and calm, and is particularly fond of the countryside, thus, having a good knowledge of flowers and trees and so on. You decide to surprise her, by having a very personal cake made for her birthday at the local *pâtisserie*.

Discuss with the penfriend what the best cake and decoration should be for this occasion and also how much you can afford to pay.

Your partner should play the part of your penfriend. Now swap roles.

READING

1 You are staying with your penfriend in July, and are quite excited at the prospect of the festivities on the 14th. However, your penfriend's father is less happy and is grumbling about so many places being closed. When this article appears in the paper the previous day, he asks you to make a note of what services are in fact open on the 14th, and how to contact them. For your benefit as much as his, you decide to make a list of what is open, and how to make contact if necessary.

Service	Contact

Ouvert et fermé le 14 juillet

Police. — Téléphone 78.00.40.40.
Service de nettoiement (ramassage des immondices). — Téléphone 78.63.40.40, Courly : bureaux fermés à 16 h 45.
Service urgence des eaux. — 24 heures sur 24 (78.93.75.50).
Syndicat d'initiative. — Place Bellecour (78.42.25.75). Fermé le 14 juillet.
Crédit municipal de Lyon. — 221, rue Duguesclin Lyon.3e (78.60.68.16). Fermé le 14 juillet.
Syndicat d'initiative de Villeurbanne. — 25, cours E.-Zola (78.89.64.42). Fermé le 14 juillet.
Syndicat d'initiative centre échanges de Perrache. — (78.42.22.07). Fermé le 14 juillet.
Caisse d'Allocations familiales de l'arrondissement de Lyon, direction et service administratif. — Les bureaux sont fermés le 14 juillet.
Caisse primaire d'assurance maladie. — (78.52.76.76). Les bureaux et services sont fermés du vendredi 11 juillet à 15 heures au lundi 14 inclus.
E.D.F. - G.D.F. service d'urgence. — (78.60.20.20) 24 heures sur 24.
Mairies, pompes funèbres. — (78.28.22.68).
Banques. — Fermées le lundi 14 juillet.
Caisse d'épargne. — Fermées lundi 14 juillet.
Bibliothèque municipale de la Part-Dieu. — La bibliothèque municipale est fermée du 14 au 20 juillet et ouvre du 21 au 5 septembre de 13 à 19 heures.
Cimetières de Lyon. — Les cimetières de Lyon seront fermés durant la journée du 14 juillet.

Le Progrès

le ramassage des immondices   rubbish collection
les Allocations familiales   child benefit
un arrondissement   administrative district of a town
E.D.F.   Électricité de France
G.D.F.   Gaz de France
la caisse d'épargne   savings bank

2 You have had to visit the doctor to be treated for a stomach upset. Luckily, this illness has been fairly minor, and easily dealt with, but has nevertheless cost over 300F.00 in doctor's fees. In order for this money to be claimed through insurance, your penfriend's family ask you to fill in this form. (Fill in as much as you can on your copy of the form.)

CERFA N°

DURÉE D'UTILISATION 15 JOURS

FEUILLE DE SOINS
(assurance maladie)

RENSEIGNEMENTS CONCERNANT L'ASSURÉ

NUMÉRO D'IMMATRICULATION _____ Né(e) le _____

NOM (en capitales d'imprimerie) _____ *indiquer le nom de jeune fille suivi de épouse X...*
(Pour les femmes mariées

Prénoms _____

Adresse : N° _____ rue _____

Localité _____

Code postal _____ Bureau distributeur _____

QUELLE EST VOTRE SITUATION A LA DATE DES SOINS ? (1)

☐ SALARIÉ : (2) Nom et adresse de votre employeur _____

☐ DEMANDEUR D'EMPLOI   Date de la fin du préavis de licenciement _____
     Date d'inscription à l'agence nationale pour l'emploi _____

☐ NON SALARIÉ : Précisez votre activité professionnelle _____

☐ AUTRE CAS : _____

☐ RETRAITÉ, PENSIONNÉ OU RENTIER : Précisez si vous êtes titulaire de plusieurs retraites, pensions ou rentes (1)   OUI ☐   NON ☐

RENSEIGNEMENTS CONCERNANT LE MALADE

S'agit-il d'un accident ? (1) OUI ☐ NON ☐   Causé par un tiers ? (1) OUI ☐ NON ☐

Si le malade est PENSIONNÉ DE GUERRE, précisez si les soins portés sur cette feuille CONCERNENT L'AFFECTION pour laquelle IL EST PENSIONNÉ (1) OUI ☐ NON ☐

---

une immatriculation   registration
un tiers   third party

3 You are perusing *Pomme*, a weekly advertising paper for the Dieppe area. You decide to send this advertisement to your parents, who will shortly be coming on holiday to Dieppe themselves. As they speak no French, they are worried about shopping. Along with the advertisement, you decide to send:

- a plan of the supermarket, showing the sections in English
- details of opening times
- a short note saying what else is available at this shop, and a comment on current developments there.

un rayon   counter, department
surgelé   deep frozen
la vaisselle   crockery
une couche (de bébé)   nappy
un entremet   ready-prepared dessert
subir   to suffer, to undergo
convenir   to suit

4 You are staying with a French family in Paris. You want to phone home, but the family are not on the phone, and you don't have the codes. In a call-box, you look at the *bottin* (telephone directory), and identify the page for Directory Enquiries. You make a note of the three numbers given, and also what each of them is for.

Number	Service

assistance à l'annuaire (renseignements)

Si vous ne trouvez pas dans cet annuaire, ou dans les annuaires de Paris, Seine-Saint-Denis, Val-de-Marne, Essonne, Seine-et-Marne, Val-d'Oise et Yvelines :

● le numéro d'appel d'un abonné
● l'acheminement ou le prix d'une communication téléphonique

composez le 12

12

Pour les abonnés de la province :
composez le 16 suivi de 1112

16〜1112

Pour les abonnés des départements d'outre-mer, des territoires d'outre-mer, de l'étranger :
composez le 19 suivi de 3313

19〜3313

Annuaire de Téléphone 1980

un abonné   subscriber
l'acheminement   series of numbers required to dial the code for a town etc.
outre-mer   overseas

5 You are staying with a French family in mid-August in Toulouse. As is not uncommon, there has been no rain for some weeks, and restrictions have been imposed on water usage. The family have gone out for the day, leaving you alone, and the father, ever concerned to follow the letter of the law, has left you instructions about the water. Scared to do anything wrong, you decide to make sure by making a note in English of what you must and must not do.

> La mairie nous a demandé de faire attention pour l'usage de l'eau aussi je vous demanderai de :
>   – ne pas prendre de douche.
>   – ne pas arroser le jardin
>   – ne pas laver la voiture
>   – ne pas faire de machine (nous en ferons une par semaine seulement)
>   – ne pas remplir la piscine.

6 You are planning a cycling holiday with a friend. Beforehand, he sends you this article, and asks you to be the group's first-aid person. Make a list of the things that you will need to do.

une entorse sprain
un garrot tourniquet
une formation training

FAITES-LE VOUS-MÊME
TROUSSE ET SOINS D'URGENCE

Partir cet été. S'offrir une grande randonnée à pied ou à bicyclette : cela se prépare. Il est prudent d'emporter dans ses bagages une « trousse d'urgence ». Et utile d'apprendre quelques gestes pour faire face, le mieux possible, aux accidents. Cette fiche vous propose quelques méthodes de secours pour accidents relativement bénins mais fréquents.

Attention ! La trousse d'urgence que nous vous proposons ici est « standard ». A vous de l'adapter. Par exemple vous n'emporterez pas de sérum contre les morsures de vipères si vous faites un stage de voile !

Préparez donc votre trousse en demandant conseil à votre pharmacien ou à votre médecin. Il vous faudra une ordonnance pour certains produits.

Faites-vous bien préciser l'emploi des médicaments avant le départ. Et notez les conseils de votre pharmacien sur chaque boîte. Attention aux contre-indications.

Ne tardez jamais à rejoindre un centre de soins : ce qui vous semble être une entorse peut être une fracture...

Notez précisément ce que vous faites : heure de pose d'un garrot, nom du médicament administré, etc. Cela peut être utile par la suite.

Enfin, pourquoi ne pas suivre (pour l'été prochain) une formation de secouriste.

Nous vous montrons ici comment faire une piqûre. Vous pouvez en effet devoir faire face à une morsure de vipère. Et il ne faut pas tarder à agir. Les injections se font sous-cutanées ou intra-musculaires ; cela est toujours indiqué sur l'ampoule.

Consultez toujours un médecin à votre retour en ville surtout si, isolés, vous n'avez pu le joindre par téléphone.

7 Deciding to take your role as first-aid person seriously, you read these specific instructions about various treatments. Write down what you have to do for each one.

une fesse buttock
une plaie wound
tamponner to dab

le saignement bleeding
une cheville ankle

une écharde splinter
une attelle splint

un abaisse langue spatula
(for looking down the throat)

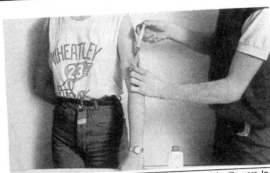

1. **Injection sous-cutanée.** Purgez la seringue (aiguille vers le haut). Désinfectez la peau et vos doigts avec de l'alcool à 90°. Pincez la peau entre le pouce et l'index et piquez dans l'épaisseur. L'aiguille doit pénétrer d'un demi-centimètre environ.

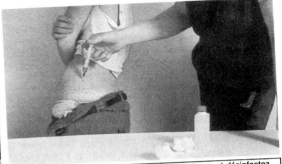

2. **Injection intra-musculaire.** Purgez la seringue et désinfectez la peau là encore. Piquez dans le quart supérieur de la fesse, assez près de la hanche. Piquez bien perpendiculairement à la peau. L'aiguille doit pénétrer de 2 à 3 cm environ.

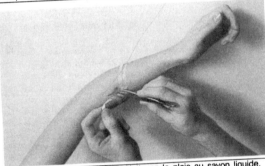

3. **Plaie un peu profonde.** Nettoyez la plaie au savon liquide. Tamponnez à la compresse stérile en cas de saignement. Rapprochez les lèvres de la plaie à l'aide d'une pince désinfectée et posez les bandelettes adhésives assez rapprochées.

4. Les bandelettes adhésives (stéristrips) referment la plaie et permettent une bonne cicatrisation. Le pansement doit rester au sec pendant 4 à 5 jours, jusqu'à la cicatrisation. On enlève les « strips » au bout d'une semaine.

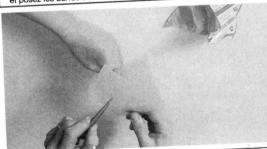

5. **Brûlure superficielle.** Nettoyez la zone brûlée au savon liquide. Recouvrez la brûlure de tulle gras et bandez. En cas de brûlure grave, enveloppez de compresses stériles et adressez-vous très vite au centre médico-chirurgical le plus proche.

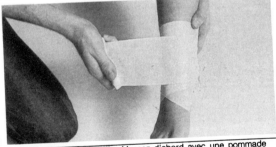

6. **Foulure à la cheville.** Massez d'abord avec une pommade anti-œdème (mais jamais sur une plaie ouverte !). Puis bandez en x autour de la cheville et, dès que possible, allez voir un médecin.

7. **Écharde.** Nettoyez à l'alcool à 90° et extrayez l'écharde à l'aide d'une pince désinfectée (en la passant à la flamme par exemple). Pour certaines grosses échardes (piquants d'oursins) il faut parfois inciser légèrement.

8. **Fracture d'un doigt.** Les fractures sont douloureuses. Il faut immobiliser le membre. Ici, posez une attelle provisoire à l'aide d'abaisse-langue que vous fixez par un bandage.
Fiche réalisée par le Dr Roques Photos : Françoise Nicol

8 Now study the suggestions for the first-aid pack. Some of the items shown are quite difficult to use. Make a list in English of the twenty items which you think are the most essential for your first-aid kit.

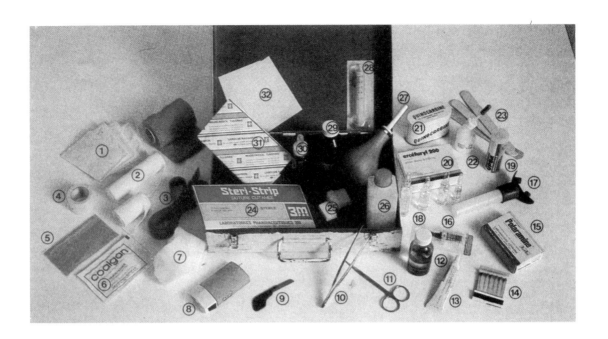

Ce qu'il vous faut :

(1) Compresses stériles « 20 × 20 » ; (2) Bandes de gaze tissu 5 et 10 cm et élastique (meilleur maintien pour foulures) ; (3) Garrot ; (4) Sparadrap ; (5) Tricostéril (pansement adhésif) ; (6) Coalgan (hémostatique) ; (7) Coton ; (8) Lampe de poche ; (9) Lime à ampoule ; (10) Pince à écharde ; (11) Petits ciseaux pointus ; (12) Alcool iodé ; (13) Pommade antibiotique ; (14) Allumettes ; (15) Polaramine : anti-histaminique (allergies) ; (16) Seringues 5 ml et 2 ml(sur ordonnance) ; (17) Canule pour respiration artificielle ; (18) Ampoules injectables * (à n'utiliser que si entraîné sauf danger immédiat) ; (19) Aspirine ; (20) Ercéfuryl ; (21) Charbon (désinfectants intestinaux) ; (22) Poudre antibiotique (plaies) ; (23) Abaisse-langue (attelle) ; (24) Stéristrip (languettes adhésives pour sutures) ; (25) Sucres ; (26) Savon liquide ; (27) Poire à lavement ; (28) Seringue 5CC (sur ordonnance) ; (29) Mercurochrome ; (30) Collyre ; (31) Tulle gras ; (32) Papier, crayon (heure de pose de garrot).
Et aussi : Epingles de nourrice ; doigtier ; thermomètre.
* Sur prescription médicale : cardiotoniques, anti-spasmodiques, sédatifs, anti-chocs (voir le détail avec un médecin avant le départ).

hémostatique   blood coagulant
une lime   file
une pommade   ointment
une canule   tube for giving mouth-to-mouth resuscitation
une poire à lavement   irrigation bulb
mercurochrome   a disinfectant for cuts and grazes
collyre   eye-drops

9 Whilst staying with your penfriend, who has lots of little brothers and sisters, you have been greatly impressed by *Algotropyl Bottu*. This is a suppository which appears to cure all sorts of minor ailments almost instantaneously!

You decide to buy some for some friends in England who have a similarly large family. However, to make sure that they understand what it is, you write down for them what it claims to cure, what the dosage is for babies and children, and how to use it!

ALGOTROPYL BOTTU
à la prométhazine

SUPPOSITOIRES
deux formes :
BÉBÉS - ENFANTS

INDICATIONS

Traitement symptomatique des affections fébriles, des affections douloureuses et des affections allergiques, par exemple :
– États fébriles, maladies infectieuses.
– Douleurs diverses, analgésie pré et postopératoire, incidents de la première dentition.
– Manifestations allergiques, prurits, urticaire, eczémas, intolérances médicamenteuses.
– Réactions générales au cours des vaccinations.
– Insomnies douloureuses et fébriles.

PRÉCAUTIONS D'EMPLOI

L'attention est appelée sur les risques de somnolence attachés à l'emploi de ce médicament ; ne pas dépasser les posologies indiquées et consulter rapidement le médecin en cas de surdosage accidentel ; ne pas utiliser de façon prolongée sans avis médical ; contient un antihistaminique, ne pas en administrer simultanément.

NE PAS LAISSER A LA PORTÉE DES ENFANTS

038-B

fébrile feverish
une douleur pain
la première dentition teething
prurits }
urticaire } itchy rashes
la posologie dosage
la prise the dose

POSOLOGIE

A n'utiliser avant l'âge de 1 an que sur avis du médecin.

SUPPOSITOIRES BÉBÉS (de 1 an à 4 ans)
De 1 an à 2 ans : 1 suppositoire 1 ou 2 fois par 24 heures, selon l'âge.
De 2 ans à 4 ans : 2 ou 3 suppositoires par 24 heures, selon l'âge.

SUPPOSITOIRES ENFANTS (de 4 ans à 15 ans)
De 4 ans à 6 ans : 1 ou 2 suppositoires par 24 heures, selon l'âge.
De 6 ans à 15 ans : 2 à 4 suppositoires par 24 heures, selon l'âge.

RÉPARTIR RÉGULIÈREMENT LES PRISES DURANT LES 24 HEURES.

A CONSERVER A L'ABRI DE LA CHALEUR

038-B

BOTTU - 52-58, avenue du Maréchal-Joffre - 92000 NANTERRE

SOPRINT - 93110 ROSNY SOUS BOIS

10 On exchange in Lyon, your family are planning to take you on holiday for a few days. The father is somewhat worried that the flat might be burgled while it is empty. Seeing this article in the paper, you decide to mention it to him, but before you do—just to make sure that you understand it for yourself—you make notes in English about what the *Service Anti-Vol* is, and how to obtain it.

Téléphone

Un service « anti-vol » : le renvoi temporaire

Vous attendez un coup de fil important ? Vous craignez l'appel malveillant d'un cambrioleur à la recherche de domiciles vides ? Et bien, partez tranquille grâce au « renvoi temporaire ».
Grâce à ce service, créé il y a environ deux ans par les Télécoms, dès que vous vous absentez, les appels sont transférés sur le numéro de votre choix que vous programmez

grâce à une simple manipulation au moment de votre départ.
Pour s'abonner, il suffit de se renseigner auprès de son agence commerciale. En 48 heures (au plus), le service est mis en place. Prix : 15 francs par mois pour l'abonnement (pour un minimum de six mois), plus une taxe de base — soit 0,77 F — lors de

chaque programmation de renvoi.
Un inconvénient : pour l'heure, le transfert n'est possible que sur les numéros de la circonscription de taxe de Lyon, c'est-à-dire sur tous les numéros commençant par 78 ou 72. En attendant le « renvoi hexagonal », prévu par les Télécoms pour début 1987.

E.C. ∎

malveillant malicious
un renvoi transfer (of a phone number)
la circonscription de taxe exchange district

11 Whilst staying in France, you are greatly impressed by the *FNAC* shops, which sell books, records, and all sorts of hi-fi equipment and related services. You toy with the idea of becoming a member, and as you subsequently study this document, you try to find answers to these questions.

1 What does *FNAC* offer as a *centre d'animation*?

2 What are the three rules of *FNAC*?

3 How long does membership last for in the first instance?

4 What are the financial benefits?

5 What is *Contact*?

6 What scope has the video hire service?

7 What courses are available?

8 What other services are available with membership?

9 What is the original charge?

10 How much cheaper is it for other family members who wish to join?

Être adhérent de la Fnac

l'informatique information technology (computers)	*l'adhésion* membership	*un amphi(théâtre)* large lecture room
la vente sales	*annuler* to cancel	*avoir recours à* to have access to
un remboursement refund	*passer au crible* to leave no stone unturned	*échelonné* staggered (payments)
en espèces in cash		*facultatif* optional

La Fnac s'est spécialisée dans les produits de culture et de loisirs : la photo, le cinéma, la TV, la hi-fi, la vidéo, la micro-informatique, les disques, les livres, les articles de sport, les voyages.

Et dans le même temps, chaque Fnac est devenue un centre d'animation. Expositions photos, manifestations techniques, rencontres littéraires, studios de la musique, festivals de films, cours pratiques sur les techniques audiovisuelles, etc., y sont organisés régulièrement.

Une organisation originale

La première règle est de vendre toujours aux prix les plus bas. Ce que permet une politique d'achat appuyée sur de très gros volumes de vente.

La deuxième règle consiste à savoir exactement ce qu'on vend. D'où l'existence d'un Laboratoire technique testant impitoyablement l'ensemble des articles.

La troisième règle se résume ainsi : dire toute la vérité sur chaque produit et, quand besoin est, dénoncer les abus et les pratiques malhonnêtes.

Tirer le maximum de profit du système Fnac

Tout le monde peut profiter des avantages et des prix proposés par la Fnac.

Mais la Fnac c'est aussi un club rassemblant 400.000 personnes qui bénéficient, en tant qu'adhérents, de conditions spéciales.

Le principe et les avantages de l'adhésion

L'adhésion à la Fnac revêt un caractère strictement personnel.

En échange de la perception d'un droit d'adhésion, la Fnac délivre pour **une durée de 3 ans** une carte magnétique personnalisée (ou un carnet renouvelable) destinée à l'enregistrement des achats.

● **La réduction de prix pour les parkings** de Fnac Montparnasse et Fnac Etoile (1 h de parking gratuit).

Cette démarche donne droit aux avantages suivants :

● **Un remboursement en espèces au bout de 12 règlements :**
– de 3 % des achats effectués dans les magasins à l'enseigne Fnac (sauf pour la librairie, les interventions SAV, la billetterie Alpha et le 2ᵉ Déclic).
– de 2 % des achats effectués dans les magasins agréés Fnac.

● **Un carnet d'adresses de magasins agréés Fnac**
De la literie au bricolage et de la maroquinerie à la parfumerie, ils consentent aux adhérents des remises importantes ou des prix nets et délivrent des bons de 2 % que la Fnac enregistre et rembourse en espèces.

La carte magnétique (ou le carnet d'adhérent) doit être présentée à la caisse à chaque règlement. Selon les magasins, l'opération s'effectue par un enregistrement automatique des achats (ou leur inscription sur le carnet d'adhésion).

La remise s'effectue uniquement pendant la période de validité de l'adhésion. En cas de non-renouvellement, les comptes des cartes périmées depuis plus d'un an sont annulés.

● **L'envoi à domicile de la revue d'information "Contact".**
Dans cette revue sont publiés les tableaux comparatifs des matériels, les tests du laboratoire de la Fnac, des bancs d'essais qui passent au crible les nouveautés, des enquêtes sur les nouvelles techniques de communication, des dossiers économiques et sociologiques...

● **Dans certaines Fnac l'accès exclusif – sans droit d'entrée – au club de location vidéo :** plus de 2000 cassettes proposées à un tarif très avantageux.

● **La priorité d'entrée aux amphis de la Fnac.**
Ce sont des cours théoriques et pratiques pour s'initier ou se perfectionner aux techniques audiovisuelles : la photo, le son, la vidéo et la micro-informatique (activités gratuites - uniquement sur inscription).

● **La réservation prioritaire** à certains programmes proposés par Fnac Voyages.

● **La possibilité d'avoir recours à des services spécialisés** facilitant le paiement :
La carte d'adhérent peut – sur demande et après acceptation du dossier – être investie d'une fonction supplémentaire de carte permanente de crédit. Cette formule appelée **compte permanent** permet le paiement échelonné et "à la carte" des achats (pour plus de détail se renseigner au service "crédit").

Les conditions à remplir

Un service adhésion fonctionne dans chacun des magasins Fnac :

● il assure l'enregistrement des demandes d'adhésion. La carte (ou le carnet d'adhérent) est délivrée immédiatement.

● il propose également à Paris et à Lyon l'adhésion facultative à l'association culturelle Alpha (40 F par an à Paris).

Cette association propose à ses membres un grand nombre de spectacles à tarifs préférentiels (20 à 40 % de réduction), elle envoie à domicile un programme d'information, elle produit ou coproduit chaque année plusieurs spectacles de qualité.

N.B. : *Les membres d'une même famille résidant à la même adresse peuvent chacun obtenir une carte d'adhésion à moitié prix.*

Coût de l'adhésion : 60 F
comprenant l'adhésion à la Fnac et l'envoi à domicile de Contact, pendant une durée de 3 ans.

Carte familiale supplémentaire : 30 F.

Renouvellement de l'adhésion
à la Fnac et de l'envoi à domicile de Contact : 30 F pour 3 ans.

Adhésion facultative à Alpha
réservée aux adhérents de la Fnac : 40 F par an (Paris).

Réf. 203 (9/84)

WRITING

1 While on exchange in France, you are asked by the French organiser for details of how much English money you brought with you, how many French francs you changed it into, and, roughly, how you have spent it. This, he assures you, is not just curiosity, but as a survey to help improve the facilities offered by the Exchange organisation. You are not all that convinced with this explanation, but nevertheless decide to co-operate.

You started your three-week exchange with £30. Make a list of what you have bought, and how much each item cost.

As the French organisers have to read it—please keep it tidy!

2 You are staying with your French partner and her family. While everyone is out one day, you feel sick and dizzy. You go to bed, leaving a note to say:

- you have gone to bed
- you feel ill
- you can't eat anything
- you will get up in the evening.

3 It is Wednesday. You have a dental appointment for Friday, but chronic toothache is making life intolerable for you.

You walk to the dentist's, but his surgery is closed. Write a short note to him, explaining that you have unbearable toothache, and that you will call first thing in the morning.

Docteur Alain GUILBERT
18 · Stomatologue   Conventionné
76, Rue Jean-Jaurès
62800 LIEVIN
62 1 03108 7 | **0 1 23 1**

	JOURS	DATES	HEURES
1	Vendredi	4/9.35	17 h
2			
3			
4			
5			
6			
7			
8			

En cas d'empêchement, prière d'aviser 24 heures avant la prochaine séance.

**DENTIFRICE MÉDICAL
AUX SELS MINÉRAUX
pour homéopathie
goût anis**

AMM 314 108-9

4 Having seen an advertisement concerning German stamps for sale you ask your French friend to find out the address for you. He tracks down the name and address, which are

Mlle Partouche, Estelle,
7 bis rue des Chèvres,
Veules-les-Roses,
76 Seine-Maritime.

Write a short letter, set out properly, saying that you are interested in the stamps, and asking if you may call to view the collection. Also, say how long you are staying in France.

5 You have been touring the South of France with friends, and you were all due to stay with a French penfriend in Paris on the way back to England.

Unfortunately, their car, a Fiat, has broken down, and it is going to take several days before the spares can be acquired, fitted, and the bill paid. You decide therefore to leave your friends, and get a train to Paris, where you will now arrive two days late. You check train times, and then send a telegram to your friend in Paris, saying that you will arrive two days late, the car having broken down, and that you will reach the *Gare de Lyon* at 14.25 next Thursday.

Use your copy of the *télégramme* form. Your Paris friend is

Dominique Benssousan,
196 avenue Daumesnil,
75012 Paris.

N° 698 TÉLÉGRAMME
Étiquettes
N° d'appel :
INDICATIONS DE TRANSMISSION
Timbre à date
Ligne de numérotation
ZCZC
N° télégraphique
Taxe principale.
Taxes accessoires
Total . .
Ligne pilote
N° de la ligne du P.V. :
Bureau de destination
Département ou Pays
Bureau d'origine
Mots
Date
Heure
Mentions de service
Services spéciaux demandés : (voir au verso)
Inscrire en **CAPITALES** l'adresse complète (rue, n° bloc, bâtiment, escalier, etc...), le texte et la signature (une lettre par case ; **laisser une case blanche entre les mots**).
Nom et adresse
TEXTE et éventuellement signature très lisible
Pour accélérer la remise des télégrammes indiquer le cas échéant, le numéro de téléphone (1) ou de télex du destinataire
TF TLX
Pour avis en cas de non remise, indiquer le nom et l'adresse de l'expéditeur (2) :
728678 Y - Cy, Paris - 7/80

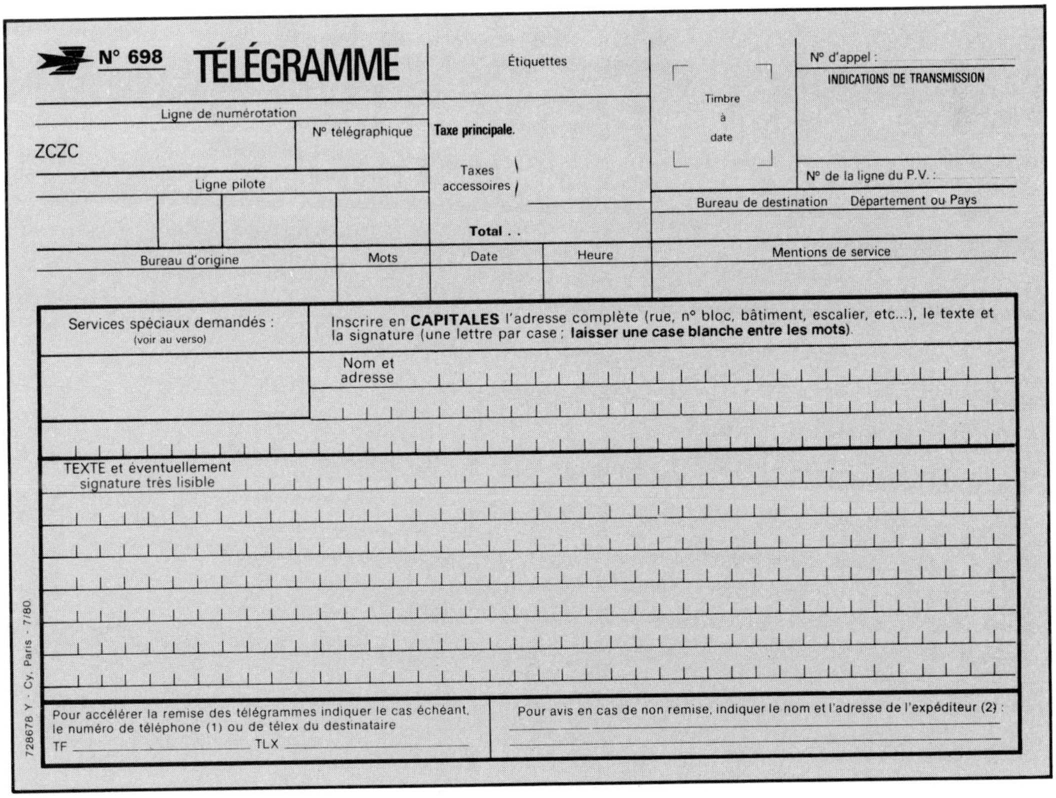

6 Having looked through the small ads in *Pomme*, the free paper for the Dieppe area, you decide to play a joke on your penfriend. Using the *Pomme* forms, write the following advertisements:

- to find a good home for your French partner's dog (see cat advert)

- to sell the furniture in your penfriend's dining-room (see 'ameublement' adverts)

AMEUBLEMENT

A VENDRE chambrée en ronce de noyer comprenant 1 lit 140 (sans literie), 1 armoire, 1 chevet. Prix 800F. Tél. 83.24.05 (après 18 h).

VENDS 6 belles chaises, rustique, sièges et dos paillés. Prix 2.000 F. Tél. (35) 86.17.56.

A VENDRE table de ferme, table ronde, meubles divers en chêne massif ou autres. Bois selon désir du client. Fabrication artisanale. Prix intéressant. Tél. après 20 h: 93.99.55.

A VENDRE cuisine formica bleu et blanc comprenant buffet avec 3 éléments haut et 3 bas + 2 tiroirs, 1 table avec rallonges, 4 chaises simili, blanches, 1 lavevaisselle Indesit 12 couverts. Tél. 85. 24. 66.

VENDS machine à laver Faure, 600 F. Camping Les POMMIERS, Sotteville-sur-Mer.

VENDS salle à manger, style Régence, chêne foncé, bahut 1 m 95, table, tirettes à l'italienne. Prix intéressant. Tél. 82.98.13 + commode ancienne.

A VENDRE lit cuivre ancien, cause double emploi, literie neuve sur mesure. Prix à débattre. Tél. 85.25.75.

VENDS salle à manger Henri-II, buffet, table 2 allonges, 6 chaises. Tél. 97.70.93 (heures repas).

A VENDRE table de nuit ancienne chêne. Tél. 83.30.69 (heures repas).

A VENDRE 6 chaises en chêne, dossier sculpté, dessus canné. Tél. 85.91.47.

VENDS salon beige et marron, bois marron, convertible, 2.500 F (acheté 5.000 F). Tél. 97.58.65 (après 18 h). St-Riquier.

VENDS chambrée chêne 140, table de chevet + lit de fer 115. Tél. 85.85.84.

ANIMAUX

DONNE châton noir et blanc (2 mois) contre bons soins. Tél. 82.21.85 (heures repas).

7 When you get home from France, you discover that somehow you walked out with your penfriend's dental appointment card. When you send it back, add a brief letter saying that you are sorry to have taken the card, that you hope the treatment doesn't hurt, and that you too have to go to the dentist soon.

```
CABINETS DENTAIRES
de la Société de Secours Minière
DE BULLY-GRENAY
Ouverte tous les jours de
8 h à 12 h 30 et de 13 h 30 à 18 h 30
Sauf le Samedi

M _____
a rendez-vous le _____
au cabinet dentaire de _____
```

	JOURS	DATES	MOIS	HEURES
1	Jeudi	2	Mai	10 H
2	Jeudi	23	Mai	9 H
3	Jeudi	20	Juin	10 H 30
4				
5				
6				

NOTA : Un rendez-vous doit être tenu - Conservez toujours cette fiche
Prévenir à l'avance en cas d'empêchement

040   Brossez vos dents matin et soir, vous les conserverez

8 Your French partner's family in Paris turn out to be real anglophiles!

They are planning a dinner party for a number of English friends who live in France, and have gone out to do the shopping, leaving you to answer the phone if it rings.

Of course, several of the friends do phone, and as you will have to be out when the family returns, you must leave written messages in French.

Here are the messages you take, about which you must leave a note.

- John Smith called to say that he smashed up his car; it's going to cost a fortune to repair, and he can't get there without it.

- Stan Brown's wife phoned to say that Stan has been severely bitten by a dog, rabies is suspected, and he's been put in an isolation unit. He can't come.

- Jean Simpson's husband phoned. Jean has been mugged in the métro, and is too upset to see anyone. She sends apologies.

- Carole Brettell phoned to ask if she can come early and stay the night. Can an appointment at a nearby hairdresser's be made for her on the morning of the party? Please phone back.

- Pete Holland will try to come but he can't guarantee it. One of his central-heating pipes has burst, and his house is flooded. He'll get there if the plumbers and builders have repaired everything in time for him to safely leave the house.

9 A French friend of yours, who is planning to tour Britain by car shortly, has written to ask you about the price of petrol in the UK. The day that you receive the letter, you see this article in *The Times.*

Write back, giving current prices of petrol, but also telling your friend how prices have varied recently, even from region to region. Don't forget to invite your friend to stay with you for a few days too.

10 This unfortunate event happens to you and a friend while you are briefly visiting Paris. Later, you recount the event in a letter to your French penfriend.

Petrol reaches 164.6p as companies lift price

The average four star gallon of petrol is now 164.6p after BP, Esso and Mobil, yesterday followed Shell by increasing the price by 7p.

The companies blamed fierce competition on the forecourts for the rise.

But motorists are likely to face further increases within weeks.

BP warned of another rise before the end of the month as higher crude oil costs work their way through the system.

Since last week's decision by the Organization of Petroleum Countries to curtail production, oil has risen from below $10 to $13.50 a barrel but this is not yet reflected in petrol prices.

The increases by Shell, BP and Esso took effect from midnight.

In South Wales, and the North-west and North-east, where petrol has fallen as low as 140p, motorists could face increases of up to 20p per gallon. In contrast, London and the South-east and Scotland, which have not enjoyed a cheap petrol bonanza, may see only small increases.

The increase still leaves petrol well below the January average of around 195p.

MULTI-SKILL TASK

Whilst on a motoring holiday in France with friends you witness the following accident.

Someone phones for the police and when they arrive they interview you. Using the picture above, and making up some responses, answer the questions as best you can. The policeman gives you a blank map to help you describe what you saw. Show your partner what happened.

Pretend your partner is a second police officer taking notes *in French* to pass to the officer in charge. (The tape should be paused between each question.) You should then swap roles so that you make the notes in French.

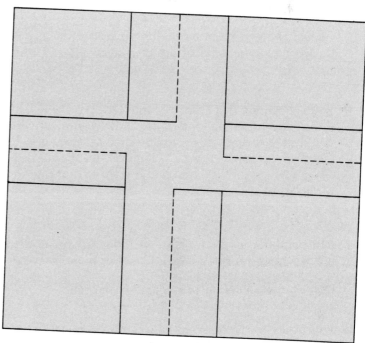

11

France Journal

Porte Ouverte

 LISTENING

1 You are travelling by car through the Ardèche region, when you hear these emergency announcements on the radio. As the cases are serious, and it will help you to keep alert to what is happening around you, you note down the following for each of the announcements:

- what you should be looking for
- what the person concerned must do
- why they should do so.

2 You are in your French penfriend's home, and have a free weekend ahead of you. On the local radio, a synopsis of what's on is given after each hourly news bulletin. Make a list of events, times and places, for later discussion with your friend.

3 You are staying with your French friend. One of his school assignments for Geography is to keep notes for a week on weather conditions in three areas of France.

As he has to be out one evening, he asks you to take down the details from the radio weather report.

Region	Midday temperature	Minimum temperature	Hours of sunshine	General detail
Le Nord				
Le Centre				
Le Sud				

4 You are staying in a French home. One day, whilst alone, the radio gives horoscope forecasts. To help with conversation later, you decide to write down the predictions for yourself and the four members of your penfriend's family. You should be able to note down one good thing, and one bad thing that is going to happen to each one.

Their Zodiac signs are:

penfriend—Aries   her father—Capricorn
her brother—Taurus   her mother—Virgo

Don't forget to note down your own as well.

5 This interview with an old lady, who has recently been mugged, is broadcast as part of a news bulletin.

As you have friends in the police at home, and are horrified by the brutality of the attack, you note down the following details for later use in discussion:

- where the attack happened
- what damage was done
- what was stolen
- the reaction of the victim, who is now in hospital.

6 You are on exchange in Brest. Shortly after returning from the Town Hall reception, the local radio plays interviews with several of the French exchange partners.

You had not known that these interviews were taking place, and decide to make notes about what each person says. This will be particularly useful, as later it will be you who has to write a report on the exchange for the school magazine.

7 Listen as a French friend explains to you the main characteristics of some national newspapers.

Make a note for your own use of his main comments about each one.

8 Your penfriend, with whom you are staying, is a great fan of Bob Dylan. When you hear on the radio that he is going to play several gigs in France, you note down the dates and locations, as well as the cost of tickets. Also, you make a note of which other countries Dylan will visit, as this is part of a World Tour.

Some comments are also made about his new LP. You write these down too, as you know that your penfriend will enjoy arguing against any criticism of Dylan!

9 Whilst staying in France, you have been instructed to keep your eye on developments in these three areas:

- the Basque problem
- attitudes towards the nuclear industry
- Ecology politics.

You listen to a weekly news report, in which each of these three subjects is mentioned. Make notes on developments this week, for use when you return to your studies.

💬 SPEAKING

1 You are stopped in the street in Perpignan by a market researcher, asking you about your ideal radio station.

A new local radio station is planned.

Your partner will take the role of the market researcher. When you have answered the questions to his/her satisfaction, reverse roles.

1 Vous écoutez la radio beaucoup/assez souvent/rarement?

2 Vous êtes sélectif, ou écoutez-vous là où vous tombez?

3 Pour l'idéal, combien de musique rock aimeriez-vous écouter par jour? Et combien de musique classique?

4 A quelle fréquence devrait-on passer les actualités?

5 A quelle fréquence devrait-on passer les bulletins du météo?

6 A quelle heure préféreriez-vous écouter les documentaires?

7 Vous serait-il important de pouvoir écouter 24 heures sur 24?

8 Quelles émissions préférez-vous la nuit?

9 Vous écoutez soigneusement la publicité?

10 Vous écoutez plus pour vous informer ou pour vous distraire?

2 You, and a group of friends in France, are interviewed about TV in England, for a radio discussion programme.

One of the group should take the role of the interviewer, and should ask such questions as:

1 Quelles sont les émissions les plus populaires?

2 Combien de chaînes y a-t-il?

Pouvez-vous expliquer comment elles sont différentes?

3 Chez une famille typique qu'est-ce que les enfants regardent de préférence? Et les parents?

4 Est-ce qu'on regarde beaucoup la télé le matin?

This should develop into free discussion. If this goes well, it would be valuable, once rehearsed, to present this to the whole class.

3 This time you are interviewed about the English press. With one group member acting as interviewer, you and your friends are asked about the different newspapers.

Each one of you needs an English newspaper, and should be able to say, when asked, what each section is about, and who might be most likely to read this paper.

4 Your French penfriend's mother is browsing through a woman's magazine which you have brought her from England. She asks you to explain to her what some of the 'Problem Page' letters are about.

When you have done so, you go on to discuss each problem.

Your teacher, French assistant or partner can play the role of your penfriend's mother.

They want me to wait

I'm 17 and my boyfriend is nearly 24. My parents like him, but as he's been married before and has two children, they are concerned about what would happen if I married him. I've talked to my priest and he's said that we could marry in church — the wedding I've always dreamed of. But my father said he wouldn't give me away at my wedding if I married before I was 20. He hasn't got anything against my boyfriend, apart from the fact that he has two daughters. I know I would be very happy if I married him. My boyfriend has asked me to move in with him. I feel I will have to go against my parents' wishes on this.

Do I have to look after her?

A few years ago when my father died, my sister and her husband informed me that, as she was younger, I was responsible for my mother. It makes me mad that my mum and dad were always at my sister's beck and call, but I have done all the worrying. My conscience is clear, but I still wonder, though, if there is such a law assigning all responsibility to the eldest child.

Suggestive remarks

I love my job, except for one thing which is making me very tense. The other two girls I type with like the radio on all day. It just drives me mad. Not only that, but they like Tony Blackburn and he is always making jokes I find offensive. When men come into the office, they make suggestive remarks, along with him. I could leave but my parents are ill and for me to be out of work would put extra pressure on them. I can't concentrate because of this and have been reprimanded by my supervisor as well.

READING

1 You have friends who are shortly due to travel to France by car with their young children.

As you know that they are lax in their use of safety-belts, you write to the kids, telling them about this McDonald's campaign concerning car safety for children. You tell them as well to point out to their parents the financial(!) and other benefits of having them get involved in this campaign.

Bouclez votre ceinture avec Mc Do

Mc Donald's s'est associé à la Sécurité routière pour mener une grande action pour la sécurité des enfants en voiture: En priorité, le thème de la ceinture de sécurité!
Moins de 10% des enfants utilisent un dispositif de retenue (ceinture ou siège homologué) Or, l'utilisation d'un système de retenue réduirait de 90% le taux de mortalité.

Programme d'action:

Dans tous les restaurants Mc Donald's de Lyon, vous recevrez 4 auto-collants, à l'effigie de Ronald Mc Donald's, portant la mention «La ceinture, bien sûr!».
— Ces auto-collants sont destinés à être placés sur les attaches des ceintures de sécurité afin de vous rappeler de boucler votre ceinture.
— Une carte de «Promesse» imprimée au dos des auto-collants, attestera que vous avez bien respecté les consignes de sécurité. Les participants devront cocher l'une des 7 cases qui figurent sur la carte, lors de chaque déplacement en voiture. Chaque carte, remplie et signée, sera échangée contre quelques frites et un cadeau surprise.
Une fiche de conseils pratiques sur le transport des enfants en voiture sera remise aux parents, en même temps que les auto-collants et la carte de promesse. (A Lyon, 3 restaurants Mc Donald's: place Bellecour, rue Victor-Hugo, Part-Dieu).

Le Progrès des Enfants

taux de mortalité (m.)   death rate
auto-collant (f.)   car-sticker
boucler   to fasten
attester   to bear witness
cocher   to mark off

2 Partly for amusement, and partly for your own edification, you decide to note the following:

- the five different answers given by people in the street to the question:
  'What is the 14th July?'
- the particular significance of 14th July in the three years mentioned in the article.

le défilé   (military) march past

Oh la belle bleue !

Chaque 14 juillet, 7 000 à 8 000 feux illuminent le ciel de France, 100 tonnes de poudre et 1 milliard d'étoiles s'envolent en fumée !
Mais le 14 juillet c'est quoi ?
Quelques réponses prises sur le vif :
— C'est la fête, c'est la danse !
— C'est le débarquement en Normandie !... ». (oh !!!...)
— C'est le défilé.
— C'est la seule nuit où on peut faire du bruit sans problèmes...
— C'est le feu d'artifice !!!
Réponses pour le moins fantaisistes pour expliquer le plus célèbre des jours fériés français !

Le 14 juillet, mais c'est la prise de la Bastille, bien sûr !

Le 14 Juillet 1789, les révolutionnaires détruisent la sinistre prison de la Bastille, symbole de la monarchie et de l'arbitraire royal (on y envoyait n'importe qui sur simple décision du roi).
Et depuis ce jour mémorable, on célèbre, on n'en finit pas de célébrer !... chaque année à la même date, mais de façons variées et parfois même insolites, au fil des ans et des siècles :
14 juillet 1798 : Illumination des monuments de la capitale et envol spectaculaire d'un ballon dirigeable dans le ciel de Paris !
14 juillet 1802 : Défilé de « mamelouks » !!! (anciens esclaves égyptiens ralliés à Bonaparte pendant sa campagne d'Egypte).
14 juillet 1880 : Date historique ! Institution officielle de la fête nationale : le 14 juillet ! Institution officielle de la fête nationale dure 8 jours ! 8 jours de danses et de chansons dans toute la France.
C'est le début de l'âge d'or du 14 juillet ! Que la fête continue !...
vive le feu d'artifice !!!

3 Your penfriend's grandparents are very interested in the British royal family. One day they show you this cutting in their scrap book. As your grandparents also follow the activities of the royal family closely, you decide to write and tell them what the French press said in the summer of 1986.

échiquier (m.)   chess board
au grand dam de   to the detriment of

GRANDE-BRETAGNE
Jeux de dames

En haut : Elisabeth II et Margaret Thatcher en période de « cohabitation » difficile. En bas : Sarah Ferguson et Lady Diana, futures belles-sœurs princières.

Les princesses s'amusent, la reine règne et le Premier ministre gouverne. Mais l'Angleterre, à quelques jours du mariage d'Andrew et de Sarah, se passionne soudain pour deux parties de dames, jouées sur des échiquiers bien distincts.

D'un côté, l'escapade que se sont offerte les deux princesses, Lady Diana et Sarah Ferguson. Cela pour le sourire.

De l'autre, l'opposition ouverte entre la reine Elisabeth II (souveraine du Commonwealth); et le Premier ministre, Margaret Thatcher, hostile à toute sanction contre l'Afrique du Sud au grand dam de nombreux Etats-membres du Commonwealth... L'été anglais oscille entre le beau temps et les orages.

4 With time to spare one day, you are browsing through the newspaper, and are pleased at how well you understand, amongst other things, the weather forecast.

As your parents will be coming to France shortly, you decide to show off by sending them a summary of the current weather in the 'four corners' of France, plus the Paris area. You even decide to send them an English key to the map!

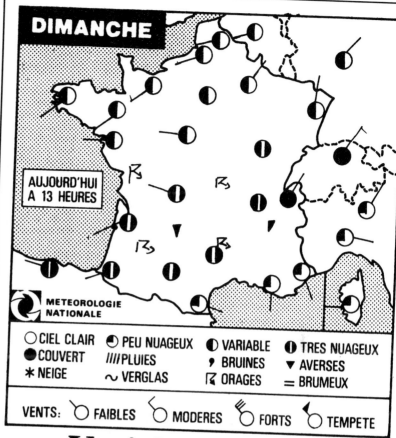

DIMANCHE

AUJOURD'HUI A 13 HEURES

METEOROLOGIE NATIONALE

○ CIEL CLAIR   ◑ PEU NUAGEUX   ◐ VARIABLE   ❶ TRES NUAGEUX
● COUVERT   //// PLUIES   ❞ BRUINES   ▼ AVERSES
✳ NEIGE   ∼ VERGLAS   ℟ ORAGES   ═ BRUMEUX

VENTS: ○ FAIBLES   ○ MODERES   ⟩ FORTS   ⟩ TEMPETE

Variable au nord
orageux au sud

Où trouver le soleil ? L'Espagne est, à son tour, touchée par les orages. L'Italie, la Corse et la Sardaigne vous attendent toujours sous un ciel bleu. L'Angleterre profitera d'une belle accalmie et d'éclaircies durables. Toutes les autres régions autour de la France restent sous un ciel mi-figue mi-raisin avec des températures encore agréables pour la saison.

En France

Région parisienne. — La matinée sera brumeuse. Le ciel gardera encore souvent un voile blanc formé de nuages très hauts. D'autres petits nuages se développeront en dessous et se partageront la journée avec des moments plus lumineux. Il fera encore un peu moins chaud : 10 à 11 degrés le matin, 23 degrés l'après-midi.

Quart nord-est. — Des nuages épais le matin de la Haute-Normandie à la Picardie, au Nord et aux Ardennes, des nappes de brumes et de brouillards ailleurs. Dans la journée, ciel très favorable avec prédominance des éclaircies sur les nuages. Les températures resteront très modestes pour la saison entre 21 et 24 degrés.

Quart sud-est. — Dans l'ensemble, le temps lourd nuageux et orageux se renforce un peu, après un rayon de soleil matinal. Le temps nuageux et les risques d'averses et d'orages n'épargneront que le proche littoral de la Méditerranée qui conservera soleil et chaleur à plus de 30 degrés. Des ondes orageuses du Roussillon aux Cévennes et aux Alpes, elles seront plus fortes en soirée.

Quart sud-ouest. — Les nuages seront plus épais qu'aujourd'hui, les risques d'averses et d'orages seront plus forts aussi. Du Limousin à la région toulousaine, il pourrait bien y avoir quelques averses de grêle. Des pluies passagères assez faibles sur toute la région. Les températures seront en baisse sensible, redescendant aux environs de 25/27 degrés.

Quart nord-ouest. — Ciel très nuageux et petites pluies côtières le matin. Amélioration lente et progressive en cours de journée avec des éclaircies de plus en plus belles. Mais les nuages resteront encore assez abondants et il fera un peu plus frais.

nappe (f.) covering
renforcer to strengthen
onde (f.) wave
épargner to spare

Avec l'aimable autorisation du journal Le Figaro. Copyright Le Figaro 1986

5 You have friends who are planning to visit the Basque area shortly. When you see this article about Bayonne and its *Musée Basque*, you write to them, listing the wide range of exhibits relating to the Basque way of life that can be seen there.

PAR MARIE STEINBERG

Bayonne : traditions et chocolats

Si l'on veut tout connaître sur le Pays basque, avant de s'y promener, il faut faire un tour à Bayonne, au musée basque. C'est un des musées folkloriques les plus intéressants que je connaisse. Dans un ancien couvent, à l'architecture très typique, donnant sur les quais, chaque région est représentée avec ses meubles, ses costumes et ses traditions. On y voit des collections de makilas (cannes taillées et sculptées directement sur pied dans du bois de néflier), d'espadrilles (les Basques disent sandales), de pelote basque avec ses différents types d'accessoires. Évocation des stars de la pelote (photos de personnages moustachus et délicieusement désuets), reconstitution d'une maison basque, salle du chocolat avec ses instruments et le matériel de fabrication, évocation de la pêche à la morue et à la baleine et maquettes de caravelles, pirogues, chalands et pinasses. amusante évocation de la sorcellerie au Pays basque rapportée par un cônseiller au parlement de Bordeaux en 1612, qui avait beaucoup d'imagination.

Enfin, une salle est consacrée aux écrivains qui furent les hôtes du Pays basque. Pierre Loti, qui possédait une maison face à Fontarabie ; Francis James, qui s'installa à Hasparren de 1921 à sa mort en 1938, et Edmond Rostand, dont on doit visiter la villa Arnaga, à Cambo, où il vécut quatorze ans.

En sortant du musée, il faut aller flâner dans les vieilles rues, autour de la cathédrale. Rue des Faures, c'est le quartier des antiquaires. Dans la très pittoresque rue du Port-Neuf se trouvent, côte à côte, deux célèbres chocolatiers : Daranatz, qui fait aussi du touron, et Cazenave (salon de thé très rétro, comme sa clientèle) où l'on trouve les « Kanougas », caramels au chocolat.

CHOCOLATIERS

- **Daranatz**, 15, Arceaux Port-Neuf. 59.24.03.55.
- **Cazenave**, 19, Arceaux Port-Neuf. 59.24.03.16.

la morue   cod
la baleine   whale
maquette (f.)   model

LYON Music festival/86

Renaud tout foulard dehors !

№ 1842

EN ACCORD AVEC **ARTMEDIA**

Rainbow Concerts
PRESENTE

RENAUD

LYON   Théâtre antique
(Lyon Music Festival)
Dimanche 20 Juillet 1986 - 21 H 30

110 F

6 You are staying near Vienne, and have just been to a rock concert to see Renaud. With the help of this article, write to a friend, telling her about the concert, and giving details of Renaud's next appearance. Ask if you should get tickets for your friend as well, as she will be joining you soon.

Rien ne manquait, hier soir à Fourvière, pour le dernier concert du Lyon Music Festival organisé par Rainbow concerts. Ni le public — plus de cinq mille personnes, beaucoup avec autour du cou un foulard rouge —, ni la lune, ni le décor — un super bateau — ni surtout, Renaud.
Un Renaud qui, dès son entrée en scène entame le dialogue avec son public : « ça va, les gônes ? C'est sympa d'être revenus me voir. Alors, vous m'aimez ? ». La réponse fuse : une immense clameur monte des gradins. Le courant passe tout

de suite. Pendant plus de deux heures il ne disjonctera pas. Des histoires de matelots, de potes, mais aussi des « beaufs », Mona, Pierrot, Manu et, bien sûr, Mme Thatcher, tous sont au rendez-vous. Entre chaque chanson Renaud parle, « engueule » ses musiciens, raconte des histoires belges, ramasse les foulards lancés par le public.
La nuit avance, les étoiles clignotent. Le service de sécurité offre de l'eau aux spectateurs du premier rang, les briquets s'allument. Tout seul, un tourne-

sol fait une tâche dans le pubic. Les grands-parents et leurs petits enfants, les jeunes mères tits enfants, les jeunes mères bon chic bon genre et leurs filles reprennent les refrains en chœur.
Soudain on se laisse embarquer par un flot de tendresse et d'émotion. Le capitaine Renaud est à la barre. Il n'y a plus qu'à... marcher à l'ombre.

F.F. ■

Renaud chante à Vienne le 2 août, au théâtre antique.

entamer   to initiate
gradin (m.)   stepped row of seats
disjoncter   to trip
pote (m. or f.)   pal
engueuler   to abuse (vulg.)
clignoter   to twinkle
à la barre   at the helm

7 One of your friends in England is fascinated by phones, and is often experimenting with them. You think this article will interest him, so you send it to him. His French is limited, however, so you also write to explain what a *bidouilleur* is, and what it is used for.

GRENOBLE
Téléphone : le clan
des « bidouilleurs »

La police grenobloise a arrêté quatre spécialistes du commerce des « bidouilleurs », ces boîtiers électroniques qui permettent avec une pièce d'un franc de téléphoner sans limite de temps dans le monde entier.

Depuis plusieurs mois, les utilisateurs des cabines téléphoniques grenobloises se voyaient proposer ces petits boîtiers fabriqués à Hong-Kong — qu'il suffit d'appliquer sur le combiné pour les faire fonctionner — à des prix variant de 1 000 à 3 000 francs.

Les services des Télécommunica-tions ont mis au point une « parade » dont le détail technique est bien sûr tenu secret.

Le « bidouilleur », avant sa légère modification pour l'utilisation téléphonique frauduleuse, sert à un tout autre usage dans le domaine de la bureautique. Bien des personnes le connaissent sous la forme d'« agendas électroniques ».

Dans le commerce, il coûte environ 300 francs. Il a donc fallu que dans le « milieu » grenoblois un esprit imaginatif le transforme en objet de délit.

Le Progrès

8 You have strong views about the death penalty. You write to a friend outlining the case described in *Lyon Matin* and add your own opinion about the sentence passed by the judge.

ETATS-UNIS
Une condamnée à mort
de 16 ans

Une jeune fille, âgée de seize ans, est devenue vendredi, la première mineure à être condamnée à mort aux Etats-Unis, un juge d'un tribunal de Crown Point (Indiana) lui ayant imposé cette sentence pour le meurtre atroce d'une veuve de 78 ans.

Paula Cooper avait plaidé coupable, en avril dernier, pour le meurtre en 1985, de Ruth Pelke qu'elle avait poignardée à plus de trente reprises avec un couteau de cuisine. Trois autres mineures ont été inculpées de complicité. Les quatre jeunes filles avaient prétendu s'intéresser à l'instruction religieuse que Mme Pelke dispensait, pour gagner sa confiance. Après le meurtre, elles lui avaient dérobé dix dollars et sa voiture.

Avant de prononcer la sentence, le juge James Kimbrough a déclaré : « Je ne crois pas en la peine capitale (...) mais la loi m'impose de l'appliquer pour cet acte prémédité et odieux ». La sentence sera soumise d'office à l'examen de la Cour suprême de l'Etat d'Indiana.

poignarder to stab

9 After seeing this series of articles in *Le Progrès,* you make a brief note of the problems that have affected and are affecting each of the areas mentioned. Your parents are planning to tour France shortly, and will want to avoid these areas.

LA ROUTE

Les premiers bouchons du week-end

Les premiers bouchons du week-end du 14 juillet ont commencé à bloquer la circulation en milieu d'après-midi aux sorties ouest et sud de Paris et sur l'axe Beaune-Valence.
Bison Futé, attend sept millions de personnes sur les routes entre le 11 et le 14 juillet, et a invité les vacanciers à ne pas partir samedi, mais dimanche.

Circulation interdite dans les forêts des Bouches-du-Rhône

La circulation des personnes et des véhicules a été interdite à partir de vendredi dans tout le massif forestier des Bouches-du-Rhône par un arrêté pris par la préfecture de région.
Cet arrêté fait suite aux incendies qui ont fait rage depuis lundi dans ce département, où 4 000 hectares de garrigues et de forêts ont été détruits par le feu.

INCENDIE

En Lozère et dans le Gard aussi

Si les Bouches-du-Rhône et le Var, où 7 500 hectares ont été ravagés par les flammes depuis dimanche, n'ont pas connu de feux importants vendredi, la Lozère et le Gard ont été à leur tour touchés. En Lozère, une reprise d'un incendie de forêts qui s'était déclaré jeudi au sud-ouest du département, a parcouru plus de 50 hectares de chênes verts et de pins. Dans le Gard, trois départs de feu ont eu lieu vers 15 heures dans la région d'Alès, combattus par plus de 200 hommes avec cinquante véhicules, un hélicoptère

et cinq bombardiers d'eau, le sinistre, qui pousse par des rafales de 8 à 10 nœuds, se propageait rapidement dans une zone de forêt. Il était toujours en activité vendredi au début de la soirée.

MONTAGNE

Une mère et sa fillette emportées par un torrent sous les yeux du père

Une vacancière originaire de Morsang-sur-Orge (Essonne) et sa fillette ont été emportées jeudi par un torrent près de la Chapelle en Valgaudemar (Hautes-Alpes), sous les yeux du père qui a assisté, impuissant, à leur disparition. Elles n'avaient pas été retrouvées vendredi soir.
M. Claude Deleglise, 48 ans, avait voulu photographier son épouse Claudine, 37 ans, et la petite Coralie, 4 ans, au bord du torrent « Les eaux du diable ». Au cours de l'opération, la fillette a glissé dans les eaux du torrent et a été emportée, suivie par sa mère qui avait voulu lui porter secours.

POLLUTION

Nuage de chlore sur Toulouse

Un important nuage de chlore, dont le volume n'a pu être évalué, s'est développé hier matin dans le ciel de Toulouse, à la suite de fuite accidentelle survenue dans une usine au sud de la ville. Aucune victime n'a été recensée.
Cet accident est survenu quinze jours à peine après l'annonce de la prochaine diffusion auprès de 30 000 Toulousains habitant cette zone, de consignes à appliquer en cas d'émanations toxiques accidentelles.

Le Progrès

BATELLERIE

Cotes prises le 11 juillet à 7 heures. — Besançon : 2,10 m ; Verdun : 1,22 m ; Chalon : 1,70 m ; Mâcon : 1,68 m ; Ternay : 0,92 m.
Débits moyens du Rhône à Seyssel. — Hier : 630 m³/s ; prévu aujourd'hui : 550 m³/s.
Débits moyens de l'Ain à Allement. — Hier : 12 m³/s ; prévu aujourd'hui : 12 m³/s.
Débits de la Saône à Couzon à 7 heures. — Hier : 250 m³/s ; aujourd'hui : 200 m³/s.
Débits moyens de l'Isère à Pizançon. — Hier : 420 m³/s ; prévu aujourd'hui : 430 m³/s.

fuite (f.) leak
rafale (f.) blast (of wind)
recenser to register

10 Feeling quite confident now with a lot of French printed material, you try your hand at some of the short items of news published in the daily paper *Le Matin.* How successful are you?

1 How much can you understand about Johannes Naegeli?

2 Who exactly was involved in the Paris drug-bust yesterday?

3 What happened to the three million embezzled francs?

4 What exactly was found in the Creil forest?

5 What has been happening to the 'Zerhoun'?

6 What was the steam-roller doing in New York?

7 What theory is being put forward in the USA about the origins of life on earth?

SOCIETE

RETROUVE CONGELE SOIXANTE-DOUZE ANS APRES SA MORT

Le corps congelé d'un alpiniste suisse, Johannes Naegeli, a été retrouvé dans un glacier du comté de Berne soixante-douze ans après sa mort. Sa mort, à l'âge de soixante-six ans, remonterait à 1914, alors qu'il avait été abandonné en difficulté dans un refuge par le guide de l'expédition à laquelle il appartenait. En allant chercher du secours le guide avait appris dans un village le déclenchement de la Première Guerre mondiale et il s'était aussitôt engagé. Naegeli avait disparu avant que les secours n'arrivent sur les lieux. □

OPERATION ANTI-DROGUE

Près de 400 personnes ont été contrôlées, hier après-midi, au cours d'une opération anti-drogue menée par la police parisienne dans le quartier de la Goutte-d'Or et dans deux foyers pour résidents dans les 20e et 15e arrondissements. Deux dealers, onze usagers et quatorze étrangers en situation irrégulière ont été interpellés. □

L'EMPLOYE DE BANQUE DETOURNE TROIS MILLIONS DE FRANCS

Un employé d'une agence du Crédit agricole mutuel d'Angers (Maine-et-Loire) a été écroué lundi pour avoir dérobé trois millions de francs, en six ans, à une de ses clientes. Serge Chenevier, quarante et un ans, conservait en fait les fonds versés par sa victime qui souscrivait des bons anonymes ; en échange il lui remettait des bordereaux fictifs. Selon le magistrat, qui l'a inculpé d'abus de confiance et d'escroquerie, le seul point obscur de l'affaire réside dans l'utilisation que l'escroc a pu faire de l'argent détourné. □

MYSTERIEUX CADAVRE EN FORET DE CREIL

Le cadavre d'une jeune femme entièrement nue a été découvert lundi dans la forêt d'Halatte, près de Creil (Oise), enroulé dans un drap de lit de couleur rose. Selon les premières constatations du médecin, la victime serait âgée de quinze à vingt-cinq ans et serait originaire du Maghreb. Le décès remonterait à plusieurs semaines. □

CANNABIS, DEUX MATELOTS ECROUES A CALAIS

Deux matelots d'un cargo marocain, le *Zerhoun*, ont été placés en détention hier à Lille pour « *importation et transport de stupéfiants* », après la saisie, vendredi dernier à la frontière franco-belge, de 138 kg de résine de cannabis. L'enquête a permis de remonter jusqu'au navire, qui aurait transporté la drogue dissimulée dans sa cargaison de concentré de zinc. Le *Zerhoun* était toujours consigné, hier, dans le port de Calais. □

LA VIE ET LES EXTRA TERRESTRES

Une conférence scientifique réunie à l'université de Berkeley, aux Etats-Unis, va chercher à déterminer quel rôle des éléments extraterrestres, apportés par des météores ou des comètes, ont pu jouer dans l'apparition de la vie sur notre globe, il y a un peu moins de 4 milliards d'années. Les biologistes se demandent si les éléments ainsi apportés ont joué un rôle plus important que ceux qui existaient sur Terre et qui ont probablement donné naissance, par des réactions chimiques, aux premiers êtres vivants. □

ON ECRASE BIEN LES FAUSSES « CARTIER »

Deux mille fausses montres Cartier ont été écrasées mardi à New York par un rouleau compresseur. La scène se passait à l'angle de la 52e Rue et de la 5e Avenue, c'est-à-dire en plein quartier chic. Fabriquées à Hong-kong, ces montres contrefaites auraient été vendues dans la rue entre 300 F et 700 F. □

---

le déclenchement starting, launching
écraser to crush

11 These articles outline three events which took place in the Lyon area recently. Write out the main details of what took place in each one, for later use in a talk which you will have to give, showing that although geography and politics may differ, many day-to-day occurrences are similar everywhere.

Mionnay

Une voiture lyonnaise s'encastre sous un camion : un mort

A 5 h 50 sur la RN 83 au lieu dit « La Marfondière » à Mionnay, un ensemble routier des transports Tenoux de Bourg conduit pr M. Daniel Marmont domicilié « Les Maros » à Branges (Saône-et-Loire) qui circulait en direction de Lyon était violemment heurté par un véhicule Citroën.
Le choc fut effroyable et le véhicule piloté par M. Ageorges Gaston, 53 ans, domicilié rue

Laënnec à Lyon, s'encastrait contre le côté gauche du poids lourd et était projeté, sous la violence du choc, près de la glissière de sécurité où il s'immobilisa. Quant au poids lourd, il continua sa course pour finir dans un champ de blé bordant l'accotement.
Des tôles, laminées, les sapeurs-pompiers devaient désincarcérer, après 45 minutes d'efforts, le corps du malheureux

conducteur, tué sur le coup. Le conducteur du poids lourd légèrement blessé devait être transporté à l'hôpital de Fleyrait à Bourg-en-Bresse.
Le constat était effectué par la gendarmerie de Saint-André-de-Corcy aidé par la compagnie de Villars-les-Dombes. La circulation devait être rendue à 10 h 15 après le dépannage du poids lourd.

Sainte-Foy-lès-Lyon

Le gang des « bleus de travail » pille une « supérette »

Quatre individus, vêtus de bleus de travail, le visage dissimulé sous une cagoule, armés de fusil de chasse, ont attaqué, jeudi, à l'heure du déjeuner, une « supérette » de Sainte-Foy-lès-Lyon.
Il était environ 12 h 30, lorsque des intrus ont fait irruption dans les locaux du magasin « Cordial », situé 28 avenue Maurice

Jarosson, maîtrisant aussitôt personnel et clients.
Après s'être emparé du contenu des différentes caisses, les gangsters prenaient la fuite avec un butin, évalué à plusieurs dizaines de milliers de francs, à bord d'une voiture « R 20 » marron clair, faussement immatriculée.

L'alerte donnée, les officiers de police du commissariat de permanence se rendaient aussitôt sur les lieux, afin de procéder aux constatations. Ils étaient bientôt rejoints par leurs collègues de la section criminelle de la Sûreté urbaine de Lyon, chargés de la poursuite des investigations.

Meyzieu

Une automobiliste tuée dans un accident

Tragique accident de la circulation jeudi, vers 11 heures, à l'intersection des rues Molière

et Girardin, située à proximité de la zone industrielle de Meyzieu.
Pour des raisons que les enquêteurs s'efforceront de déterminer, deux véhicules sont entrés en collision : une « R 12 » et une « R 18 ». Après le choc, la « R 12 » a fait un double tonneau.
La conductrice du véhicule, Mme Paulette Allardon, 61 ans, demeurant rue Louis-Saunier à Meyzieu, est décédée pendant son transport à l'hôpital dans l'ambulance du S.A.M.U. qui

s'était rendue sur les lieux de l'accident en même temps que les sapeurs pompiers de Villeurbanne et de Meyzieu.

Quant à la conductrice de l'autre véhicule, Mme Viana Consuelo, de Meyzieu également, elle ne fut que choquée, mais fut hospitalisée par mesure de précaution.

Les policiers du corps urbain de Meyzieu, sous les ordres de l'inspecteur Bonnafous, ont procédé aux constatations d'usage.

effroyable   frightful
s'encastrer   to be embedded
tôle (f.)   sheet metal
une supérette   mini market
maîtriser   to get the better of (overpower)
s'emparer   to seize
faire un tonneau   to roll over

Le Progrès

12 You are on holiday with your family in Provence. The experiences recounted here seem not far removed from your own. Write to a friend, making similar comments to those made here.

LE GRAIN D'SEL
de Jean-Michel Royer

Carte postale

Cher papy :
Nos vacances se poursuivent comme elles ont commencé, c'est-à-dire le mieux du monde. Nous avons quitté Sainte-Ursule-les-Flots : les coups de soleil de maman s'étaient transformés en brûlure au deuxième degré ; les coups de fusil de l'hôtelier et des commerçants avaient vidé le portefeuille de papa (au fait : n'oublies pas de nous envoyer le mandat promis), et la mer était tellement polluée que nous avons tous la peau couverte de boutons bizarres...
Nous nous sommes donc réfugiés dans la Provence intérieure, merveilleusement poétique avec ses ifs noirs, ses oliviers d'argent, et sa sonorisation assurée par les cigales...
Bien sûr, le mistral souffle comme un dingue, les touristes sont au moins aussi nombreux que sur la côte, et les embuscades tendues un peu partout ont achevé de nous ruiner (s'il te plaît, penses au mandat !)...
Mais, ici au moins, tout est parfaitement sain et naturel. Les méchants « écolos » prétendent que nous nageons au milieu des retombées de Tchernobyl. Ce sont sûrement des menteries. Jamais la lavande et le romarin n'ont été plus odorants, jamais les grillades aux herbes de Provence n'ont été plus savoureuses...
Nous t'attendons avec impatience, cher papy. N'oublies pas d'apporter ton carnet de chèques — et à tout hasard ton compteur Geiger.
Gros bisous.

Le Progrès

if (m.) yew tree
cigale (f.) cricket
comme un dingue like mad
embuscade (f.) ambush

13 Write to a friend, reflecting upon whether Château-Chinon will join Colombey-les-deux-Eglises in French history books.

LE GRAIN D'SEL
de Jean-Michel Royer

Colombey Bis

Les habitants de Château-Chinon ont bien de la chance. Pendant des années, du fait de la personnalité de leur député-maire, le moindre d'entre eux fut une vedette nationale. L'hôtel du Vieux-Morvan, résidence (secondaire) de François Mitterrand, faisant des affaires d'or. Bref, la France avait en Morvan sa capitale bis...
Depuis que l'illustre élu local est devenu « le roi François », on parlait beaucoup moins de sa cité favorite : les hauts-lieux du règne étaient désormais son appartement parisien de la rue de Bièvre et sa thébaïde landaise de Latche, sans parler bien sûr du palais de l'Elysée...
Pour consoler ses anciens administrés quelque peu frustrés après avoir été tant caressés par les sourires de gloire, l'ancien maire de Château-Chinon vient de leur faire un cadeau royal : les cadeaux qu'il a lui-même reçus de tous les grands de la terre. Ceux-ci sont exposés depuis hier dans les trois étages d'un musée sis devinez où ? Rue du Château...
N'ayant pas l'esprit mal tourné, je me garderai de souligner que la décision d'organiser cette exposition permanente est une pierre (précieuse) dans le jardin du précédent locataire de l'Elysée. Je me bornerai à signaler aux amateurs de pèlerinages un musée où son également montrés des présents fort émouvants, reçus jadis par un chef d'Etat français. Cela s'appelle « La Boisserie ». Adresse : Colombey-les-Deux-Eglises (Haute-Marne)...

Le Progrès

la thébaïde retreat
jadis formerly, once

14 When you return from your holiday in France, one of the topics that you will have to study is the problem of drug abuse. Make notes on these three articles, for future reference.

Le Journal du Rhône

FAITS DIVERS

Drogue : opération coup de poing hier à Lyon

Sur instructions de M. Chalandon, ministre de la Justice, M. Salavagione, procureur de la République, a lancé lundi à Lyon en fin d'après-midi une opération de contrôle contre les revendeurs de drogue.

Ainsi, ce lundi à 18 heures précises, cent policiers en tenue ou en civil, appartenant à la P.J. à la Sûreté urbaine et au corps urbain ont investi les deux quartiers les plus réputés de Lyon pour abriter des dealers ; en l'occurrence le secteur de la place du Pont (rue Paul-Bert, rue Moncey) et les alentours de la place des Terreaux (rue Sainte-Catherine, montée de la Grand-Côte) où les bars ont été fouillés, les voitures contrôlées et les identités vérifiées.

Cette opération déjà menée à Toulouse par exemple et également hier à Lille et à Paris s'inscrit dans le cadre de la guerre anti-drogue déclenchée sur le territoire par la Chancellerie.
Parallèlement aux stupéfiants, qui restaient donc le principal objectif, les services de police placées sur le terrain sous l'autorité du commissaire Menez (P.J.) et du commissaire Guenot (S.U) devaient procéder à des vérifications pour port d'arme prohibé ou interdiction de séjour. Les résultats de cette opération de contrôle seront communiqués aujourd'hui à la presse.

Le Progrès

fouiller to search
contrôler to check
déclencher to start, launch

DROGUE
Les « sniffettes » du showbiz

Les enquêteurs de la brigade des stupéfiants et du proxénétisme arrêtent un « très gros bonnet » et deux de ses dealers.

La route de la cocaïne est coupée pour certains amateurs dans les milieux du showbiz à Paris : la brigade des stupéfiants et du proxénétisme (B.S.P.) a, pendant le week-end, saisi cinq kilogrammes de cocaïne et mis la main sur un important fournisseur et ses deux principaux revendeurs.

Les enquêteurs ont saisi également tout un stock d'un nouveau gadget américain qui vient de faire son apparition sur le marché français des « cocaïnomanes » : une sorte de petit sablier qui permet de « sniffer » la « coke » avec une discrétion garantie.

« On ne parlera plus de « lignes de coke » (le plus souvent les toxicomanes utilisaient une paille) mais probablement de « sniffette » ou de « coup du sablier », explique un enquêteur. Ce gadget est en vente libre aux États-Unis, où il se présente par paquets de cinq. Mais c'est la première fois qu'il apparaissait à Paris.

Exploitant un renseignement obtenu fin juin, les hommes d'Olivier Foll, le « patron » de la B.S.P., ont remonté la filière orchestrée par Gérard Faure, 40 ans, marchand de vêtements né à Fez (Maroc), qui vit depuis plusieurs années du trafic des stupéfiants.

Interpellations en série

Les enquêteurs ont d'abord mis la main, jeudi dernier, sur Peter Murphy Shaun, 24 ans, Britannique né à Liverpool, qui évoluait dans les boîtes de nuit parisiennes et avait été recruté par Gérard Faure.

Peter Murphy Shaun a reconnu, qu'ayant des difficulfés financières, il avait fait plusieurs voyages en Hollande pour son patron et qu'il revenait chaque fois avec quatre cents ou cinq cents grammes de cocaïne dans ses bagages. Une perquisition, samedi, dans le pavillon de Gérard Faure, à Versailles (Yvelines), a permis de découvrir 4,7 kilogrammes de cocaïne.

Une « descente » simultanée à Paris, chez un autre revendeur, Elie Manka, toxicomane notoire, a permis à la B.S.P. de compléter sa prise avec trois cents grammes de cocaïne, dissimulés dans un faux-plafond et cinquante « sniffettes » cachées dans une porte creuse. La valeur marchande moyenne du stock de cocaïne saisi dépasse les cinq millions de francs.

Le frère de Gérard Faure, Georges, 41 ans, qui possède une résidence en Espagne, a été également interpellé à Paris pendant le week-end.

Dix toxicomanes évoluant pour la plupart dans les milieux du showbiz (notamment un compositeur connu), ont été interpellés au cours de ce coup de filet mais laissés en liberté.

Une autre affaire

Toujour pendant le week-end, un autre coup de filet contre les

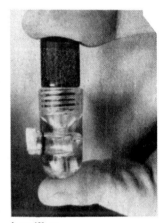

La sniffette

revendeurs de cocaïne a été opéré par un groupe spécialisé de la B.S.P., dit « de voie publique », qui a remonté une filière colombienne.

Le Progrès

---

sablier (m.)   sand box
la filière   line
une perquisition   thorough search

Boy George héroïnement drogué

Et oui c'est une surprise !
Boy George, pour ceux qui ne le connaissent pas est un chanteur pop, avec son groupe Culture Club il est régulièrement en tête des hits parades radiophoniques. Mercredi, le jeune artiste (25 ans) a été attrapé par la police anglaise. Il serait devenu dealer de drogue.
Il semble que ce soit son père qui

ait informé les forces de l'ordre par amour pour son fils. Boy George a été mis sous « contrôle médical constant ».
Mettez-vous à la place des journalistes. Ils se sont butés contre un médecin car Boy George veut rester seul pendant un mois, le temps que les esprits se calment.

LIONEL ■

Le Progrès des Enfants

15 You are in France for several weeks in the summer, and seeing this article you decide that you might well stay to see Prince play in Paris at the end of August. You write to a friend in England, who is also a fan, suggesting that she join you for the concert, and telling her:

- the possible dates and venues of the concert
- what comments this article makes about the state of Prince's career
- what comparisons are made in the article with recent achievements of other artists.

débusquer to drive from under cover
bousculer to jostle
braquer to aim

L'Attila de la pop music arrive à la fin du mois
Prince, à Paris, hésite entre plusieurs palais

VIENDRA, viendra pas ? Après un suspense de plusieurs mois, l'événement que n'osaient plus espérer les amateurs de rock arrive. Prince sera à Paris dès la fin du mois d'août. Mais sur la date exacte et le lieu de ce concert unique la valse hésitation continue.

Il était question du 25 août au Zénith puis ce matin, du 31 août au Palais des Sports.

Aux dernières nouvelles c'est à Versaille le 29 août qu'il faudrait aller débusquer la star.

Autant dire qu'il s'agit là d'une promotion torride pour l'arrivée de son film « Under the cherry moon », tourné sur les hauteurs de Saint-Paul-de-Vence et dont il est également le réalisateur.

Mais s'il a été le Prince triomphant, l'Attila de la pop music de l'année 1985, le « Kid de Minneapolis » gardera-t-il sa place en cet été 1986 ?

Nouveaux albums

Après une formidable tournée à travers les Etats-Unis, il avait laissé entendre il y a quelque temps qu'il renonçait à la scène pour se consacrer au travail en studio. Passionné par l'image, auteur de quelques clips savoureux, son but était effectivement de s'imposer au cinéma comme il s'est imposé dans la musique. On se souvient du succès de son premier long métrage « Purple Rain » où sa recette magistrale entre rock dur, swing sexy et frime sado-maso, avait mis le feu aux poudres ainsi que son disque du même nom qui, comme les cinq précédents — douze disques d'or — fit flamber tous les box-offices.

A vingt-trois ans, le petit Prince (1,60 mètre), géant de la provoque, génie du rock épicé, poly-instrumentiste surdoué, voyait son règne arriver et bousculait du même coup toutes les stars consacrées de l'Amérique.

Qu'on en juge : juillet 1984, il arrive par surprise à contre-pied de tout ce qu'on peut attendre alors que le monde du show-biz a les yeux braqués sur Kansas City où Michael Jackson démarre sa phénoménale tournée et Minneapolis où Bruce Springsteen fait son grand come-back à la scène. C'est encore Prince le petit timide, à la paranoïa aiguë, qui rafle tous les suffrages en s'installant en tête des ventes de disques et en focalisant tous les regards sur ses affiches cinéma. Un film à petit budget pourtant, mais réalisé par un jeune loup qui voit clair et qui signe avec « Purple Rain » son premier long métrage.

Aujourd'hui, avec deux nouveaux albums, le très psychédélique « Around the World in One Day » et « Parade » sorti en mars dernier et qui apparaît comme un avant goût de son nouveau film « Under the Cherry Moon » Prince marque son retour dans un style toujours aussi rock funky sexy, mais avec l'accent sur le cuir noir et les tenues légères de ses débuts, beaucoup plus que sur les jabots et les dentelles.

Monique PRÉVOT

Échec aux enfants détrousseurs de touristes

Après l'arrestation de quatre « protecteurs » des petits vide-goussets yougoslaves, les policiers de la Brigade de répression du banditisme espèrent pouvoir enfin enrayer le fléau.

.es policiers auraient-ils dé- de s'attaquer avec détermi- .n à l'un des fléaux de l'été à .s ? En arrêtant mardi dernier .re gitans du clan Hamidovic, .otecteurs » d'enfants qui pil- .es sacs et les poches des .istes, les hommes de la bri- .e de répression du bandi- .e (B.R.B.) ont, en tout cas, .é un coup sévère à ce que .a coutume d'appeler la .ugo connection » (nos édi- .s du 14 août).

L'un des hommes arrêtés .t encore sur lui 40 000 francs .devises étrangères : la recette .quelques heures de fructueu- .déambulations, remise par les .ants qu'il avait récupérés en .ure aux abords du Palais- .al. Des gamins de cinq à dix .dressés pour voler, et qui le .t avec une redoutable effica- .e en employant toujours les .mes méthodes.

Totalement impuissants

La plus fréquente est celle du .ournal » : une bande de qua- .ou cinq enfants, dépenaillés, .sutes, geignards, entoure sa .time, la noyant sous un flot de .roles d'autant plus incompré- .nsibles pour elle qu'il s'agit en .néral d'un touriste étranger. .endant que le pauvre Japonais . Allemand essaie de compren- .e ce qu'on lui veut, l'un des .tits voleurs glisse la main dans .poche ou le sac en le cachant .ans un journal. La scène dure .oins d'une minute et l'habileté . ces petits gitans est telle que, .en souvent, le touriste voit les .fants s'égayer et continue sa .omenade sans réaliser ce qui .ent de se passer.

Une bousculade, des enfants qui s'égaillent... En quelques secondes, ce touriste aura perdu son portefeuille.

Grâce à cette efficacité ce sont plusieurs dizaines de milliers de francs qui changent de poche, chaque jour, à Paris, pendant l'été. La rue de Rivoli et le Palais-Royal restent les endroits de la capitale où les risques de vol sont les plus grands mais les « petits Yougo » opèrent aussi dans le métro, rue du Faubourg-Saint-Honoré, près des grands magasins et sur les Champs-Élysées.

Ces enfants, bien sûr, ne gardent pas leur butin. Ils le remettent à des adultes, et c'est en cela que le coup de filet de la B.R.B. est intéressant. Les hommes arrêtés mardi seront au minimum inculpés de recel et passeront quelque temps en prison. Les policiers estiment que frapper leurs « protecteurs » est le seul moyen d'endiguer l'activité débordante des petits voleurs.

Contre ceux-ci, en effet, policiers et magistrats sont désarmés. « Ils ne sont qu'une centaine, nous les connaissons et pourtant nous sommes totalement impuissants, commente un inspecteur. *Nous les arrêtons de temps en temps pour nettoyer le paysage – certains sont passés plus de dix fois chez nous – mais ce sont des enfants et au-dessous de treize ans, les mineurs ne sont pas pénalement responsables. Ils le savent parfaitement et, bien qu'affirmant ne pas parler français, la première chose qu'ils nous disent c'est leur âge. Certains, bien sûr, mentent et ont au moins quatorze ou quinze ans. Mais comment le prouver ? Ils n'ont aucun papier d'identité, donnent de faux noms et de fausses adresses. Ces en-*

fants sont de petits fauves. Ils font partie d'une organisation qui éventuellement les a achetés en Yougoslavie, les a formés, les a *dressés*, et même s'ils sont battus, parfois sauvagement, ils sont incapables de vivre ailleurs que dans leur milieu. Les juges ont renoncé depuis longtemps à les placer dans des établissements spécialisés : ils se sauvent. »

Cette analyse est confirmée par les magistrats : « Quoi faire de ces enfants habitués à vivre totalement en marge, élevés pour devenir délinquants dès la petite enfance, qui ne savent ni lire ni écrire mais sont de redoutables voleurs ? explique un juge pour enfants. Toutes les tentatives de placement se sont soldées par des échecs. La meilleure solution est bien sûr de s'attaquer aux adultes qui les font « travailler ». Mais même cela ne résoudra pas le problème, car les intérêts en jeu sont trop importants : il y aura toujours quelqu'un dans le clan pour remplacer ceux qui sont sous les verrous. »

Un espoir cependant : les nouvelles lois sur la sécurité vont permettre d'expulser les étrangers qui « menacent l'ordre public ». Les policiers espèrent que les « protecteurs » des petits gitans entreront dans cette catégorie. Trois ou quatre expulsions bien choisies suffiraient, paraît-il, à les persuader que la guerre est engagée et qu'il vaut mieux renoncer.

Ces hommes ont en effet des sources de revenu beaucoup plus « juteuses » que les enfants et n'hésiteront pas à sacrifier une activité, certes lucrative, mais secondaire, pour se faire oublier des policiers.

Catherine DELSOL.

vide-gousset (m.) pickpocket
enrayer to bring under control
fléau (m.) scourge
dépenaillé ragged
geignard (given to) whining
butin (m.) booty
de petits fauves small game
dresser to prepare
juteux juicy

16 Before visiting Paris, you have been warned several times about pickpockets. You decide to make the following notes about this article, thinking that they will be useful in classroom discussion when you return home:

- the sums of money involved
- who the 'pickpockets' are, and how they are 'run'
- the methods they use
- how things are made more difficult for the police
- how it is hoped to solve the problem.

WRITING

1 Spending a holiday in Nice, you read an article about a survey of tourists, which asks you to list, from 1 to 10, in order of preference, ten things that you like about France. You are asked to do the same for ten things about France which you dislike.

2 You decide that you would like a penfriend in Monte Carlo. Write out the request and description of yourself as a small ad; then incorporate this into a letter to *Presse Monte Carlo*, asking for the ad to be printed as soon as possible.

3 You are due to return home to England after a holiday near Bordeaux, and you are broke! You come to the conclusion that the only way that you can afford to get home, is to sell your new expensive rucksack, carry your things home in carrier bags, and then to get a lift.

You write two small ads to be printed in the local paper:

- describing your rucksack, offering it for sale, and stating the price you want, and where you can be contacted
- asking for people who will be driving to England, and who can offer you a lift, to contact you.

4 Your parents want to spend their holidays in Clermont-Ferrand. They want to investigate the possibility of exchanging their home with a family in that town. Your father asks you to write a letter, for publication in *La Montagne*, the regional newspaper, inviting families who are interested in exchanging to contact him. You include in the letter a description of your house, and the area in which you live.

5 Returning to England after a stay in Dieppe, you decide to write a letter of thanks to be published, hopefully, in *Paris-Normandie*.

You have been particularly touched, not only by the kindness of your French friends but by the helpful and friendly attitude of all the people you have met. A few comments about the excellence of the food, and some of the interesting things that you have seen would also be appropriate!

MULTI-SKILL TASK

1 Whilst on an exchange visit to Lyon you see an advertisement put out by FR3, the local radio station.

Attention aux Jeunes!

Vous connaissez bien un pays étranger?
Vous êtes peut-être étranger ou vous y avez habité?

Si vous vous intéressez à participer à un programme à la radio sur la vie à l'étranger, adressez-vous à Monique Legros à FR3 tél. 22–30–51 ou bien écrivez-nous chez FR3 à la Part-Dieu à Lyon.

étranger foreign
à l'étranger abroad

2 You decide to write and answer this advertisement as you are not French.

3 A few days later you receive the following phone call.

4 Phone back and leave a message agreeing.

5 During the phone-in programme the following questions are asked. Listen to each one and tell your partner your answer. (The tape should be paused at appropriate points.)

Le français chez nous

Porte Ouverte

 MULTI-SKILL TASKS

1 You have got a holiday job working in the office of a company manufacturing computer components. One of your tasks is to sort out the mail and put it on the appropriate person's desk. One day this letter comes.

1 Who would be the most suitable person to pass this letter to?

- the works' manager
- the personnel manager
- the managing director
- the canteen manager

2 The person to whom you decide to pass the letter knows no French so you add a brief note saying what the writer wants.

3 You are then asked to write out a few more details about the writer so that the relevant manager can make a decision.

4 The manager is interested and asks you to write a brief letter requesting further details.

informatique (f.) information technology (computing)
un stage (training) course

Michel Roué,
5 rue des Lilas,
18 000 Bourges.

Bourges, le 8 juin 1986

A l'intention du chef du personnel de "BRM COMPUTER COMPONENTS" Ltd.

Monsieur,

Etant en ce moment étudiant en informatique, dans la branche robotique, il est très important pour moi de faire un stage en Angleterre. A cet effet, je recherche un poste d'été dans une entreprise spécialisée dans l'informatique.
J'aimerais savoir, par conséquent, s'il vous est possible de m'employer temporairement chez vous cet été.

Dans l'attente de votre réponse, je vous prie d'agréer, monsieur, l'expression de mes sentiments distingués.

M. Roué

2 Your exchange partner's teacher writes you this letter. Write back giving the information requested and answering any points in the letter.

Je m'appelle Patrick Duverger et je suis le professeur de français d'Isabelle, ta correspondante. Je m'excuse de t'écrire comme cela, puisque je suis un inconnu pour toi, mais, moi, je te connais bien par Isabelle, qui m'a beaucoup parlé de toi et m'a communiqué ton adresse, en me disant que tu serais assez gentille pour me rendre service. . . .

Voilà : je suis professeur, et je vais séjourner dans ta ville pendant un trimestre, dans le cadre d'un échange. Pourrais-tu me dire quelles sont les possibilités de distractions offertes là-bas (cinémas, théâtres, concerts, tourisme, loisirs, sports, etc. . . .) ?

En espérant te rencontrer bientôt, je te remercie d'avance et j'attends ta réponse

Patrick Duverger.

3 You are working at the tourist office in Haverfordwest in South-west Wales when this letter arrives. As you can read and write French you are asked to deal with the matter.

You decide which of these properties might be suitable and send a brief letter describing them and answering any points in the letter from France.

Paris, le 6 mars 1986.

Mme. Charlotte Duval,
29 rue Descartes,
75008 Paris,
FRANCE.

Monsieur,

Ayant l'intention de passer mes vacances dans le comté de Dyfed, j'aimerais savoir si un gîte serait disponible là-bas entre le 1er et le 14 juillet, si possible à proximité de la mer et à une distance raisonnable des magasins. Ce serait, donc, pour 4 personnes : mon mari, mes deux enfants et moi-même.

Auriez-vous l'extrême obligeance de m'envoyer les prix des gîtes et les détails d'hébergement ?

Je vous remercie à l'avance, et vous prie d'agréer, monsieur, l'expression de mes sentiments distingués.

P.S. Pourriez-vous nous envoyer une réponse en français, si possible, car nous ne savons pas lire l'anglais. Merci.

hébergement (m.)   accommodation

Coastal Cottages of Pembrokeshire

A very special selection of 150 coastal cottages scattered along the quieter areas of the Pembrokeshire coast. The following properties are an extract from our 1986 brochure.

Member of British Tourist Board, Wales Tourist Board and South Wales Tourism Council.

MARINE WALK, Fishguard

Ref. 544L Sleeps 4 (2 Bedrooms) PRICE CODE 10

A cottage situated in a very sheltered sunny position facing South beside the Pembrokeshire Coastal Path. Extremely peaceful but just 400 yards from the shops. Not on a road, but path wide enough for vehicular access and parking. Magnificent panoramic views of the Old Harbour at Lower Town and the Preseli Mountains. There is a small pebble beach about 200 yards down the path, but many sandy beaches are within the immediate area.

The cottage is furnished with antique pine and offers very comfortable accommodation. Sitting room with French windows to sheltered Patio with table and chairs. Kitchen/dining area with electric cooker and fridge. Bedroom 1 has a 4-poster double bed. Bedroom 2 has twin beds. Cot. Bathroom. Colour TV. Night storage heating is provided free in the main living area and bedrooms. Additional electricity is obtained through a 50p slot meter. Linen is provided for the beds which have continental quilts. Pets are only accepted by prior agreement.

ABEREIDDY,

Ref. 513 Sleeps 8/9 (4 Bedrooms) PRICE CODE 16 Friday Booking

A perfect dream cottage, set quietly back off the beach with peaceful sheltered garden and sitting-out area at Abereiddy. Carefully restored and now offering a good standard of extremely comfortable accommodation comprising: Large olde worlde sitting room with comfortable old settee, chintz covered and feather filled, and 4 other easy chairs. Two oak corner cupboards compliment the oak coffee table and the gateleg table. Colour Tele-vision. The chimney breast is made of stone and slate, also the fireplace with slate alcoves for flower arrangements. Logs for open fire usually plentiful on beach, (saw provided). Kitchen/dining room well equipped, electric cooker and fridge, pine table and chairs. Hall with archways decorated with pebbles from the beach.

Bathroom. Bedroom 1: Double bed, beamed ceiling, wash basin with h & c recessed into the stone wall, delightful view of grassy slopes and old cottages through the window; Bedroom 2: Double bed, wash basin, h & c, pine panelling, radiator; Bedroom 3: Twin beds, beamed ceiling, two sunny aspects, a delightful room; Bedroom 4: (with access through Bedroom 3) Pair bunk beds plus 'Zed' bed and cot and high chair. Bed linen is not provided for the beds. Electricity is supplied by 10p slot meter. We regret that pets are not accepted at this cottage.

NEVERN, Newport

Ref. 563L Sleeps 4 (2 Bedrooms) PRICE CODE 10

Nevern is, perhaps, the most restful and charming village in the whole of the Pembrokeshire National Park. There are so many interesting walks around the village. Up the lane you would follow in the footsteps of Pilgrims who, a 1,000 years ago, carved a 'Cross' in the rocks and peacefully knelt in prayer beneath it, en-route to St. Davids. Climb over the stile, which is a rock, worn away by footprints. The 'peace' of times past is still here today. At the far end of the village (about a ¼ mile away) is the local Pub. This cottage is the secret gem of the village. Completely secluded by high hedges, the garden is an absolute delight. Spring and summer flowers smother stone walls and banks that separate the garden into individual secluded areas around the cottage.

The cottage itself is just as enchanting as the surroundings. The front door leads into the open plan Sitting/Dining areas. The old beamed ceilings and log-burning stove (logs in the shed) and cosy settees, and intimate dining area with French antique style anthracite stove, all combine to make the whole cottage something very special. The Kitchen is well equipped with split level cooker and hob, and refrigerator. Bathroom. The 2 bedrooms upstairs each have a pair of twin beds. Linen is provided for the beds. There is night storage heating in the living area. Electricity is charged according to use. Colour television. Pets strictly by prior agreement.

ABERCASTLE, Nr. St. Davids

Ref. 530 Sleeps 6 (3 Bedrooms) PRICE CODE 11

Abercastle is a small sheltered haven about midway between St. Davids and Strumble Head. There is a seal colony at the entrance to the creek, also badgers, foxes, ravens, falcons and herons inhabit the vicinity. The hills and cliff pathways abound with Spring and Summer flowers. At low tide it is possible to visit the island at the end of the creek and explore the cave.

The Cottage is a traditional fisherman's cottage, detached and facing south, quietly situated up a small cul-de-sac track about 300 yards from the beach, with beautiful views across the sea to summer sunsets. The accommodation is comfortable and comprises: Entrance to large 28ft. main living area with beamed ceiling, inglenook fireplace with log burning stove. Settee and armchairs, dining table and chairs, electric cooker and fridge. Bathroom. Sun lounge/3rd bedroom with 2 single divans and easy chairs. The 2 upstairs bedrooms are approached from the main living area by spiral staircase and sleep 1 double and 2 single beds. Cot. Bed linen is not supplied for the beds. Colour television. The meter will be read and electricity charged as used. Pets by arrangement.

Terms: *Winter weeks from £55 (short breaks £45). Spring/Autumn from £60 per weeks. Summer from £125 per week. Pets are welcomed at most properties. All properties are approved by the Wales Tourist Board, many with Special Awards.*

If you would like a full brochure please call or telephone our office at Abercastle.

Coastal Cottages of Pembrokeshire

Abercastle, Nr. Haverfordwest, Pembrokeshire. SA62 5HJ. Tel (034 83) 742.

4 The manager of the company for whom you are working on a
Training Scheme knows that you are quite good at French. One
day this letter arrives from France.

1 At a glance you can see that they want to . . .

2 Naturally, the manager is very interested and asks you to jot
down a few notes about what is in the rest of the letter.

3 The manager then asks you to write out a letter ready for
typing. This letter should give the information that large
saucepans are £3000 per thousand, small ones £1500 per
thousand and frying pans £3500 per thousand.

```
Posy Pots Ltd.,
Unit 6,
Industry Way,
Bilston,
West Midlands.
ANGLETERRE.

Monsieur,

Etant, depuis longtemps, le plus grand magasin de produits
domestiques de notre région, nous avons l'intention de proposer
à nos clients, le choix le plus étendu possible de produits
domestiques.

Ayant récemment pu inspecter votre gamme de casseroles au Salon
de la Cuisine à Paris, nous avons décidé de nous renseigner.

Pourriez-vous, monsieur, nous envoyer votre liste de prix de
vente en gros? Il s'agit d'une commande importante (au moins
mille casseroles par an si le prix nous convient.)

Dans l'attente de votre réponse prochaine, veuillez, monsieur,
agréer l'expression de nos sentiments les plus distingués.

Richard Grégoire.
```

```
"Le Chic Domestique",
Avenue du 8 Mai,
76001,
Dieppe,
FRANCE.
```

---

vente en gros (f.)   wholesale

5 As part of a market research exercise for your local tourist board, you are asked to undertake a survey in your local town. You need to find out where the visitors come from, how long they are staying for, how they travelled here and how they are getting about, what they have been doing and what they think of the locality as a place to stay.

1 Working with a partner practise the sorts of questions you will need to ask. Your partner should make up answers at this stage. Swap roles so that you each have the chance to ask the questions.

2 Some French friends of yours were over in the town last week and you decide to write and ask them their opinions. Write out, in French, the questions you wish to ask.

3 You receive the following answer from your friends which, eventually, you will need to incorporate into your findings.

Vannes   le 26 juillet

Chers amis,

D'abord, il nous faut beaucoup vous remercier de nous avoir si gentiment reçus chez vous la semaine dernière.

Vous nous demandez de vous préciser nos impressions au sujet de votre ville. Alors - - - - - c'est une très belle ville avec beaucoup d'ambiance — surtout dans les "pubs" dit Georges! Nous avons beaucoup apprécier ces lieux ainsi que les jolis magasins et les sites historiques que vous nous avez faits visiter.

Le fait qu'on soit venu en voiture a beaucoup facilité notre visite car nous n'aimons pas du tout les transports en commun bien que, chez vous ils soient assez commodes.

La prochaine fois, nous espérons pouvoir rester plus longtemps pour mieux connaître votre ville — une semaine n'est vraiment pas assez longtemps.

Merci encore mille fois. Nous attendons avec impatience votre visite à Vannes au mois d'octobre

Amitiés à tous,

	Origin	Mode of travel	Length of stay	How travelling around	Activities	General impression

4 You have interviewed six French people and recorded their answers on tape. The tourist board have asked you to collate the information on this form. Fill in your copy of the form according to the headings given and the answers on the tape. (Don't forget your friends' letter.)

5 The tourist board is preparing a multi-lingual brochure, extolling the virtues of your town. You are asked to make a list, in French, of the positive points made by visitors for inclusion in the brochure.

Sem. : HS 482 F BS 413 F
Pers. suppl. : 15 F par jour
Jours suppl. : 120 F
Réservation : S.R.

 500 m 10 km

BLUNAY
N° G 77/27 : 2 épis. A 90 km de Paris et à 10 km de Provins. Maison indépendante comportant deux gîtes. Gîte du premier étage. L'accès se fait par une pièce au rez-de-chaussée pouvant être une cuisine d'été dans laquelle se trouve un escalier par lequel on accède au gîte. Chauffage électrique. Terrain vaste, commun aux deux gîtes. Grand séjour/salon mansardé avec coin cuisine. Salle de bains, W.C., 2 lits 2 pers. (4 adultes).

3 km / 2 km
 2 km / 3 km / 2 km
10 km / 3 km / 10 km

6 Your next door neighbour is planning a *gîte* holiday in France.

1 One evening she arrives with the details of some holiday homes in the area she wants to visit. She asks you to help her to sort out which *gîte* will be the most suitable. The family consists of two adults and three children, one boy, one girl and the youngest only a baby.

- Read through the details and decide which *gîtes* might be suitable.
- Jot down details of the suitable ones so that your neighbour can discuss them with her husband.

SOLERS
N° G 77/22 : 2 épis. A 30 km de Paris et à 15 km de Melun. Maison indépendante dans village comportant deux gîtes. Gîte du rez-de-chaussée, vaste terrain commun à trois gîtes. Petit gîte studio adapté pour 4 personnes maximum. Chauffage électrique. Village non loin de Melun, propriétaires proches. Petit séjour avec coin cuisine, salle d'eau, W.C., 1 chambre (1 lit 2 pers., 1 divan 2 pers., 4 adultes).

 3 km / 10 km
 100 m / 30 km
 15 km / 15 km
 2 km / 2 km
 500 m / 15 km

Sem. : HS 482 F BS 413 F
Pers. suppl. : 15 F par jour
Jours suppl. : 120 F
Réservation : S.R.

Sem. : HS 1006 F BS 926 F WE 384 F
Pers. suppl. : 15 F par jour
Jours suppl. : 120 F
Réservation : S.R.

VILLIERS SUR SEINE
N° G 77/23 : 3 épis. A 90 km de Paris et à 12 km de Bray sur Seine. Maison indépendante dans un village. Terrain clos, jardin et meubles de jardin, garage. Maison sur deux étages, les propriétaires habitent le village. Chauffage électrique. Maison de charme, abords fleuris. Au rez-de-chaussée grande cuisine, salle à manger/salon avec cheminée, salle d'eau, W.C., au premier, 3 chambres (2 lits 2 pers., 2 lits 1 pers., 1 divan 2 pers., 8 adultes).

 4 km / 18 km
 4 km / 1 km
 10 km / 4 km
 4 km / 2,5 km
1 km / 10 km

2 When they have reached a decision about which *gîte* they would like to book, your neighbour comes round again to ask you to write the booking letter. She would like to go from 12th August to 26th August.

3 About ten days later your neighbour receives the following letter from the owner of the *gîte*. She asks you to tell her what is in it. Again make some notes so that she can consult her husband.

Versailles le 2 avril

Monsieur,

Nous accusons réception de votre demande de réservation concernant "VILLIERS SUR SEINE".

Nous vous informons avec regret que ce gîte ne sera disponible qu'à partir du 19 août en raison d'aménagement. Vous serait-il possible de prendre vos vacances à partir de cette date? Ceci étant le cas, veuillez nous le communiquer aussitôt que possible, pour que nous puissions confirmer cette nouvelle réservation.

En attendant de vous lire dans le prochain futur, veuillez nous accorder l'honneur d'accepter nos salutations les plus distinguées.

ALBERT J BENSAID.
DIRECTEUR.

Relais Départemental des Gîtes,
Rueaux des Yvelines,
Hôtel du Département,
2 Place A.Mignot,
78012 Versailles,
FRANCE.

---

4 They are quite happy to make the necessary alterations to their plans and your neighbour asks you to phone the number on the letter to say that this is all right.

5 She then asks you to write a letter confirming the new details.

7 Your young cousin has been taking part in an exchange visit and at the moment there is a young French boy staying with the family. One evening your aunt phones to ask your help. The boy is refusing to eat and clutching his stomach. You go immediately to your aunt's house to see what you can do to help.

1 When you get there and have asked the boy what the difficulty is, he is so relieved to find someone who can speak French that he pours out all his problems. You listen carefully and jot down the main points to explain to your aunt.

2 Your aunt then asks you to explain to Jean-Marie that the family is going to visit some friends on Saturday; that they will leave about 9 am and travel for about an hour. They will have lunch with the friends and in the afternoon everyone will either go shopping or to a football match. She asks you to find out what Jean-Marie would prefer to do. After tea they will set off for home and be back about 8 pm.

Pretend that your partner is Jean-Marie and give this information. Don't forget to find out Jean-Marie's preference.

3 Jean-Marie asks you if you could please jot down the information for him in French to help him remember what will be happening.

8 One day you are in a chemist's shop waiting for a prescription to be filled. A young woman comes in and tries to make herself understood to the pharmacist. You realise that she is French and offer to help.

1 She tells you what she wants and you jot down the details for the pharmacist.

2 Having told the pharmacist what was required he asks you to tell her the following:
- All medicine he sells is taken orally.
- He can offer junior paracetamol and some children's cough mixture.

3 The young woman agrees to take these medicines and asks you to jot down the instructions on dosage etc. in French.

angiers JUNIOR
PARACETAMOL TABLETS
Angiers chewable, peach flavoured paracetamol tablets relieve pain and reduce fever in many conditions including colds and flu, toothache, headache and general aches and pains.
DOSAGE
Ages: 3 months-1 year: 1 tablet
1-6 years: 1-2 tablets
6 and over: 2-4 tablets
The dose may be repeated at the end of 4 hours.
Do not exceed 4 doses in 24 hours.
Do not exceed the stated dose – an overdose is dangerous: Medical attention should be sought immediately.
Do not give for more than 3 days without consulting your doctor.

CONTAINS PARACETAMOL

P   Each tablet contains Paracetamol BP 125 mg
Do not give to children under the age of 3 months except on doctor's advice.
KEEP ALL MEDICINES OUT OF THE REACH OF CHILDREN.
Angiers is a Trademark Authorised user Bristol-Myers Co. Ltd
Station Road, Langley, Slough SL3 6EB
Robinhood Ind. Est., Clondalkin, Co. Dublin
© 1985

PL 0125/0168   PA 48/39/3

Benylin*
Paediatric

is indicated for the relief of cough and its congestive symptoms and for the treatment of hayfever and other allergic conditions affecting the upper respiratory tract.
It is specially formulated for children.

Dosage
CHILDREN: 1 to 5 years, One 5 ml spoonful every three hours; 6 years and over, Two 5 ml spoonfuls every three hours.

Warning
If symptoms persist please consult your doctor, or pharmacist.

Keep bottle tightly closed. Store below 30°C. Keep out of reach of children.

WARNING:
May cause drowsiness. If affected, do not drive, or operate machinery. Avoid alcoholic drink.

125 ml.

9 On a three-week work-experience placement from school you are working in the offices of a company which manufactures exclusive hand-made chocolates.

1 One day the following letter arrives and the manager, knowing that you are studying French for GCSE, asks you to make a note about its contents.

---

le dix décembre

Classy Chocs,
Unit 9,
Hogsbury Trading Park,
NORTHAMPTON
Angleterre.

Monsieur,

Ayant récemment vu votre publicité au cours d'une visite à Londres, nous serions très intéressés par les oeufs en chocolat (500 grammes) que vous proposez pour la saison de Pâques.

A la suite d'une consultation avec la direction, nous voudrions en commander 500 (cinq cents), pourvu qu'ils puissent nous être livrés avant la fin du mois de février.

Veuillez nous préciser aussitôt que possible, si vous pourrez satisfaire à cette demande.

Dans l'attente de vous lire, veuillez accepter nos salutations distinguées.

Alphonse Mozziconnacci,
Propriétaire.

Au Bon Bonbon,
67 Avenue de Gaulle,
60391 Senlis,
FRANCE.

---

2 Unfortunately some key people are away at the moment so there is likely to be some delay. The manager asks you to phone and leave the following message on the client's answering machine:

You are calling on behalf of 'Classy Chocs' of Northampton. Unfortunately, there will be a three-week delay on the order sent since some essential workers are ill. Tell them a letter will follow. You should apologise and give the number of your firm (Northampton 369404) in case they want to ring back. (Remember that the French split phone numbers into pairs.) If they do phone they should ask for you. Leave your name and spell it out. (Make a few notes in French if you like to help you and then record the message. Do not write out everything you are going to say.)

3 The manager now asks you to write out the letter confirming the phone message so that the typist can type it up.

10 You are on a work experience placement in a garage which is the main dealer for French cars in a town in the South of England. One of your jobs each morning is to listen to the telephone answering machine and note the messages on a telephone pad. You then pass the messages to the appropriate person. Inevitably there are quite often messages in French.

1 One morning there are no fewer than five messages in French. Make the necessary notes about each one in English.

2 Two of the messages asked for someone to phone back. The manager asks you to call back with the following messages:

- **For Renault in Calais**

  We need a set of wheels for a Renault 5 special as soon as possible. It is very urgent. A letter follows.

- **For M. Lefèvre**

  Would be delighted to see him when he arrives. Will meet him from the 2 pm train. The hotel is arranged.

3 The manager now asks you to write out the letter to Renault so that the secretary can type it. It must be complete as he understands no French.

```
To _____
Date _____  Time _____
WHILE YOU WERE OUT
Name _____
of
Tel N⁰ _____

┌─────────────────────┬──────────────────────┐
│ TELEPHONED          │ PLEASE CALL BACK     │
│ CALLED TO SEE YOU   │ WILL CALL AGAIN      │
│ WANTS TO SEE YOU    │ URGENT               │
└─────────────────────┴──────────────────────┘

MESSAGE
_____
_____
_____
_____

TAKEN BY: _____
```

11 You have a holiday job in the Grand Hotel in Climpton-on-Sea. Normally you are a simple 'chamberperson' but from 9th to 16th August the manager asks you to act as host/hostess whilst an international convention is on in the town. Your job is to be available in the mornings and late afternoons/early evenings to help those attending the convention and their spouses with their enquiries. You sit at a desk in the entrance hall wearing a badge proclaiming that you speak French (your colleagues are taking care of the other languages).

Working with a partner who will check what you are saying, answer the questions asked of you on Tuesday 10th August. Use the information sheet opposite as a basis for your answers. (The tape should be paused at appropriate points.)

CLIMPTON-ON-SEA
INFORMATION BULLETIN

INTERNATIONAL CONVENTION

9th to 16th AUGUST

Shopping

Early-closing day—Wednesday. Shopping hours 9 am to 5.30 pm; late night shopping Thursday until 8.00 pm.

Garages

A and A Automobiles—Ford specialists.
  Tel: Climpton 369572

Davis Motors—Repairs all makes.
  Tel: Climpton 796352

Stans Autos—Foreign car specialist. All makes, V.W., Honda, Citroën, Renault and Datsun.
  Tel: Climpton 314960

XYZ Motors—All kinds of repairs and adjustments. Agent for Skoda.
  Tel: Climpton 712192

Theatres

Alhambra—'Run for your Wife'—8 pm daily, Sundays 2 pm and 8 pm.

Grand—'Where the Wild Wind blows'—7.30 pm daily Sundays 6.30 pm.

Cinemas

Odeon, ABC, Ritz, Gaumont. Varied programmes, ring cinemas for details.

Exhibitions

Civic Hall—Renaissance Art—9 am to 5.30 pm—entrance free.
Maritime Museum—10 am to 8 pm—entrance free.
Museum and Art Gallery—special exhibition of local art and artefacts 9 am to 6 pm—entrance free.

Doctors

Dr P Smith—17 The Avenue—tel Climpton 639716
Dr S Malik—6 The Parade—tel Climpton 794358
Dr J Washington—76 George St—tel Climpton 252126
Dr K K Singh—21 Major Road—tel Climpton 232411

Chemists

Green and Hope, 19 The Parade
Jackson, 24 Arthur Street
Pradey's, 35 Rushworth Boulevard
C G Claud, 32 Workhampton Road

Transport

Buses—hourly to Hopton Sherwood and Barville
    —half-hourly to Jamestown
Trains—hourly to London (from 6.30 am) and to Norwich (from 7.20 am)
    every 2 hours to Barville (from 8 am) and to Hopton Sherwood (from 8.40 am)
Taxis—Joe's Cabs—tel Climpton 747576

12 You are working in the tourist information centre in Stratford-upon-Avon. Inevitably there are a lot of foreign tourists, many of them French or French-speaking. One morning you have to deal with a series of French-speaking tourists requesting directions and information.

1 Using the map provided and working with a partner, give the directions requested. Your partner should use the blank map and mark the position of the various places of interest according to your directions. Then compare maps to see how well you gave directions and your partner followed them.

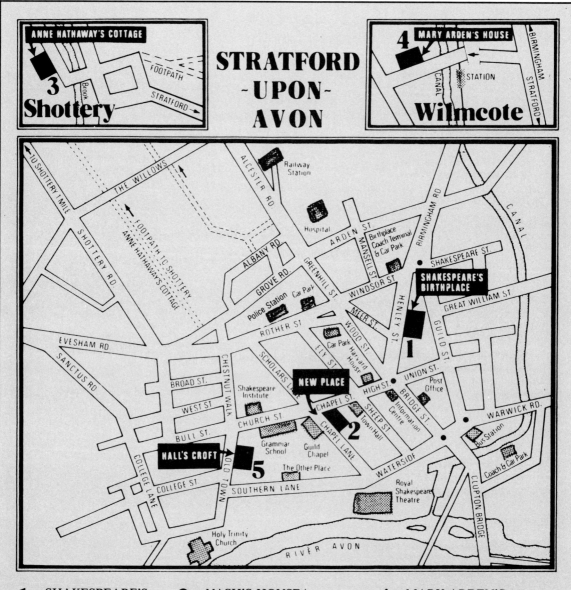

1 SHAKESPEARE'S BIRTHPLACE AND SHAKESPEARE CENTRE HENLEY STREET

2 NASH'S HOUSE/ NEW PLACE CHAPEL STREET

3 ANNE HATHAWAY'S COTTAGE (one mile) Buses leave Bridge Street for Shottery at intervals and a field path from Evesham Place provides a short walk to the Cottage.

4 MARY ARDEN'S HOUSE (three miles) Trains, calling at Wilmcote, leave the station at intervals. Stratford to Birmingham buses pass the Wilmcote turn one mile away.

5 HALL'S CROFT AND FESTIVAL CLUB OLD TOWN

⊙⊙ 2 Some tourists want information about the various places of interest. As you have no French brochures available you jot down in French the details they want for them, using the English brochure.

The Shakespearian Properties

The world's most famous dramatist was born at Stratford-upon-Avon in 1564. His mother was the daughter of a prosperous local farmer; his father was a glover and wool dealer who rose to become Bailiff or Mayor of Stratford. In Shakespeare's time the town's Grammar School, which still remains, provided pupils with an excellent classical education. Although Shakespeare spent his professional career in London he kept his connection with Stratford, purchasing, in 1597, New Place, one of its largest houses, where he later retired. He died there in 1616 and was buried in Stratford's Parish Church.

THE SHAKESPEARE CENTRE

The Shakespeare Centre, a building of striking modern design and construction, was conceived as an international tribute to Shakespeare on the 400th anniversary of his birth in 1964. It provides the headquarters for the Shakespeare Birthplace Trust whose main tasks are to preserve and maintain the Shakespearian properties and to advance Shakespearian knowledge. The Trust maintains a Shakespearian library and a records repository, available for the use of students.

SHAKESPEARE'S BIRTHPLACE

The house in Henley Street where Shakespeare was born and spent his early years is a half-timbered building of a type common in Elizabethan Stratford. In Shakespeare's time part of his family home was used by his father in connection with his trade as a glover. Today, one half of the property, including the living-room, the kitchen and bedrooms, has period furnishings which re-create the atmosphere of a middle-class home of Shakespeare's time. The other half contains an exhibition illustrating the life and work of the dramatist, as well as the history of the property itself.

NEW PLACE AND NASH'S HOUSE

The site and foundations of New Place, a handsome house where Shakespeare spent his retirement and died in 1616, are preserved in an Elizabethan garden setting occupying the corner of Chapel Street and Chapel Lane. The entrance to the site is through Nash's House adjoining, which belonged to Thomas Nash, the first husband of Shakespeare's grand-daughter, Elizabeth Hall. The house is furnished in period style. It is also a museum of local historical material.

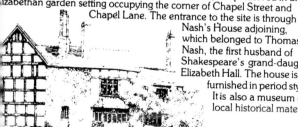

HALL'S CROFT

Situated in Old Town, Hall's Croft was the home of Shakespeare's daughter, Susanna, and her husband, Dr. John Hall, who had an extensive medical practice. It contains some exceptional Elizabethan and Jacobean furniture. Of particular interest is the dispensary, complete with apothecaries' jars, herbs and surgical instruments and an exhibition illustrating Dr. Hall's career and the medical background of his time. The beautiful walled garden is a special feature of the property.

MARY ARDEN'S HOUSE

This Tudor farmstead, with its old stone dovecote and farm buildings, was the home of Shakespeare's mother. It is situated at Wilmcote, three miles from Stratford. The house contains rare pieces of country furniture and farming utensils and the outbuildings accommodate a unique museum of old farming implements and other bygones, most of which were associated with the outlying Warwickshire countryside.

ANNE HATHAWAY'S COTTAGE

The picturesque thatched home of Shakespeare's wife, before her marriage, is at Shottery, just over a mile from Stratford. In Shakespeare's time the 'cottage' was in fact a twelve-roomed farmhouse, the home of the Hathaway's, a substantial yeoman family. The kitchen, with its open fireplace and a bake-oven still intact, and the dairy or buttery are vivid reminders of the property's long history as a farmhouse. The exterior view of the Cottage is justly famous, with its old-fashioned garden and adjoining orchard.

ADMISSION CHARGES

Shakespeare's Birthplace £1.30 (child 60p). Shakespeare's Birthplace including costume exhibition £1.50 (child 60p). Anne Hathaway's Cottage £1.20 (child 50p). Mary Arden's House £1 (child 40p). Hall's Croft and Nash's House/New Place 80p each property (child 30p each property). Inclusive ticket to all properties and costume exhibition £3.80 (child £1.50). Special rates available for school and educational groups. Tickets are obtainable at each of the properties.

OPENING TIMES

			November–March	April–October
☐ Shakespeare's Birthplace Anne Hathaway's Cottage	Weekdays		9am–4.30pm	9am–6pm†
	Sundays		1.30pm–4.30pm	10am–6pm†
Mary Arden's House Hall's Croft New Place	Weekdays		9am–4.30pm	9am–6pm†
	Sundays		not open	10am–6pm†

☐ Includes the BBC Television Shakespeare costume exhibition.
† Until 5pm in October. Last admissions are normally 20 minutes before closing times shown above. The properties are closed on Good Friday morning. Christmas Eve, Christmas Day and Boxing Day.

3 In the post this morning there is a letter in French requesting
information about accommodation. Your superior asks you to
have a look at it and sort out what exactly is required. Make
notes in English.

Calais, le 14 mars

Monsieur,

Je vous écris dans l'espoir de pouvoir visiter Stratford cet été avec mon mari.

Nous sommes un couple retraité et mon mari souffre d'une difficulté à marcher, surtout dans les escaliers. Donc, nous voudrions être logés, si c'est possible, pas loin du centre-ville et dans un logement au rez de chaussée.

J'éspère que ce sera possible de nous trouver quelquechose qui convient et à un prix pas trop élevé. Pouvez-vous donc me faire parvenir une liste des logements avec les prix?

En vous remerciant d'avance

Mme Dupardieu.

4 You decide to send the list of guest houses with a covering letter, in French, drawing attention to any accommodation you would consider particularly suitable.

The Coach House, 17 Evesham Road, (0789) 63975
Number of bedrooms 5D,2T,2F,1S,2PBS. Prices from £10.50.
Comfortable family-run guest house convenient to town centre.
Families welcome.

Hamlet House, 63 Broadway, (0789) 29333.
Number of bedrooms 4D,1F,1PBS. Prices from £10.50.
Quiet location, close theatre/town. Colour TV. Tea/coffee making all rooms.

The Romeo, 21 Alcester Place, (0789) 20496.
Number of bedrooms 2D,1T,1F,1S. Prices from £7.50.
Family-run guest house, evening meals, quiet setting, outskirts of town.

Avon Lodge, 37 Alcester Place (0789) 66616.
Number of bedrooms. 6D,5T,3F,6S. Prices from £8.50.
Warm welcome. Private facilities. Town centre position.
Ground floor rooms available.

The Othello Guest House, 2 St Gregory's Way.
(0789) 29227.
Number of bedrooms 3T,1S,1F. Prices from £9.
Quiet residential area, 5 minutes to centre, TV in all rooms.

D = double	F = family	PBS = private bathroom/
T = twin	S = single	shower